MARIA CALLAS

MARIA CALLAS
Diaries of a Friendship

Robert Sutherland

CONSTABLE · LONDON

First published in Great Britain 1999
by Constable and Company Limited
3 The Lanchesters, 162 Fulham Palace Road
London w6 9ER

Copyright © Robert Sutherland 1999
ISBN 0 09 478790 5

The right of Robert Sutherland to be identified as author
of this work has been asserted by him in accordance
with the Copyright, Designs and Patents Act 1988

Typeset in Linotype Janson 11pt by
Rowland Phototypesetting Limited
Printed in Great Britain by
St Edmundsbury Press Limited
both of Bury St Edmunds, Suffolk

A CIP catalogue record for this book
is available from the British Library

This book is dedicated to
Bernard,
and to Beryl, John and Norah

CONTENTS

LIST OF ILLUSTRATIONS

ACKNOWLEDGEMENTS

In the preparation of this book I have been helped by several people, some who have simply asked me pertinent questions at the right time, others in more positive ways. In particular I would like to thank Felix Aprahamian, Ringland Boyd, Jackie and Andreas Calogeropoulos-Stathopoulos, Daniel Donovan, Adrian Edwards, Dietrich Fischer-Dieskau, The Earl of Harewood, Joel Honig, Geoffrey Land, Helen Leitch, Marvin David Levy, Mario De Maria, Ferruccio Mezzadri, Mary Morris, Louis Parrish, Elena Pozzan, Catharine Robinson, Rocco Serini, and lastly, in alphabetical order but *primus inter pares*, Bernard Varley, who deserves my very special gratitude.

I thank Carol O'Brien who was courageous enough to commission a still unwritten book and who, in a difficult time when a reprimand was expected offered instead understanding, kindness and persistent encouragement. My thanks also to Rivers Scott for his diplomatic guidance, and to Ilsa Yardley whose enthusiasm and eye for the niceties of the English language I greatly appreciate.

The value of a good photographer in our modern lives is too often overlooked. For the prints reproduced in this book I thank the artists involved. Some I have been unable to trace but if they will make themselves known I will make amends.

I

FIRST MEETING

'I NEED advice on an unusual proposition,' wrote Ivor Newton on the card I received on 20 July 1973. I knew that Maria Callas had been present when Ivor accompanied Giuseppe Di Stefano in a recital at the Royal Festival Hall some weeks earlier and I had heard rumours of her return to the singing world. My curiosity was aroused. Could Ivor's proposition possibly involve the famous prima donna?

Over a glass of sherry in his Belgravia house Ivor told me of a proposed tour which Callas and Di Stefano were planning, performing in a number of European capitals, the USA, Canada, then Japan and other countries in the Far East. Unusually for Callas, the concerts would not be accompanied by orchestra but by a pianist. Di Stefano had persuaded her that with a pianist life would be easier. They need not be bound by a fixed programme, nor even a fixed key. The choice and order could be flexible. Ivor Newton, who had played for Di Stefano for many years, seemed the obvious choice of accompanist, but had recently suffered serious health problems, which were known to the insurance agents of the tour. Not happy to provide cover for a tour featuring an octogenarian with a heart condition, they stipulated that a younger man, someone who could take over at short notice, should be engaged as well. A decision not to be taken lightly, Ivor spent a good while looking around. He knew something of my work and had only recently sent me congratulations on good reviews I had received after a performance of Schubert's *Winterreise*. To be absolutely sure, he asked the opinions of several other notables on London's musical scene. Their responses must have been favourable. He invited me to come on the tour as his deputy.

He talked to me at some length about the stars he had accompanied in the past, many with names famous beyond the musical world, but in the tone of his voice I could hear that nothing compared with this new project. To accompany Maria Callas would be the crowning glory of his career and he was keenly aware of the value to a younger colleague of such an association. 'I'm giving you the opportunity to work with the greatest prima donna of our century – but remember, dear boy, I shall do everything in my power to prevent you performing with the artists,' he said. I knew where I stood.

When I was a student at the Royal College of Music in the early Fifties, two accompanists dominated the London music scene: Ivor Newton and Gerald Moore. Gerald became the doyen of recital partners. The career of an aspiring young recitalist would be triggered off with considerable kudos if the eminent Gerald Moore could be persuaded to accompany a Wigmore Hall début. With his writings and playing, Gerald opened the eyes and ears of the concert-going public to the importance of the pianist in such a partnership. Thriving success meant he was able to choose the work he found most rewarding, the 'serious stuff' – Schubert, Schumann, Brahms, Hugo Wolf et al. – a rich repertoire of songs composed originally for voice and piano alone. Gerald no longer played 'arrangements' for opera singers. That field was left to Ivor.

Newton had grown up in the music theatre and had a well-honed appreciation of its attractions. Nothing pleased him more than to appear on the stage with a glamorous woman in a gorgeous evening gown. Men were all right too, as long as they were famous and could draw a crowd. Ivor revelled in the theatricality of the occasion.

Born in the East End of London, he had spent a happy childhood there. His father owned a building business which provided a comfortable living for his family. At the age of six Ivor could have piano lessons without stretching the family budget, unlike another musical child three generations later, Maria Kalogeropoulos, whose father thought such things a waste of money. Ivor began his career playing in the band pit of local variety halls, where such legends as Vesta Tilley and Marie Lloyd appeared. He was alert, clever and better than most at his job, so he soon moved up to the West End theatres. This led to engagements in the salons of the famous society hostesses, where his wit and good looks proved an advantage. He became the darling boy of the duchesses and fashionable ladies who gave musical soirées. As so often happens in the musical world, where artists are pigeon-holed according to their success in some style, technique, or even one composer, Ivor found his niche. He became known as pianist to the stars. Many of the famous names chose him – Dame Nellie Melba, Clara Butt, Lotte Lehmann, Tetrazzini, Kirsten Flagstad, Gigli, Björling, Chaliapin, most of the great voices and some of the most illustrious instrumentalists, such as Casals, Menuhin, Piatigorsky – incidentally enhancing his own reputation. At the same time some good fortune in his private life, coupled with an acute business sense, brought him enough wealth to enable him to emulate the domestic style of his stage partners. He bought a house in Belgravia, conveniently situated for the West End theatres, and engaged a manservant.

In 1973 Ivor's appearance was not that of a conventional musician. He was short, had a strong nose, smooth pink cheeks and wore glasses over his bright eyes. Hair grew on the sides of his head, but none on top. He was not simply bald. The skin on his head was tight, smooth and shiny, as though it had been buffed up regularly by Andrew, his ever dutiful manservant. When he left his small but well-situated house in Belgravia, in his Savile Row three-piece suit and pin-striped shirt with white stiff collar, he could easily be taken for a man of the city – not an ordinary broker, of course, rather the company chairman. Impeccable, urbane, he could mingle smoothly as an equal in the society life he so much enjoyed. This was the person Maria Callas knew, a grown-up Little Lord Fauntleroy and a perfect English Gentleman.

A few days after our meeting Ivor announced that he was going over to Paris for some preliminary work with Callas and Di Stefano. I would not be needed. I could remain in London, he said. Instead, I took advantage of the warm summer weather and left town to enjoy the pleasures of the English countryside for a few days. When I returned I found an express letter and several telephone messages from Ivor begging me to come immediately to Paris. I contacted Sander Gorlinsky, his agent, who said he would speak with Ivor, but on the phone from Paris Ivor pleaded with me not to wait for Gorlinsky's decision. He had been given unfamiliar and difficult music, and was expected to rehearse twice a day. 'Please come immediately,' he said. 'You mustn't be nervous.' I thought it strange that while seeming to show concern for me, he was reluctant to help by giving details, or even the titles, of the music they were working on. I took the next plane.

That balmy August evening as we dined alfresco together, Ivor confirmed his reputation as a raconteur, regaling me with stories of the foibles and failings of the famous – amusing stories and some naughty tales better left to verbal recounting than committed to print. Mostly he talked of his long association with Di Stefano and his affection for him. A natural, instinctive singer who cared little for the niceties of a composer's notation, the tenor could bring an audience to the edge of their seats with the charm and intensity of his singing. Ivor spoke of his great generosity, how he was in his element hosting a party of friends and entertaining them with his inexhaustible fund of witty and amusing stories. I had heard of his famous open-handedness and how, during the run of an operetta in San Francisco, he had taken the whole cast to Las Vegas for a weekend at his own expense. I was warming to this man, looking forward to meeting him, when Ivor said, 'Be on your guard, though, he has a fiery temperament!' He had little to say of Callas, except that he had once turned pages while Sir Malcolm Sargent accompanied her at the piano at a soirée in St James's Palace. 'Don't be nervous,' he said again. I was not nervous, merely concerned at the thought of sight-reading music which the two artists had performed innumerable times, perhaps even recorded. If Ivor had been more forthcoming about the music being rehearsed, I could have done some preparation in London. Now it was too late.

At the end of the meal Ivor produced a crisp, folded 500-franc note saying, 'Oh, my dear boy, you see how I have no change. Why don't you just pay the bill and I will repay you – but you must remind me of it.' Something told me a reminder would be unwelcome. In all the time we worked together the new banknote, or its equivalent in another currency, remained intact.

Next morning we left the Hotel Belles Feuilles in good time for our noon appointment. As we strolled round to nearby avenue Georges Mandel at Ivor's leisurely pace, the sun, in a cloudless sky, was already hot. It was going to be a scorcher. Still talking of Di Stefano Ivor said, 'Do be careful with him. When he flies into a temper just remember he is a Sicilian peasant – that explains all.' Of Callas he could only repeat, 'You'll find her very sweet.'

An Italian maid showed us into the music room where, after a few minutes, Di Stefano made his entrance. Darkly southern and handsome, he carried himself like a man who knows his own worth. Without any ado he gave me a song to transpose. Ivor sat beside me at the piano, ostensibly to turn pages but continuously butting in on my concentration with whispered suggestions.

Suddenly Maria Callas appeared at the door. With quick long strides she crossed the room to me. 'Sutherland, eh, are you Australian?'

'No,' I answered. 'Nor are we related.' Joan's name was not mentioned, but my allusion to the famous prima donna with whom I share a surname was not missed. A man may have only one prima donna in his life.

Callas could see I had chosen my camp. There were smiles all round and what little trace of tension there had been was gone.

'Would you like some tea?' she asked – a thoughtful concession to my arrival from England. The reviving drinks arrived almost immediately – fruit juices in cut crystal and my tea in fine white porcelain, with linen napkins. Callas was evidently fastidious in her care for such details, which I found comforting as well as heart-warming.

As we sat around exchanging small talk she was open, positive, friendly and polite. Curious about me, she showed no inclination to start the rehearsal, remarking how disagreeable she found work in Paris in such hot weather. She was wearing a long flowing summer dress in a red, orange and yellow floral pattern, and some gold chains around her neck. From one hung a gold fob-watch. Once during the rehearsal, when an alarm in the watch tinkled, she left the room for a short time. I learned later that this was the signal for her two-hourly eye drops. Once we had become more familiar, she would put them in without leaving.

When we had finished our refreshments Di Stefano stood up and announced *Faust*. He looked up to the ceiling as though unwilling to make a choice of pianist. Ivor indicated that I play – it was a tricky piano part. I knew that to some extent I was on trial so it was reassuring to hear Callas remark after a short while that I was 'very sensitive to the voice'. We played through a variety of operatic duets, all chosen by Di Stefano. Callas let him dictate and seemed content to go along with his choice.

Eventually Di Stefano remarked, 'It's so hot in Paris we've decided to go for a holiday in San Remo.'

Ivor said, 'How nice, when will you go?'

Di Stefano answered, 'Now, right now. We're waiting for the car.' So ended our first rehearsal, although when Callas reappeared a little later, wearing a hat, she asked me to leave my London and country telephone numbers.

As they drove off, Di Stefano at the wheel of the Mercedes, Ivor and I made our way to a nearby restaurant. During lunch I ventured to remind him of Callas's compliment.

He said, 'Oh, you don't want to take much notice of what they say' – an ungenerous remark, I thought. Then he went on, 'Flattery is like smoking a cigarette: so long as you don't inhale it does you no harm.' Which was amusing and slightly more palatable.

In the afternoon we returned to the apartment to sort out the music. Ferruccio, the butler, a handsome gentle Italian, let us in. He brought us coffee and stayed to talk. He did not know how long they would be away, perhaps a week, maybe two, but he would not be surprised if they returned tomorrow. He shrugged his shoulders, suggesting he had not yet become accustomed to Di Stefano's unpredictable presence in the household. When he left us I took a leisurely look around the room.

Cream-painted panelled walls, the mouldings and rococo decoration touched in gold leaf, were hung with classical landscapes and paintings of allegorical scenes. Above a richly-carved Louis XV marble fireplace a fitted mirror was framed to match the panelling, with elaborate ormolu wall-light brackets on either side. From the fireplace a large Empire-style Aubusson covered most of the floor. In the centre of the room two sofas, upholstered luxuriously in a soft golden silk velvet, with lush overstuffed cushions to match, were separated by a glass-topped ormolu coffee table. Four wood-carved and gilded Louis XV fauteuils were placed conveniently around the room should they be needed. A major feature of the décor were the curtains. In a vibrant burgundy-red velvet the pelmet stretched across most of the wall, golden cords holding back the heavy material to disclose an inner pair of oyster-coloured raw silk. White voile nets covered each window. The impression was rich, warm and somewhat theatrical, suggesting the proscenium curtains of a grand opera house.

Around the room consoles and small tables held *objets d'art* and lamps, one made from an antique porcelain vase on an ormolu base, another the typical Bouillotte lamp, with adjustable japanned tin shade in the French Empire style. Most of the *objets* were antique Chinese *cloisonné* and bronze – model elephants, pagodas, vases. The eye was held constantly interested and amused. Opposite the fireplace a Steinway grand stood against the wall, the light from the windows falling on the music stand. Above it hung a framed page from the manuscript of *Lucia di Lammermoor* and on top, among other mementos, an interesting old first edition of the vocal score, bound in red morocco.

The role of Lucia was one of Callas's greatest successes in her gallery of romantic heroines. She sang it for the first time in Mexico City on 10 June 1952. She had been coached in the role by the eminent Italian conductor Tullio Serafin, an authority on the bel canto operas of Donizetti, Bellini and Rossini, but before daring to offer her work to him Callas had taken her usual course when learning a new piece. With a resolution seldom encountered in an opera singer, she embarked on a period of intense study. Meticulous and methodical, note values had to be academically accurate. 'Strait-jacketing,' she called it. Words were learned and pondered separately. Every aspect was scrutinised. She would reach back beyond the libretto to the original book. (In the case of *Lucia*, how she handled Sir Walter Scott's turgid prose no one can tell, though probably she had a good go at it.) She researched the costumes of the period. She read about previous productions and about the singers who sang in them. Franco Zeffirelli, versatile man of the theatre, said Callas was likely to know more about an opera than anyone else involved – including the producer.

She would attend orchestral rehearsals, partly because being short-sighted she could not rely on cues from the conductor, but also, as she said, 'It helped me to live into the music.' Even the first stage performance, she felt, was only a beginning. 'It is after the first performance that the real good solid work begins. You have made a rough sketch and now you start to mature the role.' Each time she took up a role again her performance was enriched by re-study, the psyche of the character embedding itself deeper into her own subconscious. Other artists might sing the part but no one understood a Callas role better than she did. Her study did not stop with her own character. She knew the other roles in the opera too, sometimes better than her colleagues who were singing them. Di Stefano recalls how in ensembles she would nudge him with her elbow, prompting his next entry. In the Mexico City *Lucia* he, too, was singing his role for the first time.

After Mexico, Callas returned home to sing in Italy and prepare for her London début. She chose *Norma* for the Covent Garden audience. In that production the small role of Clotilde was sung by a young Australian soprano, Joan Sutherland who, some years later in 1959, sprang to international stardom overnight in a new production of *Lucia di Lammermoor*. Her coach and conductor was Tullio Serafin. Learning that Maria Callas was present at the dress rehearsal did little to alleviate the nervous tension of the occasion, though in Joan's words Callas was 'most complimentary' afterwards in the dressing-room. At lunch with Elisabeth Schwarzkopf and her husband Walter Legge, Callas agreed that Sutherland would have a great success. 'But,' she said to Walter, 'only you and I know how much greater I am.'

Sutherland went on to sing other 'Callas' roles: the heroines in *Traviata*, *I, Puritani*, *La Sonnambula*, *Norma* and *Anna Bolena*. While Callas was 'La Divina', Sutherland became 'La Stupenda'.

With her first words to me earlier that day in her music room (about my nationality and possible relationship to the Australian soprano), Callas had grazed a momentous chunk of operatic history. I had noticed the score of *Lucia* and now, with time to reflect, I could better appreciate its significance. On the piano beside it stood two silver-framed photographs: one of Tullio Serafin signed simply, the other of Di Stefano caught in a dramatic operatic pose, the whole print hardly discernible under an elaborate dedication and signature in a large flamboyant hand.

Despite the grandeur and formality it was a friendly room, a place to be lived in. Only later did I learn how practical it could be. Behind the curtains hung stereo loudspeakers, one either side of the windows, easily uncovered. An antique commode housed a barrage of hi-fi equipment. This included the tape-recorder which was one day to be my salvation. When necessary, the whole room could be converted in a few moments into a musician's studio. Now it was a comfortable, enhancing environment, with no hint of the aloof inhospitable chill of many formal rooms. There was an extra-ordinary air of ease, everything radiating an atmosphere of warm opulence.

In 1952 Callas said in an interview, 'The most important room in my house is the music room, where I have my piano and where I work and practise. This room knows all my happiness and my anxiety.' Now, twenty-one years later, I was to learn more about that 'anxiety'.

2

PARIS PRELIMINARIES

On 3 September 1973, while I was at the Wigmore Hall rehearsing for a lieder recital, a visitor to my home answered a telephone call from Paris. A rich baritone voice asked for me. My house guest offered to take a message.

'Ask him to phone Maria please.'

Startled by the unexpected female name he said, 'Maria? Maria who?'

'Maria Callas,' the voice replied.

I contacted Sander Gorlinsky, Maria's agent in London, to tell him I had been invited to Paris to work. He asked me to come to his office. When I arrived, promptly at 10 a.m., a secretary offered me a chair, then after a short time announced that Mr Gorlinsky would see me. He was sitting behind a large desk at the far end of the room smoking a thick Havana cigar, a cut-crystal glass half filled with whisky within easy reach. On the wall behind him hung pictures of some of his clients: Rudolf Nureyev, Renata Tebaldi, Tito Gobbi and others. Alone on another wall a large framed poster featured a photograph of Maria Callas.

I felt I had walked into the office of a Hollywood mogul; into the realms of the big shots whose names we know from the silver screen: Cecil B. DeMille, Sam Goldwyn, Louis B. Mayer, David

O. Selznick and the like. *Emigrés*, or sons of *émigrés*, they were men of extraordinary power and influence. Sander Gorlinsky's origins also lay in Eastern Europe. Russian-born, educated in Germany, he had been settled in London for forty years. He was active in various fields of management, at one time running a 700-bedroomed holiday camp for Sir Billy Butlin in France. Then he moved into the music business, where he was known as a tricky customer, eventually emerging, his own boss, as impresario and manager of international opera and ballet stars. He first represented Callas when he persuaded her to come to London in 1952. Covent Garden had asked him if he could sign her up. He was now as influential and powerful as his counterpart in America, the renowned Sol Hurok.

In an accent heavy with the resonance of Central Europe he asked me, 'What can I do for you, Robert?' He leaned forward, peering sharply at me through thick glasses. This was our first official business meeting and he was using an old trick to show me who was boss. 'I've been trying to get her back on-stage for eight years,' he said. 'Go over for a few days and see how you get on.' On my way out the secretary handed me a flight ticket to Paris. Optimistically, I packed for a week and flew next morning.

As soon as I had settled into the comfortable small hotel near avenue Georges Mandel which she had recommended I phoned the Callas apartment.

'Madame is out,' I was told.

When, after lunch, I managed to speak to her she said, 'Why didn't you just come round and make yourself at home – you know where the piano is.'

I went at six and found her very polite and friendly, immediately offering me something to drink. She was quite relaxed and unpretentious, and in this warm atmosphere I became conscious of the pleasure of being alone with her. No Ivor. No Di Stefano. She asked me news of Covent Garden and London, a city she was very fond of. At one time, thinking she might settle there, she had viewed several properties, one a flat in the very block where I was living at the time – an agreeable coincidence. Time passed and as we sat drinking espresso coffee she showed no sign of wishing to work. Even when I broached the subject by asking if she had made any decision about programmes she gave me a vague 'Mm, yes and no', then turned to another irrelevant topic. I might have been on a casual social visit. Eventually, thinking one of us needed to be positive, I stood up and moved towards the piano. She took the hint and left her coffee. 'Let's have a look at something, then.' She sighed, taking down some piano scores from the shelves, *Don Carlo*, *Carmen*, *Cavalleria Rusticana*, *The Force of Destiny*. We began with Massenet's 'Pleurez mes yeux'.

This was my first time playing a solo aria with Maria Callas. I felt challenged, but what a thrill it proved to be! In the intimacy of her music room she sang with all the intensity of a stage perform-ance. The greatest surprise, and delight, was how responsive she was to my piano playing: the kind of rapport expected from a good lieder singer, floating in on the rhythm of my introduction as though she had been singing from the first bar and taking up after an interlude with the same natural flow. This was something I had not expected. And there was more. During the aria I experi-enced moments that musicians will recognise. Those times when a sudden, inexplicable energy makes itself felt. The performers are taken over and carried along by a greater superhuman force, uniting them and driving them forward as one. Like a kind of spiritual experience, it is something that cannot be planned or conjured up at will. It may happen two or three times during a concert, if one is lucky. With Callas it happened almost always, even in a run-through in her music room. This was surely what Shelley meant when he wrote, 'Rarely, rarely, comest thou, spirit of delight.'

When we finished the piece Maria took some moments to recover from the intensity of her performance, while I tingled with excite-ment. Then, to my astonishment, she turned to me and asked, 'Was that all right?' This surprising and unexpected question I found hard to answer. Before an artist who had received in her time every possible accolade I felt tongue-tied and could only mutter something that I hoped sounded like an encouraging reply.

'What else shall we do?' she asked. For an hour we worked, discussing the suitability of each aria for a recital. We talked of transposition, which generally means singing an aria in a key lower than that in which it was written, taking the strain out of the higher-lying passages. Although singers often take this easy way out, she did not like the idea. 'It isn't fair to the composer to change the key for your own convenience – that's cheating – I've got to be honest to the composer. Am I right?' she asked, looking hard at me for confirmation. She was so surprisingly girlish. As I sat at the piano she stood with feet together and hands clasped before her, looking directly at me, like a tall, meek, schoolgirl in a lesson. It took some time to adjust to the feeling she gave me that *she* was depending on *me*. I had gone with an open mind, not knowing what to expect, but excited and eager. I could never have expected how modest and self-effacing she would be.

Not until later, reflecting on the session, did I realise that there had never been any disagreement about the tempo of an aria. She always took my tempo, then all I had to do was listen and I knew what she wanted. There was never any doubt about the shape of a phrase, or where it was going. As we approached the climax I could hear exactly her intention and was able to build up the sound and tension underneath, helping her to achieve it. Even as the music relaxed there was complete control of the line. This mutual response was the extent of any rehearsal we ever had. It worked and she was happy.

We fell into a pattern of work. I went at ten in the morning, practising while I waited for Maria to emerge. When she came in at about eleven we drank coffee and chatted. The talk was of commonplace things: the news of the day, the gossip from Covent Garden, whatever came to mind. Often two dogs were with her, miniature poodles, white Pixie and brown Djedda. While she fussed affectionately they showed their devotion by licking her face and nose. I was curious about the name 'Djedda'.

'It's a place in Saudi Arabia. My boy-friend was there on business at the time he gave the dogs to me.' I was learning the domestic language. When she spoke of Onassis Maria used 'boy-friend', never 'ex boy-friend'. Among the servants he was always '*mon Oncle*'. The dog with the less original name, Pixie, could be troublesome. When Maria sang anything above the middle range of the voice, Pixie would point her little chin into the air and sing along in a sustained wail. This became a party game. It worked every time. But when Maria could no longer find an excuse to delay our work Ferruccio and one of the two maids would come and take the dogs away, Maria stroking them and making reassuring noises like a mother sending her two children off with a nanny.

Sometimes she would talk about old times and past experiences. I gave her time, for her reminiscences were certainly fascinating, before seizing an opportune moment to get her to the piano. Once there, however, her reluctance to sing quickly disappeared and for an hour or so we were deep into the music.

A second session usually started at about six o'clock in the evening and was open-ended. If I stayed to dinner we would return to the music room for coffee. 'Shall we listen to some music?' Music meant Callas. Nearly always she played pirate recordings or tapes made by friends of a live performance. She listened with intense concentration, making occasional comments almost to herself, or in a strangely detached, uninvolved way, drew my attention to something that pleased her – 'Don't you think I sang well that night?' – her smile of pleasure, or pride, dissolving into shadows of wistful sadness.

This was an exciting time. Even though, as Maria would say, 'The voice doesn't always obey,' the musical intensity of her singing and the creative phrasing were inspiring. We were enjoying making music together without the distracting presence of other people. I could not imagine a musician's life more fulfilled. I needed to express my appreciation, to show her how I felt. I took some roses. Elena, the Italian maid, brought in a vase, but while Maria was arranging the flowers a thorn pricked her thumb. 'Uh,' she said. 'Just like life – there's nothing without a thorn. Just when you think everything is going OK there's trouble somewheres [*sic*] in the background – somebody waiting to stab you in the back.' The old-fashioned American English sounded quaint but there was a bitterness in the delivery. After the usual procrastination we began a session that lasted into the late evening. I returned to my hotel, tired but elated, eager for our next meeting and more of this exhilarating work.

It was a distraught voice I heard on the other end of the phone next morning: 'There will be no work today.' A tired, empty voice. The previous evening, after I had gone, her friend Gina Bachauer, famous Greek-born pianist, phoned to ask if Maria had heard the news that a few days after Maria's date at the Royal Festival Hall Renata Tebaldi and Franco Corelli were to give a recital of solos and duets in the Albert Hall, blatantly copying the format of Maria's concerts with Di Stefano. Flabbergasted, she could not believe what she heard. Such an unexpected blow from the past could hardly have been more painful had it been physical. Amidst all her misgivings about the tour – the uncertainty of her singing technique, about Di Stefano's true motives, about her own desire, or even need, to go through with it – came this awful, irrelevant revival of an irritation that had bedevilled the years of her singing career, the infamous rivalry between the two great prima donnas of the Fifties and Sixties, Maria Callas and Renata Tebaldi. Even on the phone I could hear how disheartened she was. 'I can't sing today.' I sensed she was waiting for my reaction so, at the risk of being thought presumptuous, I offered to visit her, work or not. I felt she wanted to talk and needed some support. She welcomed my suggestion eagerly.

I found her tense, bleary-eyed, sapped. She had been awake all night, weeping and wrestling to find a solution to this tormenting situation. Most hurtful was the knowledge that Gorlinsky, her own agent, had arranged the Tebaldi concert. Already the newspapers were busy resuscitating the old feud. Once again, she was being used to boost box-office sales, by a man from whom she could surely have expected loyalty. She felt betrayed. 'I'm tired of being used like this,' she cried. 'It happened so often in the past – gossip, vendettas, intrigues, the opera world is rotten. I thought I'd put it all behind me. . . .' She seemed as helpless as a child, needing reassurance and, above all, affection. 'You won't leave me, will you?' she pleaded.

In our few weeks of acquaintance I had always given her the respect due to a much-admired figure. There was warm friendliness but not yet the candour that comes with intimacy. Now I felt swept into her passionate crisis, uncertain of the part I was expected to play. It was then that my natural Scottish reserve broke. I opened my arms and she fell on my shoulder, weeping bitterly. Through her tears she asked what she should do. Cancel everything, tell the press that she would stand aside to allow Madame Tebaldi to have her day, thereby letting her public share her indignation at being used in this way – and promise that she would sing later? Or should she ignore the whole palaver and carry on as though nothing had happened? Gorlinsky, who had promised her every support for the tour, was a target for scorn. 'I'll take another agent,' she said angrily.

I wondered if she could find an agent who would offer her the loyalty she expected and asked, 'Do you know another agent?'

Maria drew herself up out of my arms, stretched her back, grew some feet taller and in a haughty, incredulous tone exclaimed, 'For Callas?!' Her whole appearance had changed. She was no longer the weak, vulnerable little girl whose distress was so deeply touching. Instead, here was my first glimpse of the much reported prima donna whose walk-outs and tantrums had scandalised the avid readers of popular tabloids and gossip magazines, the opera singer who had caught the imagination of the public in a manner unrivalled in her day.

To them she was the embodiment of the mythical opera diva; a difficult, capricious, self-obsessed woman, prone to hysterical outbursts and temperamental tantrums. As she jetted her way around the world the media waited for her at every airport, adding a little spin here or a twist there to anything she might say. I was familiar with this image, of course, but this was my first encounter with the reality, my first experience of 'La Callas'. I trembled.

I stayed with Maria the whole day and into the late evening, unable to do much more than act as a sounding-board and try to avoid another *faux pas*. I knew now I was dealing with two personalities: Maria Kalogeropoulos, a well brought-up, ingenuous girl who respected a strict, old-fashioned moral code and on the other hand the operatic legend known as 'La Callas', a formidable adversary, shrewd (some might say shrewish) and sharp of wit. My task was to perceive which persona might respond. My contributions to the conversation became more considered.

There were frequent long telephone calls to Di Stefano in Italy. He also was angry with Gorlinsky. He promised to arrive in Paris next day. An air of unease pervaded the apartment, the servants moving around silently, more than usually attentive, exaggeratedly caring, as though there had been a death in the family.

Di Stefano, with Devereux Danna, an American friend and one-time secretary, arrived in the early afternoon. Rooms could not be found in any convenient hotel so Maria offered to put them up. Once their accommodation had been settled the serious business of the tour could be discussed. Maria's whole behaviour, her carriage, her tone of voice were much more assured in the presence of Di Stefano. She moved with the confidence of a woman in the calming protection of her spouse. He hardly sat still, but strutted around, exercising his machismo. He telephoned Gorlinsky, threatened to punch his nose and demanded that he come to Paris, hanging up with, 'And bring money!' He turned to me. 'That dirty dog – he only gave me $2000 for the Festival Hall concert.'

I had gone round expecting there might be some singing, but as there was no sign of it I quietly suggested I would leave. 'Oh no, stay, Roberto,' Maria said, with a new tenderness in her voice, suggesting I had been accepted into the family circle.

Di Stefano was scathing about Tebaldi and Corelli, saying they had simply stolen his idea, quickly arranged a tour, got bad notices all over America and now needed this publicity buzz to boost sales in London. He did not believe Gorlinsky's protestations that he thought Maria would not mind, claiming that he could not refuse when another promoter, Denny Dayviss, asked him to come in on the deal. Here was Di Stefano in his angry mood, not averse to a touch of lurid language, and leaving us in no doubt about where he would shove Gorlinsky's cigar. 'Lighted,' he said. I found it hard not to flinch. Maria simply pretended not to hear. Although very distressed and nervous, she was obviously greatly comforted by his presence.

The atmosphere next morning at Georges Mandel was electric. Gorlinsky was coming. He arrived at about one and was told Madame was at lunch. He was asked to wait in the music room. Knowing he was there, Maria, Di Stefano and Dev loitered over the meal for nearly another hour. In the meantime I arrived, hoping we might do some work. Gorlinsky put his cigar into the ashtray and greeted me with a sweaty palm. On the table stood his offerings, two packets of favourite dog biscuits not available in France and, from the duty-free shop, a bottle of brandy. Maria rarely drank brandy but it came in handy when there were visitors and his concern for her brood might be helpful in placating her anger.

When the others joined us, there were 'darlings' all round, everyone putting up a nervous pretence of light-hearted affability. Dev and I went into the salon, leaving them to talk, but there was much coming and going, Di Stefano leaving Maria to talk earnestly with Gorlinsky; then Maria joining us while Di Stefano contended with him. About an hour later Gorlinsky left. Di Stefano was jubilant. 'That'll show him we mean business!' Business was a clear $50,000 for the first London concert. It was to be televised by the BBC and recorded by EMI. The contract was in Maria's name, Di Stefano's share paid by her.

There was a general air of relief and at last we could make some music. Di Stefano produced a song for me. No courtesies such as 'Let's try this', or 'Do you know this?' or any other kind of introductory small talk. He raked through a pile of music while I sat waiting at the keyboard, pulled out something that took his fancy and put it up on the music stand with a dead-pan face. He began to sing, but was musically so erratic I could only assume he was simply concentrating on warming up his voice. This was not the singing I knew from his recordings. As we reached the end, he started up again in the middle of the song so that I had to find him and carry on playing. (This was to become the norm in our work, a game he enjoyed, making it ever more difficult for me. He once handed me his music case and without a word started to sing. He kept going while I searched through the sheets, hoping to catch up with him before the end.) Now in glorious voice and so obviously relishing his vocal freedom, he gave me more songs. I was rather perplexed when, still singing, he started walking around the room, sometimes through the double doors into the salon where Maria and Dev sat talking and occasionally shouting an odd word of encouragement at him. In one song he was so wildly free with the time and rhythm, making such illogical unexpected changes in dynamics and tempo, that I began to despair for the concerts. Ivor had warned me of his highly erratic temperament, but I would not have believed his singing could be so wayward and unmusical. I would have understood what was happening had I known that some minutes earlier, out of my hearing, Maria had been complimentary when expressing her opinion of my sensitivity as an accompanist. Di Stefano had countered with 'Really? Well, we'll see if I can catch him out!' At the time I could not understand why Maria called from the salon, 'Bravo, Roberto, I'm proud of you!'

Di Stefano then discreetly began to encourage Maria to sing as he took up the score of *Don Carlo*. I had practised the piano part of the famous duet, 'Io vengo a domandar', which came off to my satisfaction and they were both in excellent voice. I seldom heard them produce such an exciting performance. In Maria's music room, with only Dev as audience, they sang as though they were on the stage of La Scala. Congratulations all round and coffee was served. I sensed a tacit agreement that fate should not be tempted by taking up another duet. Maria was happy, so therefore were we all around her.

I decided to leave. The run-through of *Don Carlo* had been truly exciting and Di Stefano's behaviour explained, but even as we shook hands and he told me we were gong to 'have fun together', the musician in me could not help wondering what the concerts would be like.

Some time later Edith, Gorlinsky's wife, smiled when she told me of her husband's return home that evening. She was surprised to find him in such high spirits. 'I've got it!' he cried, patting the inside pocket of his jacket. He could afford to be content, even smug. For months Maria had resisted any commitment in business terms and now, for the first time, he had inveigled her into signing a contract for the tour. She would receive $20,000 for each concert after London, $5000 of which she would pass on to her partner Di Stefano – rather more than the £250 she was paid twenty-one years earlier for her first appearance at Covent Garden. Most important for Gorlinsky was that he would have to deal with Di Stefano no longer. He knew which singer the public would come to hear. They would have equal billing but the whole onus of the concerts was on the shoulders of Maria Callas. This was to prove a clever move. He was relieved. For the first time in months his mind was at rest. As Edith poured him a whisky he reached for a fresh Havana and relaxed into his armchair, another strenuous day over.

Next day, in Paris, work began again in earnest. Not that there was anything that ever approached a normal rehearsal. All our time was spent working on Maria's voice. She needed help and encouragement to rebuild her technique. The trouble was that Di Stefano wanted her to sing as he did, but basically she could not understand his method. Their techniques were so different. His was a God-given voice and, though without academic training, he had the instinctive musicality that is an integral part of being a great singer. In his youth he had never needed to struggle with the voice, to work for a technique. The enthusiastic guidance of a wise teacher was all that was necessary. Maria's was also a supreme talent, but hers was an enormous voice which needed long, rigorous training. For five years she had applied herself to the demanding

principles of bel canto, a highly schooled method of voice production in which the singer must conquer all the basic techniques,
scales, arpeggios, trills, etc. as an instrumentalist would. 'A whole
vast language on its own,' Maria called it.

No two singers could have been further apart in their methods
or attitudes to work. She spent her career searching for perfection.
He believed he was born with it.

Some days his coaching would have good results, but not without
much badgering and cajoling and, if he lost his temper, which was
often, some verbal abuse. His persistent call was, *'Aperta, la gola!'*
(open your throat). Though it may explain much about his singing,
it puzzled Maria. She was confused, not understanding what he
meant. 'Look at her,' he said to me, 'the greatest singer in the world
and she doesn't even know how to open her throat!' I wondered how
she could put up with this harassment but she took it all quietly
with patience. She was willing to try anything if it meant regaining
her technique.

There was a limit, however. Things came to a head during a
session which had been unusually long and stressful. Without let-up
Di Stefano was persisting in his demands – 'No, that's not it! *Aperta,
la gola*! Keep your throat open!'

Suddenly Maria could take it no longer. She froze for a second,
then exploded. In a rage she railed at him, spewing out invective
with the voice of a navvy, her face distorted, teeth bared, huge
black eyes flaring like a caged animal, her long fingers with their
blood-red varnished nails curled like the talons of an eagle. The
bright, sunlit room became grey and cold. An elemental force was
at work. Confronted by this demonic power Di Stefano stood trans-
fixed, unable to move, his jaw dropped, mouth open in shock. He
seemed not to be breathing. Neither was I. The hair on the back
of my neck pricked up erect. My hands, in the shape of the chord
I was about to play, trembled over the keyboard. Hardly compre-
hensible, Maria was screaming in a coarse Italian dialect. But the
meaning was clear. Having failed to sense her simmering tension,
Di Stefano had overstepped the unknown limit. Her fighting spirit

was aroused, anger and frustration uncontrollable. If I thought I had seen La Callas on the day of the Tebaldi crisis this was something different. Not simply an indignant prima donna, but an angry wild beast, the celebrated 'Tigress' of the popular press.

Despite its vehemence the tirade did not last long. As the tension in her body eased, Maria hung her head, eyes downcast. The fury was spent. The end of the session seemed to have come, but then, as though nothing had happened, Maria picked up the work from the point where we had stopped. The sun was there again, bright and warm, and we could breathe freely. But all three of us were now carefully polite, deferential, preserving an air of exaggerated mutual respect.

3

IN MILAN WITH THE DI STEFANOS

Twelve days after having packed my suitcase for a week I began to think of London. I could take an early plane, recharge and be back in time for an evening session at Georges Mandel. As I was suggesting this to Maria, Di Stefano cut in with 'Oh, you can't do that. We're all going to Milan this afternoon.' Till that moment I had had no inkling of this move. Putting aside my thoughts of London I packed, checked out of my hotel and returned with my suitcase at the appointed time. Maria was at the door, in a blue denim trouser suit, flat-heeled shoes, her long chestnut hair hanging loosely down her back. She could well have been taken for any ordinary Greek girl – albeit accompanied by her maid Elena, a sensitive Italian girl from Milan, who was carrying some light hand luggage. Soon Ferruccio arrived in the Mercedes and drove the four of us to catch our flight. A Sunday evening and the airport, full of homebound Italians giving free rein to their effervescent emotions, was as colourful and noisy as a fairground, the screaming children, anxious rushing late-comers, joyous meetings, tearful partings contributing to the general clamour. With all the excitement, babble and gesticulation we might have been already in Italy. But all was not well for us. The planes were full and we had no tickets. As we stood, looking at one another, Maria, calm and decisive, said, 'Wait here' and strode off in the direction of Olympic Airways. She returned with a rather nervous and excited official in tow, took her jewel box from Elena and said, 'Let's go.' The airline representative guided us through Customs and led us out across the tarmac to the waiting plane.

All eyes were on us as we entered the cabin, everyone curious to see who would take the places of the four passengers enticed off with the promise of another night in Paris. Di Stefano, in the lead, was the first to be recognised. An excited whisper spreading among the passengers became a gasp of surprise when they spotted Callas. As we were shown to our seats at the back of the cabin some tried to stand up, twisting on half-bent knees in the cramped tourist-class space in an attempt to get a better view. Ignoring the 'Fasten Seat-belts' sign, Di Stefano took his place behind Maria, standing with his hands on the head-rest of her seat, his black eyes glaring defiantly. He was silent but the message was clearly 'keep off'. He might have stood there for the duration of the flight had the stewardess not requested him to sit down and belt up. Maria held her jewel box on her lap for the whole journey. Luckily the pilot was able to take off just in time to save his slot. When the plane touched down in Milan we scrambled like the others to gather our things together and get off.

In Milan, Di Stefano's wife, also called Maria, greeted us at the door of their home in via degli Omenoni, but Di Stefano was not inclined to linger. 'Let's sing,' he said, taking us straight into his studio. He was singing before I could get out of my coat. We took up our work where we had left off in Paris as though we had just had a break for coffee.

The studio was a large room, decorated in grand style, with some important-looking pieces of antique Italian furniture, oil paintings and a tapestry covering nearly all of one wall. A venerable old Steinway grand in one corner had a friendly air about it but, unlike Maria's impeccably maintained piano in Paris, it was badly out of tune. I disturbed a thin layer of dust as I opened the lid. This studio had not been in use for some time.

[25]

Di Stefano was not in best voice when our session began. As he reached for his first climax I crashed down on the dramatic diminished-seventh chord. The poor piano responded with a cacophonous jangle, which was matched by his high note as he charged it like a bull. He pointed to my hands and yelled, 'He played a wrong note!' Immediately Maria said quietly, 'No he didn't. It's your piano, it's out of tune.' Di Stefano's jaw dropped as he stared at her in disbelief. Knowing nothing of how our relationship had developed in Paris, he seemed astonished that she should defend me against him. He walked away from the piano to the far side of the studio, sulking for a while, then left.

Maria looked at me and shrugged her shoulders. 'You see,' she said. 'I told you!' A few days earlier she had hinted, I thought jokingly, that 'The Sicilian' was becoming jealous of our relationship, but being completely innocent I thought no more of it. Our music making drew us close and we were friendly, but nothing else. Maria said, 'He knows that we have our music together and he can't compete in that. It makes him jealous.' I asked her, for the sake of peace, not to side with me if such a situation should arise again. Thus ended our first session in Milan. A car came to take me to my hotel, the Marina Scala adjacent to the famous opera house. A few steps away in the same building as La Scala was the Biffi Scala, the restaurant which sustains the hungry celebrities from next door.

As the days passed I met Mrs Di Stefano again with her two teenage daughters, Floria and Luisa. Her son Pippetto was not around. They were polite but distant, leaving me wondering about the famed Di Stefano hospitality. I could feel a tension which left me uncomfortable. There seemed to be something unhappy in the household. I discovered part of the answer one morning when I walked into the living-room with Di Stefano and found Luisa there. I was startled to see that she was completely bald. 'Now you know,' she said defiantly. That is how I learned of her cancer and the chemotherapy she was undergoing. I felt sick at the thought of such a young and beautiful girl being stricken, but she was a brave patient who took a positive view of her illness. If she had no hair, she would take advantage of the situation. She bought beautiful wigs in different colours and played with them according to her mood – curly blonde one day, she would be a wild redhead the next. Her good looks carried them all well. But her worsening condition was a strain on all the family and the continued presence of a distinguished guest, who expected a lot of attention, did nothing to help. I began to understand the anxiety in the air. Later I discovered another cause. After Aristotle Onassis, the great love of her life, married the widow of the president of the United States of America, Callas had spent more and more time with Di Stefano. Together, he and his wife Maria had thought to help her by breaking the monotony of her existence and her loneliness. She spent two summers with the family, in Milan and at their apartment in San Remo. When she was not with them in Italy Di Stefano was with her in Paris 'working'. Her presence in their lives meant that the Di Stefano family saw less and less of their father and, with Luisa in danger, resentment grew. They hardly spoke to her. It could not have been easy for Maria Di Stefano, but she demonstrated her marital rights by always being with her husband and Maria when they were in the public gaze.

In this atmosphere I was left very much to my own devices. When not rehearsing at the studio I took to the tourist trail, each day visiting at least one of the sights. I clambered up the 500 steps to the marble-paved roof of the Cathedral to find myself in a forest of slender saint-topped spirals and pinnacles stretching up to the heavens, an endless variety of decorated finials, niches with praying priests and nuns, putti, fruits, masks and fantasy creatures, hardly a surface left unadorned. Another day I searched out the monastery refectory of the Santa Maria delle Grazie where the beauty of Leonardo's *Last Supper* shone through the disintegrating plaster on the wall. In the evening I joined the *passegiata* in the *Salotto di Milano* – the Milanese drawing-room – as the Galleria Vittorio Emmanuel is affectionately known, observing the young women, secure in arm-locked groups, as they glanced sideways at the cocky young bloods whose ribald observations were safely out of earshot.

In these days of mass tourism many cities the world over are instantly recognisable by one image. Sydney has the Opera House, London Big Ben, Paris the Eiffel Tower, New York its skyline. Milan's symbol may be its Gothic Cathedral, but the true heart of the city is the Galleria where the Milanese as well as visitors meet, walk, talk, shop, drink aperitifs or coffee or eat ice-cream, or dine at Savini's. Covered by the high-domed wrought-iron and glass roof, like a great conservatory, the arcade makes an ideal spot for the *passegiata* whatever the weather. The rich effect of the Renaissance-style façades is enhanced by a floor of multicoloured marble set in elaborate patterns. Near the central coat of arms of Savoia, within a mosaic medallion of laurel, a rampant bull is portrayed in detail. With its brilliant azure background it was a delight to the eye, although I could not have known that this would be my last opportunity to view the lively animal complete. Since that time a misguided simpleton had the unfortunate idea that luck would be his if he placed the heel of his shoe on a certain sensitive part of the bull's anatomy and swivelled around on it. The idea caught on and over the years the tesserae depicting that part have been ground away, leaving only a circular hole in the exposed fixing cement and an emasculated bull. Sadly, there are no messages of thanks to a pagan god on the nearby wall so there is no way of knowing how much luck the witless destruction has brought.

Good luck was not to be with the architect of the Galleria, Giuseppe Mengoni, though he must have welcomed his good fortune when his model for the 'largest, highest and most ambitious of all shopping arcades' won first prize in the 1861 competition. He worked on the city's tribute to King Victor Emmanuel II for ten years before his luck broke. On the day before the grand opening, while high up on the scaffolding making final checks, the unfortunate man lost his footing and fell to his death on the marble *pavimento* below. Only a heart of marble could not feel for him. His masterpiece was the death of him but he left Milan with a most remarkable public venue that was to become the heart of the city.

I sat at a strategically placed café table drinking coffee and read in the newspapers of a terrible outbreak of food poisoning in Capri. For some a bowl of the local mussels had been fatal. Others were more fortunate, merely desperately ill. Sometimes I met Di Stefano and his wife strolling with Maria. In helping them choose new furniture for their living-room she was enjoying two of her favourite pastimes, shopping and decorating.

'We won't be eating mussels tonight,' said Di Stefano one day. 'We're going to the country. Come round about eight.' About eight-thirty people began to arrive at the studio in via degli Omenoni, all very jolly and creating much noisy chatter and laughter. Time passed without a drink being offered, though this spirited party needed no alcohol to relax a stiff upper lip. I was decidedly hungry when at last, at about 10 p.m., the party of fifteen or so set out in a motorcade of Mercedes, Ferraris and Porsches for the country trattoria. It was charming, an old converted farmhouse with open beams, a log fire, the smell of grilling meats and herbs, and the happy babble of people having a good time. The proprietor and some waiters greeted us at the door. In the line-up an elderly lady held the hand of a curly putto. 'That's her,' she whispered to him as Maria passed. The fervent wonder in the little boy's wide eyes could not have been greater had he seen a vision of the Virgin Mary. Maria walked through the room without comment, her head held high for all to see.

A stairway led to a private room on the first floor, where Di Stefano held court, telling endless stories with great panache, showing off and enjoying the kudos of having brought the star guest.

This was the first time I had eaten with Maria in a public restaurant. She ordered mushrooms as a first course and, in the endearing way of Greek Island hospitality, offered me the first mushroom from her plate. It had to be passed on its fork to me two places away. I wondered what to do, knowing that traditionally I should return the gesture – but I had ordered spaghetti. Thinking how difficult it can be to achieve a tidy forkful of pasta, I hoped in the hubbub of the animated conversations around us she might forget.

But no, when it arrived and I made no move to reciprocate, she called out, 'Come on, Robert, you're not really a mean Scotsman!' I set to. With all eyes on me and without the help of a spoon I spun a mouthful of spaghetti neatly on to the fork and passed it up to Maria to much laughter and a round of applause from the Italians.

During coffee one of the guests produced a number of La Scala posters announcing Callas performances. Space was cleared as Maria took up a pen, congratulating him on his collection, and autographed each one. Everything was bright and friendly until someone pointed out that on all the posters she was billed as Maria *Meneghini* Callas. Maria's mouth tightened and her mood quickly changed. 'Not any longer,' she said. Taking up the pen again, she held it like Tosca's stabbing knife and scored through the name *Meneghini* so vehemently that the paper tore and the white linen table cover underneath was stained by the ink. There was no sign of the besotted wife who told her husband in 1949 that she was 'so proud of being called Meneghini'. For a few moments a cloud passed over the table. We all felt the force of her anger. No one spoke a word. When she had finished she smiled contentedly, while the company attempted to regain the bonhomie of the evening. Fortunately the festivities had run their course and it seemed the right moment to move towards our cars.

Capri was again in the headlines next morning. I was particularly interested since Jim Goldie, a Scottish friend with a talent for surrounding himself not only with the beautiful and the rich but also the interesting and the talented, had a villa there and was expecting me down for one of his famous weekend parties. In five weeks there had been no day which I could call my own, often having to cancel an evening engagement because of late work at the studio. I thought it not too presumptuous to take a weekend off. During a suitable break in our work I mentioned the invitation to join the party on Capri. Di Stefano said, 'Oh, you don't want to go down there and get poisoned.' I hoped he was joking but he brought up the subject so often during the session that I realised he was against my leaving Milan. Maria said nothing. Nor did I.

In the morning, however, she talked about happy times sailing with Onassis on his yacht, the *Christina*, visiting the beautiful ports around the Mediterranean, Capri in particular. They had dined with the reigning queen of the island, Gracie Fields, the much-loved Lancashire lass who had sung her way to stardom on stage and screen. Then, in the sweetest possible voice she said quietly, 'It would be so nice if we could work together over the weekend.' That was it. How could I possibly refuse? Goodbye holiday break! Goodbye weekend party! Goodbye Capri! That she could not practise if I went was enough to keep me in Milan. She needed all the practice she could get. Although Di Stefano's coaching could be helpful, she was not regaining control of her voice as easily as she had hoped. Knowing she lacked impetus he bullied her. Maria Kalogeropoulos might be able to suffer this treatment (perhaps enjoy it?) but Callas resented it. Even so, if his undiplomatic manner sometimes upset her, at least he was making her sing.

As the date of the first concert approached, Maria became increasingly aware that she was not ready to perform in public. She knew her technique was not nearly able to respond to her perfectionist demands. She was in a crucifying dilemma. The opening concert, a sell-out, planned for 22 September in London's Royal Festival Hall was, as she had agreed with Gorlinsky, to be recorded by EMI and televised live by the BBC. There would be fans from all over the world, curious operatic stars, the glitterati, impresarios, the big names of music's administration and music critics from the international press. The hall was again completely sold out for the second concert on 26 November. Maria was frightened. Di Stefano was also worried. He desperately wanted to do this tour. His engagement book was not filling as easily as it had done in the past and now he had the added burden of Luisa's medical expenses. He needed the money. Maria was aware of this, believing that in agreeing to the tour she was helping him, as well as finding a solution to her own lonely existence.

Our sessions became fraught with tensions. If Di Stefano was pleased she'd cry, 'But I can't sing like that, my ears are buzzing.'

'But that's how you used to sing in the old days,' he replied, exasperated.

'Please don't be angry with me, Pippo,' she pleaded.

'OK, let's go again.'

'Again?' in a distraught voice.

'Yes again. It's only by repeating you'll get it.'

'Then let's do it just with the words, please.'

'But it's not a question of the vowels – it's a question of opening your throat. *Aperta, la gola!*' So it went on, from session to session.

When she could no longer take the strain Maria would break down in tears, hiding her face in her hands, her body quaking. To see her convulsed in such childlike sobbing was harrowing. I longed to cradle her in my arms, as I had done in Paris, but in Di Stefano's presence I dared not. Like a fly on the wall, I sat at the piano pretending not to exist, self-conscious and frustrated.

The stress began to affect Maria's health. Trouble with her hiatus hernia became more frequent, her blood pressure was low, but a more worrying problem was her glaucoma. Every two hours she dutifully dropped the medicine into her eyes – 'I could go blind, you know!' The only solution was to remove the stress and that meant postponing the beginning of the tour. The Festival Hall would be cancelled, the itinerary picked up from the Hamburg date and London fitted in later. This meant we had just over a month of extra time. There was a great sense of relief and a new feeling of quiet determination in our work. Maria stopped weeping in the studio.

Life in Milan was not just work and sightseeing. I had friends living there, and sometimes there were visiting musicians. Margaret Price came to sing the soprano solo in several performances of the Brahms *Requiem* with Claudio Abbado at La Scala. At dinner in Savini's, one of Milan's famous gourmet establishments, we had fun reminiscing about younger times and catching up with the news of her development since she had been just a promising young soprano from the Welsh valleys. Not only was she now a world-famous singer, she had also gained that larger shape which some people believe enhances the beauty of a woman's voice. Still a pretty face, she was now a fine figure of a woman.

After dinner we walked arm in arm through the streets, enjoying the brightly illuminated shop windows, past the Cathedral – the golden floodlighting bolstering D. H. Lawrence's description of it as 'a giant hedgehog' – and back towards the busy Galleria. Sensing a chill in the air, Margaret loosened the shawl which she was carrying folded over her arm and threw it around her shoulders. It was a bright piece of homely handiwork, made of small crocheted squares of different coloured wools sewn together into a larger square and completed by a fringe all round – a garment much favoured by caring grandmothers. Amidst Milan's bright shops and elegant window shoppers it did little to enhance Margaret's image as a prima donna. As the cold night air drew in, we hurried along, unaware that we had been observed.

In the morning Di Stefano pounced on me with, 'Who was that woman we saw you with last night?' He teased me as though he had discovered a dark secret, taunting me with male-chauvinistic gibes about Margaret's good looks and cuddlesomeness. When I explained the purpose of her visit, Maria said, 'I hate oratorio. I sang it at the beginning of my career because I had to, then I gave it up. It's a big bore.' Di Stefano was less interested in oratorio than the contours of my companion. Maria said, 'She doesn't have to be as big as that. I took it off.' She smiled when I suggested that not all women have the will-power of a Callas.

Ever since her early days Callas had been overweight. As a child and teenager she was plump, plain and wore thick glasses. She hated to see her reflection in a mirror. It was her sister, Yacinthy, who was considered the beauty of the family. Five years her senior, tall and slender, with chestnut hair and brown eyes, she was the daughter for whom a doting mother made pretty dresses. The second girl had to make do with plain, practical clothes. To the young Mary, as she was called then, it seemed that all the admiration, love and attention were given to her sister. Only when Mary was singing did she receive anything like maternal love. Litza, her mother, was happiest when bidding Mary to sing before friends and neighbours, or better still, encouraging her to take part in a talent competition. It was the beginning of a love–hate relationship with singing and a distrust of her mother's true motives, which was never to be resolved. Resentment grew. Oversensitive, perhaps, Mary withdrew into a world of her own and her solitude sought the comfort of food, eating great quantities to assuage the pain of the rejection and loneliness she felt. Often, in the silence of the night, she would tiptoe to the kitchen to devour some cake or ice-cream before settling down to sleep again. Of course she was pimply and plump. The more she ate the more she hated herself. It was a vicious circle. As she grew older and her singing studies took over her life, no one thought anything about her weight. Sopranos were traditionally fat. But Mary was always aware of her size.

By the time of her marriage to the Italian millionaire industrialist Giovanni Battista Meneghini on 21 April 1949, the struggle with her weight was an ongoing battle. She searched for any answer: massages, heat treatments, special baths, electrolysis and, in the case of her dumpy, ankleless legs she even consulted a surgeon, asking for plastic surgery. Nothing came of that.

By 1952, while acclaiming her achievements as a singer, critics were calling her 'the prima donna with the elephant's legs', or asking, 'Why is she so fat?' This attack on her person, as opposed to her art, hurt Maria deeply. But it coincided with her own growing frustration with a cumbersome body. Her dimensions were restricting her range and possibilities as an actress. Singing and moving on stage in a heavy sweat-inducing costume was not comfortable for an overweight woman. Soon she would start rehearsing a new production of *Medea*. Maria had to make a decision.

Our reasons for embarking on a course of action are seldom simple and sometimes ambiguous. Unwilling to admit our true motives, we hide behind a screen that suits the moment. While the new production of *Medea* might have been the trigger incident which actuated Callas, the public artist, into reducing her weight, the attacks on her personal appearance had offended the private woman's vanity. Having proved her vocal abilities, Maria now turned her attention to her appearance as a woman, creating a new figure. She could always say, half truthfully, that she did it for her art. We are all capable of a little self-deception.

Cherubini's opera based on the story of Medea, a mythological sorceress who takes revenge on her faithless husband by killing their children and burning alive his new wife, was scheduled for the Teatro Communale in Florence on 7 May 1953. The strong-willed but wronged woman in romantic opera was a type Callas found herself increasingly drawn to. In *Norma*, her favourite opera, the role she sang more often than any other, there is the conflict between duty and the heart's desire, ending in self-sacrifice. *Medea* is a tale of irrepressible primeval passions, cruel and bloodthirsty vengeance. No plump soprano, however great as a singer, could ever be dramatically convincing in such a role. Maria knew her fatty jowls would be no help in portraying Medea and make-up no answer. She needed a gaunt jaw-line and a sharp chin to express the cruelty and the tension in the character. She set herself a challenge. A rigorous diet was embarked upon – no pasta, only greens, salads and fat-free meats, usually underdone or raw – and a meticulously charted daily record begun.

At home with Meneghini she enjoyed cooking, spending much of the evening in the kitchen but, with her usual unbending discipline, refused even to taste her handiwork if her diet did not permit it. She had, however, unusual eating habits. While most singers refuse to eat till after a performance, Callas would tuck away a huge underdone fillet steak, or an enormous *bistecca alla Fiorentina* (the American T-bone) with salad and vegetables, before dressing for her role. Anyone who saw her must have wondered how she could sing with all that food restricting the free movement of her diaphragm, the most important muscle for breath control.

Since her bout of jaundice in 1951 her doctor had recommended she drink the juice of carrots and, in view of her low blood pressure, eat plenty of calves' liver. Underdone, he advised. With typical determination Callas thought, why bother to cook it at all? Her maid chopped up the meat into tiny pieces with two knives (she did not want a soup), adding a dressing of olive oil and lemon. Every morning enough fresh carrots to produce a large tumblerful were crushed into juice in the processor. At other times of the day steak tartare was the snack of choice. Also prepared with lemon and oil – no salt – the uncooked minced meat remained a favourite all her life. This was no doubt the source of the tapeworm which she endured for some time. Scandalmongers, always delighting in their fantasies, spread a rumour that she had deliberately taken a tapeworm in her obsessive desire to lose weight. This is nonsense, since the worm would have been digested by the stomach juices as is any other food. In fact, it is as an egg in the infected meat that it reaches the intestine, where it develops into the worm. With treatment the tapeworm is killed, the head being the last part to leave. In a letter from Mexico Maria tells Meneghini how relieved she is that, 'At last the head has come out.' Maria did not suffer alone. Elena, her maid who often ate the same menu, endured the ordeal on two occasions.

By 1953 the change in her appearance was beginning to be noticed and remarked upon in the press. Even her dieting brought her trouble. In an attempt to cash in on her new slim figure one of Italy's pasta manufacturers, Pastificio Pantanella, began an advertising campaign which claimed that during her slimming routine Callas had eaten pasta only from their range. Furious that she was being used by others to make money, none of which she was likely to see, Callas embarked on a court case which lasted nearly four years. She won, but by then the steam had run out of the incident and the public was no longer interested. Like her many other attempts for legal restitution, while the onset was heralded on front pages the result in her favour was relegated to a few lines somewhere on a back page.

The *Medea* in Florence was such a success that Milan demanded Callas for five performances. On 10 December 1953, at La Scala, she triumphed again in the role. While she did not yet have the svelte figure of an Audrey Hepburn, that dream was not far off. Only a few months later the success of her diet was confirmed in an unexpected way. By chance, she met a former colleague, the conductor Carlo Maria Giulini, at the artists' entrance of La Scala. One of the most distinguished of all her collaborators, he had conducted her *Traviata* in Bergamo in October 1951. He remembered the impression she made when she appeared in costume for the first-act dress rehearsal: 'Like a big beautiful ice-cream – all white and round'. Now, eighteen months later, as she was leaving La Scala he saw 'A most elegant lady, very slim, with a marvellous figure come through the artists' entrance'.

As they passed she exclaimed, 'Maestro!' He turned, surprised, to look at her. She said, 'You don't recognise me?'

'I'm sorry, no.'

'But Maestro, I am Maria Callas.' To him she seemed not only a slimmer woman but a different person; a complete transformation. It was a very proud moment for Maria, which she related with great satisfaction. Proof enough that she had successfully overcome yet another of the many challenges in her life.

This time the media were an ally, writing of the miraculous, fairy-tale-like metamorphosis. She became 'photogenic', paparazzi fighting to snap the ultimate glamour photo of the new Maria Callas. Already distinguished as a singer, she was now celebrated as a woman of beauty and her pride in her new appearance gave her a social energy and confidence she had never known.

In 1974 her weight still balanced on a fine wire. 'What shall I wear in Chicago?' We settled on the red gown. 'Oh, then I must diet for the next three days!'

During those weeks in Milan I dutifully kept in close touch with Ivor, reporting to him frequently on our work, telling him of new duets, changes of key or any other detail which might affect his practising. This information interested him little. He questioned me only on Maria's social activities: where she was going, what she was saying, what she was wearing, even what she was eating. I was unaware that he was feeding this information to a contact in a popular London evening newspaper. Meanwhile, a reporter from a rival paper came to Milan in the hope of getting an interview with me – 'Just a few questions about working with Callas,' he said, claiming to be 'an old friend of Giuseppe'. That was a mistake. Since Di Stefano's friends all know him as 'Pippo' I sensed a trick and ducked the interview.

When, eventually, I returned to London Ivor proudly showed me a headline IVOR NEWTON SAYS CALLAS IS READY. 'I don't know how they get their information,' said he, feigning bafflement. Ready or not, the date of the Hamburg concert, the first of the tour, was upon us. This one could not be cancelled. We were all due to meet in the Plaza Hotel in Hamburg on 24 October in preparation for the big night on the 25th.

4

'LA DIVINA' RETURNS

MARIA came from Paris with her maid Elena, Di Stefano from Milan with his wife. They were all to share the penthouse suite. Signora Borghi, lifelong admirer, follower and family friend of Di Stefano, travelled up from Rome. When Ivor and I arrived from London, Gorlinsky had already spent time with Kurt Collien, the agent who was to travel with us during the German part of the tour. We met them while checking in. Collien was very sombre. Without any preamble, Gorlinsky plunged into business. An unexpected problem had arisen. Di Stefano was uncertain about singing the duets without someone to prompt him – as is usual in an opera house. He wanted to send for his favourite *souffleur* from Milan, but when Gorlinsky told him he must cover the expenses himself he changed his mind and declared that I should do it. 'On the concert platform?' I asked. In the opera house the prompter sits in a little box at the front of the stage, unseen by the public but brightly lit for the benefit of the singers. He has the exacting task of indicating each soloist's next musical entry, using the words of the libretto in a stage whisper, that is, a penetrating tone which he projects through the orchestral sound. Many artists rely on him. His is the puzzling and then annoying intrusion that can often be heard in radio broadcasts of opera. His job does not exist on the concert platform. I thought that if Di Stefano had not learned all his words – Maria was not asking for a *souffleur* – we would need to find another way.

In the meantime Ivor and I settled into our rooms and prepared for the rehearsal in Saal I of the brand new Congress-Centrum, an unsympathetic ultra-modern auditorium, clinical and cheerless.

We were on the platform when Maria and Di Stefano came in through the auditorium, calling my name in greeting. Ivor pursed his lips, but his pique eased when Maria greeted him especially warmly as she reached the piano. She addressed him very respect-fully as a child would her grandfather. Even her tone of voice was that of a little girl. ('We have to be very careful with Ivor, you know. He's had two heart attacks,' she had said to me in Paris.) Ivor had seen neither artist for two months since 21 August in Paris and I was anxious that he should have a proper rehearsal with them for the concert next day. Instead, Di Stefano fell into his regular role as coach, interrupting Maria as she sang, so that Ivor seldom had the chance of playing through one item from beginning to end. The session did not last long because Maria wanted an early lunch so that she could return to a shop where something had caught her eye the previous day.

They had, in fact, already been in Hamburg for three days. Gor-linsky had enticed them to come early, ostensibly to give Maria the opportunity to familiarise herself with the acoustic of the new hall, which he had booked for three days, but really to expose her to the media and create publicity. Although the first concert was a sell-out with requests for tickets from all over the world, the bookings for the other German dates were disappointingly slow. It seemed the public was waiting for the critics' verdict on the Hamburg concert. Collien was worried. In the hotel Maria and Di Stefano were questioned by a brigade of reporters and photographers about the tour, and in a television interview Maria warned her public not to expect her to sing as she had twenty years earlier. 'We all get older, we all change,' she said. The exposure did the trick, there was an upturn in the bookings all over the country and Collien began to smile.

At lunch Maria raised her eyebrows when Gorlinsky told her
that Elizabeth Taylor was in town. Maria told us how she and
Richard Burton had been so helpful when she was making the film
of *Medea* with Pasolini, giving her useful tips about camera angles
and other techniques not used in the theatre.

'Shall we invite her to the concert?' asked Gorlinsky.

'Sure, why not?' answered Maria, then, after a telling pause,
'Well, I think not. Why should I let her cash in on my publicity?'

When Maria returned to the hotel suite she found an impressive
white orchid plant awaiting her on the Steinway grand. It was from
Elizabeth Taylor. 'She always sends only white flowers,' Maria said.

A maid came in to collect the dress Maria was planning to wear
for the concert – pale-green body-fitting silk, ankle length with a
belt, covered in chiffon. Long panels touched the floor when the
arms were outstretched. 'It only needs pressing,' she told the maid.
Biki, Maria's dressmaker in Milan, had worked for some time on
Maria's wardrobe for the tour, altering some of her favourite clothes
and producing some other original designs. With so many photographers around Maria wanted a different dress for each concert.

At about lunch-time on the day of the first recital we met in the
hall. The air was electric. Maria feigned calmness but little signs –
twitching fingers on the piano lid, or quick, nervy reactions –
betrayed her apprehension. Di Stefano, still anxious about his
entries in the duets, presented me with his solution. I should very
deliberately mouth the words – not just an occasional prompt but
all the text of his part – so that when he needed help he would
simply look at my moving lips. I was not happy but I could hardly
refuse. The rehearsal did not last long. Maria seemed reluctant to
sing, so Di Stefano took her off shopping. On the strength of his
playing in the rehearsal I suggested to Ivor that he might like to
stay and practise. I felt he needed it, but he pleaded hunger and
proposed we eat lunch, then have a siesta before the concert. Nothing had been said of the items which might possibly be sung, let
alone a running order. The printed programme said the artists
would sing a selection from a detailed list of seven duets, eleven

[41]

soprano arias and fourteen tenor arias. Among them were some we had never looked at, but that left a sizeable number which had been used in one way or another, sung through once and discarded, perhaps, or selected phrases taken as exercises for Maria. I had always kept Ivor informed about the music we were working on, assuming he would practise. Now he seemed quite unconcerned about the momentous event in which he would take part that evening. My duty during the concert was quite clear in my mind. I would look after the music, turn pages while Ivor played, and be ready to take over should he tire and be unable to continue. I would therefore be dressed in white tie and tails. On-stage, for most of the evening, the diva would be supported by three men, of three different generations, in full evening dress.

Later in the afternoon, as Maria sat watching the television, the hotel maid, all smiles, returned with the dress saying, 'We've cleaned and pressed it for you, *Gnädige Frau.*'

Maria jumped up. 'Cleaned! but I only wanted it pressed.' The stuff of the dress had lost its pristine freshness, though it remained a spectacular gown. Crestfallen, Maria told me such things happened so often to her. Eager-to-please people often overstepped her requests.

That evening Maria looked splendid in the gown. But there was fear in her eyes as Di Stefano led her towards the platform. All around her, Ivor and I and the agents felt her tension. Then, as a curtain was pulled aside and she stepped out, an amazing transformation took place. A radiant smile illuminated her face and her superb eyes gleamed as she swept forward to the front of the platform, the chiffon dress flying out behind her. She appeared not to touch the ground. A huge roar erupted from the audience as they jumped to their feet, applauding and calling out 'Maria!' 'Bravo!' 'Diva!' From my seat beside the piano I could feel tremendous waves of warmth and love coming from the auditorium and I felt happy for her. I was amazed by her courage. It was difficult to believe that this was the same woman I knew from the studio sessions. Di Stefano, handsome and buoyant, held her hand high and led her around the stage, jubilantly presenting her to the various sections of the audience – a splendid piece of theatre. It was some time before the concert got going. The programme consisted of duets from *L'Elisir d'Amore* ('Una parola, o Adina'), *Faust* ('O silence! o bonheur!'), *Carmen* ('C'est toi?' C'est moi!'), *I Vespri Siciliani* ('Quale, o prode, al tuo coraggio'), *Cavalleria Rusticana* ('Tu qui, Santuzza?'), a solo by Di Stefano from *Fedora* ('Amor ti vieta') and from Maria *Gianni Schicchi* ('O mio babbino caro'); only five duets and one solo from each singer, the rest of the evening being taken up by applause. Now I knew what she meant when Maria told me not to worry about a short programme. 'The applause will take a lot of time,' she said.

Elizabeth Taylor did after all cash in on Maria's publicity. She and a party of eight arrived late, after the first duet, and took their seats in the front row of the stalls. Cameras flashed and some people applauded. Others showed their displeasure at her late arrival by booing. Whichever way, she had succeeded in making an entrance. At the end of the recital as people were rushing down to the stage to be nearer to Maria, throwing up flowers and stretching to touch her hand, Elizabeth was among the first, offering up a red rose – this time Maria's favourite colour. From one of the many bouquets Maria took a white rose and threw it to the film star.

Later, in Maria's dressing-room they greeted one another like old friends, Maria admiring the enormous diamond which Richard Burton had given Elizabeth Taylor amidst great media publicity, and she cooing over Maria's outsized pearl ear-rings and necklace.

A festive dinner was given in another part of the complex. Maria and Pippo sat together at the large round table, the Gorlinskys, the Colliens, Ivor and I, and a few friends, making up the party. Curiously, Mrs Di Stefano was not placed beside her husband but with the German agent. During the meal I was surprised to see Maria drinking champagne, white and red wine with the rest of us. After dinner Ferruccio's arrival with her poodle Pixie prompted Maria to play her party game. Sitting the dog on my lap she took a chair opposite. I wondered if I should be bouncing the dog like a baby on my knee as Maria, in the tones of a doting mother, told Pixie how clever she was before bursting into an improvised cadenza. Pixie's miniature ears perked up. Had she been a bigger dog her response might have been a howl. As it was, she could only manage a plaintive little whine – ingenuous, but fervent. 'She loves the limelight,' said Maria.

Later, in her suite at the hotel, Maria served whisky to Gorlinsky, more champagne to the others, then dismissed her maid. She was exhausted but happy. As an event the concert had been a triumph, confirming that her public still loved her, and now that the ordeal was over she was relieved and tired. Soon the champagne took its effect. While it would be wrong to say she was drunk, she was certainly tipsy. Staggering a little and speaking incoherently, she bade us good-night and went into her bedroom. Shortly afterwards, while those who remained were chatting in hushed tones, she reappeared at the door, dressed in a revealing négligé, her eyes glazed over, oblivious of the men present. In a whimpering, childlike voice she asked for help with her hair. Mrs Di Stefano rushed up and steered Maria back into her bedroom. La Divina was tucked up in bed.

Next morning the Berlin newspapers were full of the imminent arrival of Maria Callas. Front-page photographs showed the staff of the Kempinski Hotel rolling out the ceremonial red carpet and in the afternoon cameras flashed again as the manager greeted Maria in great style, his pride and pleasure evident in his smile. It was not to last long. After only one night Pippo persuaded Maria to change hotels.

In 1966, while singing in a season of Franz Lehár's *Das Land Des Lächelns* in the Theater des Westens, he had lived in the Hilton. He liked the staff and they had learned to cope with him. He wanted to return to familiar surroundings. Next day new headlines fanfared: CALLAS LEAVES HOTEL. TOO NOISY SHE SAYS. In the Kempinski Di Stefano's apartment was on the seventh floor and Maria had the Presidential Suite on the eleventh, high above the

Kurfürstendamm, one of Berlin's busiest thoroughfares. Contrary to the newspaper headlines it was Pippo who complained when he opened the double-glazed bedroom window and heard the noise from the traffic below. In the morning he took Maria to view the Presidential Suite at the Hilton and while their luggage – including all the flowers Maria had received – was transferred from the Kempinski they went to the town hall to lunch with the mayor. Only Maria was invited to sign *Das Goldene Buch der Stadt Berlin* (The Golden Book of the City of Berlin). After lunch they returned to the Hilton, where the red carpet last used for the visit of the American astronauts Neil Armstrong and Edwin Eugene 'Buzz' Aldrin had been rolled out and a delighted manager greeted them.

Ivor and I, along with Signora Borghi, were happy to stay on at the Kempinski, enjoying the stylish atmosphere of the traditional 'Grand Hotel'. She gave us her version of how the tour originated. During a concert tour in Japan an agent offered Di Stefano a bonus if he could bring a famous soprano with him next time: $5000 for Moffo, $10,000 for Tebaldi, but $15,000 for Callas. He just happened to be in New York when Callas was giving her much-publicised masterclasses at the Juilliard School of Music, so he sent her a large bunch of roses, with a card which read, *'Felicità, Pippo'*, but no address. Maria tried all the likely hotels without success, then one day met a mutual friend who told her where to find him. When Di Stefano proposed the concert tour she laughed and said, 'Impossible.' 'But Pippo is a very persuasive man,' added Signora Borghi.

Ivor and I were often together now and I was finding him a most congenial and entertaining companion. An idea that started as a joke – that he would die of a heart attack while playing for Callas – had now developed spectacularly in his imagination. More than once he gave me instructions: should he collapse as Maria was approaching her highest note I would quickly push his limp body off the piano stool and continue the accompaniment without interruption. Having performed with all the most distinguished singers of his lifetime, Ivor would leave this stage playing for the greatest.

[45]

What a sensational exit! He need not care that in this incident was the making of one more Callas scandal. Unaware of the drama behind her and being so involved, she would carry on her performance, leaving herself open to yet another Callas-swiping headline: 'Callas Ignores Dying Pianist'. Fortunately, Ivor's last ambition of a spectacular *coup de théâtre* was not to be fulfilled.

After a merry lunch together he said to me, 'You have been in the Royal Navy, you must know what a husif is.' I recognised the traditional naval pronunciation and nodded. A 'Housewife' is a sailor's sewing kit. Usually made of denim, it holds needles, threads, spare buttons and scissors in separate compartments and can be rolled up, tied with a bow and stashed away after use. Ivor produced one from his suitcase, asking me if I would sew a button on his dress-suit trousers. He had not asked the chambermaid to help him, he said, because of the embarrassing location of the defect. The suit was probably as old as the century, made in the days when clothes were 'built' for gentlemen, and zip-up flies unheard of. Beautifully tailored, it was still going strong. I just had time to make the repair before collecting the music from my room and leaving with Ivor for the Hilton where a rehearsal had been arranged.

A young assistant manager of the hotel insisted on accompanying us to Maria's suite, making it clear that his real objective was an introduction to the famous prima donna. She was sprawled out on a sofa, wrapped in a well-worn blue-and-white-striped towelling caftan, with Di Stefano and his wife nearby, all three eating fresh pineapple with their fingers and watching television. They had forgotten we were coming. Ivor presented the young man to Maria but inadvertently forgot Pippo, who objected angrily to the supposed snub. Ivor was very worried when we left the apartment. 'Oh dear, I do hope he won't be difficult when we meet again,' he said. As we waited for the lift he added 'Callas can look so remarkably ordinary in a dressing-gown.'

They came down to rehearse about forty-five minutes later. One wall of the room, adjacent to the foyer, consisted solely of glazed doors with curtains drawn to shut out prying eyes. In the course of the rehearsal Di Stefano went over a number of times to see who might be curious and left a few openings in the curtains. Maria was discreetly coaching Ivor in the introduction to 'Suicidio', from Ponchielli's *La Gioconda*, never complaining, but gently making suggestions about tempo or dynamics. She wanted to try the aria in a lower key and sweetly asked me if I could write out the transposition for Ivor. The introduction is a series of chromatic chords difficult enough to read as printed, let alone transpose into another key. Ivor took offence at the implication of incompetence. 'That won't be necessary,' he said, plunging into the chords, misjudging the accidentals and playing so many wrong notes that Di Stefano raised his eyes to the ceiling and swallowed hard.

'Let's do *L'Elisir*,' he said. Once again our rehearsal became a vocal lesson for Maria. She took all his cajoling and protestations without complaint, repeating phrases again and again in an effort to find his way and to please him. After a while, when a little relaxation seemed in order, Ivor asked me to tell Maria of the small task he had given me that afternoon.

Maria laughed and said, 'All that damage! Did you get so excited during the concert?'

Ivor replied, 'In all my career no other soprano has done that for me.'

Maria quickly retorted, 'You mean it has only been the tenors?'

Ivor corrected himself with 'No other artist'. Maria told Di Stefano, who again had been fiddling with the curtains, stirring up interest in any passing hotel guests. Always needing the last word he said, 'At the next concert we must look under the piano and see exactly what it is he uses to put the pedals down.' Much laughter, Maria tittering like a naughty schoolgirl.

A small crowd with cameras and autograph books had gathered outside the room, among them the sad, deluded man who had been bothering Maria since she arrived in Berlin. He fantasised that she would take part in a ceremony in which he, representing the citizens of Berlin, would award Maria a carved wooden statuette of a bear, symbol of the city. Each time he appeared he was accompanied by a professional photographer who was to record the various stages of the presentation. Knowing the media's even wilder abilities in the realms of make-believe, Maria decided this was one set of pictures she did not need. She asked us to stay close. Like arresting officers, with Ivor in the rear, we frog-marched her through the lobby, Di Stefano holding one arm and I the other, almost lifting her off her feet as though we were supporting a drunk. As soon as Maria was secure in her apartment Ivor and I left to visit an English pub before dining out.

Fibreglass medieval beams establishing 'Ye Olde Englishe' décor were festooned with Union Jacks and photos of Queen Elizabeth II and Sir Winston Churchill. This was 1973, in the centre of Berlin so, not surprisingly, the customers, like the beer, were mostly British. Ivor was soon chatting with a group of young short-haired men who were dressed identically in casual shirts and jeans. They could not have been anything but soldiers, squaddies out of one uniform into another, thirsty for a flavour of home. Soon they were curious about this diverting elderly gentleman with the upper-class English accent. 'What are you doing here?' asked one.

'Shall I say?' Ivor asked me, longing to tell them of his glamorous assignment.

'Wow!' said one of the boys. 'You mean that opera bint?' His epithet for 'girl' I knew to be smart slang at the time. The other rookies 'Ooh-ed' and 'Ah-ed'. They were too young ever to have seen Callas on the stage, in the unlikely event of them being interested, but they knew her as a household name – barrack-room name now – and were impressed enough to offer us a drink. We made our excuses and left to dine in a typical Berliner *Gaststätte*.

As usual I settled the *Rechnung*, the bill. 'I'm very mean,' said Ivor, 'but not dishonest, so you must tell me at the end of the day how much I owe you.' I told him that when Di Stefano had offered to repay me some small amounts I had laid out on his behalf I had suggested we wait until the sum was worth bothering about. 'That's a mistake,' Ivor said. 'If they ever offer you money *take it!*' Other-

[48]

wise he was very entertaining, telling stories of the failings and foibles of duchesses and donnas with a verve and detail remarkable for an eighty-two-year-old. If Tetrazzini got a bad notice she would say, 'Oh, they must have sent the football reporter.' A nervous tenor said he would like an aria transposed down a bit. When Ivor asked how much he replied, 'Oh, just put it into the minor.' Some neighbours came to dine when Ivor was a house guest of Noël Coward in his chalet high above Montreux on Lake Geneva. Introducing him, Coward said, 'This is Ivor Newton, the man who has soothed the savage breasts of many sopranos over the century.'

'They are all the same you know,' Ivor said to me. 'Tenors or sopranos, male or female, they think of only one thing – themselves.' We laughed a lot together and I found him most companionable. I had grown fond of him.

About 11 p.m. we returned to the Kempinski to find Gorlinsky and Collien drinking in the lounge with their wives. They invited us to join them, but Ivor said he was tired and ready for bed, so after a few moments we left. Gorlinsky, however, had indicated quietly to me that I should come down again after Ivor had retired. Very soon after I had returned, as if on cue, Collien and the two wives excused themselves and I was left alone drinking brandy with Gorlinsky. He asked me to draw my chair nearer and immediately began to talk of Ivor. He told of their long association and how he would not like to do anything to hurt him. Did I know how Ivor felt about the remaining concerts in Germany? I told him that although he had originally said he was only interested in playing Hamburg (the first concert of the tour) and London, now that he had the bit between his teeth he seemed quite prepared to play them all: Berlin, Düsseldorf, Munich, Frankfurt, Mannheim, Stuttgart, and also Madrid, Paris and Amsterdam, should they be confirmed.

Gorlinsky went on to talk of the terrific costs involved in the tour, especially the extra expense of taking two pianists so, thinking my uniquely interesting experience had come to an end, I asked if he would like me to return to London. To my surprise he answered,

'No, not you, Ivor.' Maria had noticed his failings during the Hamburg concert and mentioned her misgivings to Gorlinsky. Now he had the difficult task of keeping her happy without offending Ivor. As Ivor had introduced me to this company I felt my loyalties were to him. I told Gorlinsky I had been encouraging him to practise. Gorlinsky went on to talk of the world-wide tour which would include twenty concerts in the USA, followed by New Zealand, Australia, Japan, etc. and for the first time actually asked me to do it. 'The artists are happy with you and your work,' he said. 'And that's good enough for me – maybe Ivor will spare me the job of firing him.'

In Maria's suite next day Ivor and I discussed with her and Di Stefano the reviews of the Hamburg concert. They were not good. In varying degrees of kindness the critics wrote of her glorious days as the greatest luminary in opera, when the power, beauty, variety and suppleness of her voice left no one unmoved. They heard now only a shadow of that voice. Though the lower register was still rich and could occasionally thrill with an echo of the old sound, the top was thin and monochrome, and easily overpowered by Di Stefano's loud singing. But all wrote of her beauty and the charismatic personality which transformed a less than satisfying musical evening into a glittering, festive occasion.

One writer, enumerating the number of concerts in the tour, doubted she would ever make it to the end, while another suggested her voice would become stronger with the run. That optimistic remark was exactly what Maria wanted to hear. 'I need to sing before my public to improve. My audiences love me and will help me,' she said.

It is true that the greatest strides in performance can only be taken before an audience. In the studio the artist may study and practise unencumbered by the presence of others, but on stage the added factor of nervous tension can be destructive. Maria believed she needed, and never doubted she would receive, the indulgence and support of her audience. Few artists would dare – or have the courage – to expose themselves in such a way. 'I don't read the critics,' she said, 'because I don't want to suffer pain. I know my failings before they do.' She may not have read all the reviews but her household did and it was through this filter that she learned what was being written about her. Ferruccio and Elena were instructed to cut out the most hurtful lines. But what she knew of the reviews had struck home. Maria was pensive, while Pippo tried to cheer her up with, 'If 3000 people received us the way they did why should we worry about the odd twenty?'

In the foyer, as we were leaving the Hilton, Ivor said that he himself had reached an age when the reviews were no longer of any interest to him. He asked me if I thought his playing was all right, or if he made too many mistakes; and then, if I minded not playing any of the concerts. I took the opportunity to hint discreetly that the second London concert could be very important for me. He stopped in his tracks: 'You mustn't be too ambitious, dear boy, you mustn't be too ambitious.' Some time passed before *die gute Laune* (the good mood) was restored. While I was buying a newspaper he disappeared. I found him in the hairdresser's shop paying for a small item which he gave to me as we left, saying, 'Here is a little present for you.' Inside the brown-paper bag was a flannel face-cloth. My consolation prize.

The Berlin Philharmonie is an intriguing example of modern concert hall design. Empty of an audience, the first impression is of an agreeable confusion of modern shapes in natural wood finishes. With its series of interlocking terraces surrounding the platform and variously shaped acoustic panels hanging like gay flying kites from the ceiling, the hall seems to be waiting for something spectacular to happen. It did that evening when Maria and Di Stefano reached the platform. The audience shot out of their seats and roared. Completely surrounded by cheering spectators as in a Roman colosseum, Di Stefano led a glowing Callas around the arena-like stage presenting her to all sections like a victorious gladiator. I had plenty of time to arrange the music on the piano and, unencumbered by the nerves of performance, sit comfortably and enjoy the spectacle. After the triumphant parade I watched how Maria controlled the audience, acknowledging the applause with a resplendent smile but standing almost motionless, then, with only a trace of a wave, inflaming the fans into near hysteria. The programme they sang was similar to Hamburg: the *Vespri* duet omitted and two others added, *La Forza del Destino* ('Ah, per sempre') and *Don Carlo* ('Io vengo a domandar'); still only one solo from Maria – 'O mio babbino caro' sung as an encore. As in Hamburg, I mouthed all the words while Di Stefano sang, feeling rather foolish and hoping not to be noticed.

During dinner after the concert Ivor reminded Maria of the time in 1961 when she sang in a concert at St James's Palace. Sir Malcolm Sargent accompanied her while Ivor turned pages for him.

IVOR   Did you like his accompanying?
MARIA   No, it was terrible.
IVOR   Yes, I remember you saying, 'Oh I do miss my orchestra.'
MARIA   But I wasn't surprised. I haven't come across a conductor yet who could accompany well on the piano.

The day after the Berlin concert we moved on to Düsseldorf where we had two days before the performance in the Rheinhalle. A wide-eyed Mrs Collien rushed to meet me as I arrived in the hotel asking if it were true that Callas was having an affair with Di Stefano. I shrugged my shoulders, leaving the interpretation to her. 'But . . .' said her husband, his expression shifting from confusion to shock, 'did you know that Di Stefano entertained a young lady in his bedroom in the Hilton?'

Again I shrugged off the question, without telling them that on the day of Di Stefano's rendezvous I had taken tea with Maria who let me know that she was already aware of it. 'I can't compete with twenty-year-olds,' she had said, and sighed.

Collien had more news for me. As I had feared, many of the audience in Berlin had noticed my moving lips, one critic even thinking it worthy of a mention. '*Der Umblätterer sang mit* (the page-turner sang along),' he wrote. I did not know whether to laugh or groan.

Maria carried Djedda in her arms as we made for an Italian restaurant where we were guests of a local Italian singing teacher. As usual, Di Stefano took the limelight and soon had us laughing at his clowning and ribald tales. 'You ought to tell some stories at the end of the concert and save us having to sing encores,' Maria said, shifting Djedda on her knee.

He waved a finger at her. 'That may come yet,' he quipped. During the lunch a young girl arrived with a bouquet of flowers which Maria received graciously. Our host then produced a large album of signed photos of famous singers, pictures of Callas and Di Stefano already pasted in, waiting to be signed. They flicked through the pages reading out the names, Toti dal Monte, Melba, Tetrazzini, etc., then Di Stefano passed it to Ivor saying, 'Here you are, they're all your pupils.' With complete disregard for table manners Djedda, on Maria's lap, silently broke wind, bringing another typical reaction from Di Stefano. 'She's an old dog, you see. The skin dries up and creases around the eyes, so the other end gets opened up.' Even with such unlikely material he tried to make yet another joke to amuse Maria, but she just turned her head, whether from distaste at the crudeness of his humour or the niff of Djedda's indiscretion was not clear.

In the car on the return to the hotel Ivor lifted the driver's newspaper saying, 'Oh dear, the newspapers are so dull today, there are no pictures of Callas.'

'Are you pulling my leg?' Maria asked.

'I wouldn't dare pull such beautiful legs,' he answered.

'Beautiful legs? If you think I have beautiful legs you'd better have another look,' she said. Silence from Ivor. Despite the fairytale success of the dieting, which transformed her into a magazine-cover beauty, Maria never succeeded in controlling the shape of her legs. With heavy ankles often as thick as her calves, a frequent duty of one of the maids was to massage Maria's legs.

Kurt Collien was also at the lunch but seldom smiled. He said he was very worried about the bad notices, which had reached even America. He told us Copenhagen, originally pencilled in, had decided against a concert and now Madrid was doubtful. He carried the whole burden of the German tour and it showed on his face, although in the event few of the concerts were less than fully booked.

On the day of the recital in the Rheinhalle we arranged to meet in the foyer at twelve-fifteen to be driven all together for a rehearsal in the hall. Maria and Di Stefano came down arm in arm, greeted us warmly, then announced that they were going shopping. 'See you about three,' he called, while Ferruccio started up the engine of the Mercedes. 'So rude,' said Ivor, as we stood wondering what to do. We went to lunch. At two-thirty we were in the hall, taking the opportunity to try out the piano before they arrived. They were late but did not sing much. Most of the time was spent on planning the lighting and considering what Maria should wear. The curtains at the back of the stage were a dowdy green colour, old and torn. The manager explained that no money was being spent here because a new hall was being built. In an easy and informal atmosphere Ivor quietly asked Maria if she had made a decision about the programme. She pointed to Di Stefano saying, 'Ask the boss,' but Ivor, fearing the 'boss's' unpredictable and explosive nature, did not dare.

The air was charged with tension that evening when Maria and Di Stefano got to the hall. Something had obviously upset them and I wondered if the arrival of Mrs Di Stefano could be part of it. Even though it was nearly 8 p.m. they sang through all of the *L'Elisir* duet in the dressing-room, while Collien, nervous about the time, fidgeted and stared pointedly at his watch. Then Maria discovered that the belt of her green dress had been left in the hotel, so Elena was driven back by Ferruccio to collect it. It was already past eight o'clock and the audience were getting impatient so Maria agreed to go on without the belt, only to discover during the duet that she had left her ruby and diamond ring, a present from Onassis, on her hotel dressing-table. I wondered what drama had so distracted her before she left the hotel.

The initial reception was tremendous, a very long, warm, enthusiastic welcome – bravos, etc. Maria had cleverly decided to wear an apple-green dress which in the stage lights glowed brilliantly against the dowdy green of the back curtains. Since our visit in the morning the tears had been mended. We left the platform with sighs of relief after the first duet to find Elena there with the belt, but we all felt Maria's much greater anxiety about the ring. Elena was immediately sent back.

I remarked on the reception to Maria. 'Yes, tremendous,' she said. 'I wish they would leave it till the end of the recital.'

Whatever had happened in the hotel that afternoon had left Pippo very disturbed. He was tense and in poor voice, taking too much time in difficult passages and often skipping quickly over high notes. After the second duet he went to change his shirt and took so long the audience began a slow handclap. 'We can't have an interval already,' the distraught Collien cried. 'It's too early.'

'Why don't you play, Robert,' Maria whispered to me during a break. She was worried about Ivor, his mistakes and simplifications. 'I can cope,' she said. 'But poor Pippo might get lost or go astray.' Ivor was not on good form, frequently making mistakes and generally playing as though he was tired. Sometimes he was not even together with the singers. He said later it did not matter very much to him any more. I did not mention the review in a Düsseldorf newspaper which complained of his over-simplifications and lack of support. 'We could have another concert with the notes the pianist left out,' the critic had written.

Di Stefano returned refreshed, and the programme continued with the *Carmen* duet. With a change of shirt there was a noticeable change of voice: he sang much better. After the interval the *Don Carlo* duet was rapturously applauded and Di Stefano surprised us by saying he would sing a solo. Maria then sang 'O mio babbino caro', which delighted the audience. Caught up in the waves of excitement, Di Stefano decided they would sing the *Cavalleria* duet, which got a wonderful reception, but much to Collien's dismay he made a cutting gesture with his hands as he left the platform saying, '*Basta.*' '*Mein Gott,*' Collien said, his teutonic discipline offended.

'No concert can be this short.' The vociferous audience wanted more, however, and after ten minutes of applause and 'getting his breath' Di Stefano announced the *Forza* duet. The evening was another great personal success for Maria.

Afterwards at the hotel fans filled the foyer, making it difficult for us to get to the lift and to our rooms to change before dinner in the hotel restaurant. When we came back I found poor Collien pacing up and down, asking why they should take so long and worried that we would be too late for last orders at eleven. Our table was decorated with some operatic symbols, a Madam Butterfly doll and a 'musical' cake with two piano keyboards and a few bars of the *Faust* duet. That morning the press officer had taken me to the kitchen where I spent forty-five minutes with the chef, showing him on paper how to write the music, then left him to translate it into marzipan and sugar icing. He produced an impressive *chef-d'oeuvre*, but it was only just noticed and barely mentioned.

A particularly delicious meal, underdone steak for Maria as usual, was served while Di Stefano entertained us. 'In three years' time when this tour is finished I'll be drawing the out-of-work pension,' he joked.

Of all our destinations in Germany, Munich was the city I most looked forward to visiting. I was delighted to learn that we would be staying at the splendid Vierjahreszeiten, a luxury hotel well out of reach in my days in Munich as an academic exchange student. I was one of a polyglot group from lands as diverse as Greece, Argentina, Finland, Italy, Scotland and of course the USA, all thrilled to be studying in this centre of culture with its great history and love of the arts. After the war, when two-thirds of the city had been devastated by bombs from enemy aeroplanes, the theatres and opera houses were rebuilt first, with the approval of the community, before the start of work on domestic housing. We all contrived to live in or near Schwabing, the bohemian quarter north of the university and the Hochschule für Musik, where we could eat cheaply in picturesque old *Gaststätte* and enjoy the avant-garde theatre and music, as well as jazz clubs and cabarets.

Work was not entirely forgotten, though, and it was in Munich that I had the good fortune to meet Claudio Arrau, the famous Chilean-born concert pianist. Over a period of months, when he often returned there to visit his wife in hospital, he gave some lucky pianists a few lessons, in a group or alone. He did not touch the keyboard while teaching, instead, when necessary, illustrating a relevant technical point with his fingers on his knee. Famous for never producing a harsh noise on the piano, he obliged his students to find their own individual sound. As his recordings testify he had a great love and understanding of bel canto, his beauty of tone and the creative imagination in his ornaments exactly what composers like Bellini and Donizetti require of their singers. A pupil with a formidable but steely technique played a Chopin nocturne as though performing on a typewriter. He let her finish, then asked her if she knew a soprano called Maria Callas. Puzzled by this unexpected question the girl replied, 'Yes, of course.'

'Find a record of her singing a Bellini aria,' Arrau said. 'Listen to it carefully, then you will know how to play Chopin.' We moved on to something else.

When we arrived in Munich we found a 'British Week' in full swing. Princess Margaret had come to add royal patronage and glamour to the event, staying in the Presidential Suite at the Vierjahreszeiten. A second suite there was occupied by the Dalai Lama and his entourage. Maria was not happy to play second – and certainly not third – fiddle and take only separate rooms. Collien flew an assistant from Hamburg to find suitable accommodation for our prima donna. He chose the Presidential Suite at the Hilton, a high-class, modern, sharp-clean hotel with nothing of the charm of the Vierjahreszeiten. My student dreams of luxurious living evaporated. The press officer at the Hilton busied himself and the newspapers headlined CALLAS CHANGES HOTELS AGAIN. They reported also that she had demanded all the electric light bulbs be changed, making it sound like the empty whim of a capricious

[57]

prima donna when it was simply a practical solution for a myopic suffering from glaucoma. Sometimes she needed bright lights around her.

Meanwhile Collien had arranged a press conference. Maria was very defensive when a reporter asked her reaction to the negative remarks of the music critics. To my dismay, I heard her repeat, 'If 3000 people receive me the way they have been doing why should I worry about the odd twenty.' Di Stefano might have spoken the words himself, her delivery and intonation parroting the remark he made in Berlin. How many times she had heard it since then could not be known. He was doing all he could to protect her and keep her happy, rarely leaving her alone. In real life and on-stage she obediently left every decision to him. I began to wonder what would happen when the break in the tour came in December and January, and Maria had time to reconsider the whole project.

The Hilton was taking an active part in the British Week festivities, Union Jacks fluttering outside and decorating the foyer inside. By the front entrance stood a Beefeater, the traditional Yeoman Warder, guard of the Tower of London. In fact, he was a young trainee hotel manager from the East End of London dressed in a rented costume and brought over for the occasion, but he added a touch of colour in a city that loves carnivals.

We were to discover more of the British theme. During dinner on our first evening we were surprised to hear the sound of bagpipes approaching the dining-room. A piper in full Highland regalia appeared at the door and proceeded to parade around the tables. The sound of bagpipes, so romantic in the open Scottish hills, can often be an ear-shattering experience when brought inside, as any Burns Night celebrant may know, but these pipes were unusually sweet and sonorous, delighting us and the other diners around us.

As we were leaving the dining-room the piper approached, asking me if the lady was really Maria Callas. 'You see,' he said, in a broad Scottish accent, 'when she sang Tosca at Covent Garden I was one of the two guardsmen who caught her when she jumped from the parapet. Could I not meet her?' We agreed he would come to the table the following evening at the end of our meal. Maria was delighted by the coincidence and next evening the two chatted for some time. He told her how he had been warned to be especially alert because of the voluminous cloak she wore. 'Yes,' she said, 'I always had the wardrobe use a lot of fabric in the cloak. I jumped high and it made a more impressive effect.' Chuffed by the encounter and her friendly reception, the soldier picked up his pipes and we watched the swing of his kilt as he swaggered off.

'It's funny, Robert,' said Maria, turning to me, 'that you're a Scotsman, yet you're not at all mean with your money.' I told her that though thrift and self-sufficiency may be known traits, the Scots are also famed for their warm hospitality and friendliness. Meanness is global, I pointed out. 'I know you're from Glasgow,' she said, 'but it's Edinburgh I've been to. That's where they tried to pull a fast one on me.'

'The Scots?' I asked.

'No,' she replied. 'La Scala . . .'

Early in 1957 Callas looked at her heavily booked diary and found there was only one period when she could take a holiday and enjoy some swimming in the sea – a week at the beginning of August. She deserved a break after a long unbroken period of recordings and performances in international opera houses. The travelling and intense work were beginning to affect her health. An invitation came, however, which she found difficult to refuse – to give a concert in the Herodes Atticus Theatre during the Athens Festival. She told Meneghini she would sing without a fee, but instead he employed his standard technique when impresarios asked for Callas. Whatever fee they might offer he would reply, 'That's out of the question.' The Athenian administration was startled but could only agree when he demanded a sum equal to the largest fee she received in the USA. When the time came to travel to Athens, Callas was tired and unwell. Despite the advice of her doctor, who told her she was exhausted and needed a rest, she felt she could not disappoint her compatriots. But when she arrived in Athens, instead of being honoured and fêted as she might have expected, she found herself in the eye of a political maelstrom, the opposition accusing Karamanlis's government of squandering much-needed public money on the extravagant expenses and fees of a ruthlessly greedy singer. The hot polluted air of Athens in summer did little to alleviate the flagging state of her health. Callas simply lacked the energy to sing and to the fury of the Athenians cancelled the first concert. She was attacked and vilified from all quarters. As usual, Meneghini tried to comfort her, but when she made her entrance on to the stage of the ancient theatre some evenings later, what she needed more than anything else was courage. If she had dreamed of acclaim on her return to Greece she found only polite applause from a resentful audience. Enough to break the will of an ordinary artist, Callas saw in their attitude the stuff of a battle – another challenge. As the concert progressed each aria was received with longer and louder applause until at the end the audience roared their approval and the final piece had to be encored. She had proved her indomitable spirit and won them over – a glorious victory.

The stress took its toll, though. Her doctor in Milan ordered complete rest. 'What about the Edinburgh Festival? They're expecting me,' she objected. The doctor explained she had the symptoms of severe nervous exhaustion caused by overwork and fatigue, and advised thirty days of complete rest from work and society. A certificate was sent to the administrator of La Scala, who answered that the guarantee of Callas's name was the basis of his contract with Robert Ponsonby, Director of the Edinburgh Festival. Rather than cancel and have to face another 'scandal' as in Athens, Maria departed for Edinburgh. She had signed a contract for four performances of La Sonnambula and felt she must fulfil her commitment. But Ponsonby's contract with La Scala was for five performances of La Sonnambula with Callas, and he used her name in all his publicity and ticket sales. La Scala did not tell him that she had signed for only four performances, nor of her stipulation that she would not sing a fifth.

Maria arrived in Edinburgh to find yet another conflict brewing.

Ponsonby was astonished when she showed him her contract for only four performances. He remonstrated with Luigi Oldani, the La Scala administrator who was travelling with the company. Oldani was disgruntled that Callas would not give way to what he considered a *fait accompli*, while she was furious at being used in such a devious way. He begged her to save the face of La Scala. Phone calls were made to Antonio Ghiringhelli, General Manager of La Scala in Milan, Oldani asking for help in persuading Maria to sing, and Maria demanding that he exonerate her by clarifying the situation to the press. He said he would look into the matter but took no action. Maria was adamant. She had fulfilled her part of the contract and was preparing to leave Edinburgh. A desperate Oldani managed to persuade her to announce to the press that her departure was due to bad health, thus saving the face of La Scala and the Edinburgh Festival Administration, but at the same time exposing herself to attacks from a press only too willing to discount the truth for the sake of an eye-catching headline. No one remarked on the curious fact that the soprano who took over the fifth performance of *La Sonnambula* was no ordinary understudy. In case their ruse would fail, La Scala had another soprano of calibre up their sleeve. Renata Scotto sang. 'Maria Callas walks out on the Edinburgh Festival,' the press wrote. 'I didn't walk out,' Maria said to me. 'I had other things to do.'

The Edinburgh scandal was exacerbated out of all proportion when the press learned what those 'other things' were. From Edinburgh Maria, with her husband, flew directly to Venice where she was an honoured guest at a grand party in the Danielli Hotel organised by the American columnist and international society gossip Elsa Maxwell. Maria was photographed at the party looking beautiful and happy – and *healthy*. Too ill to sing but not to dance into the early hours, Callas was harshly condemned by an incensed international press. Elsa Maxwell did little to ease the situation when in a moment of vainglory she boasted to the press that Callas had cancelled a performance in Edinburgh in order to attend her party. Ghiringhelli never did keep his promise to admit the truth of the part played by La Scala in the Edinburgh hullabaloo.

In Venice Maria took the opportunity of having a holiday at last. After the party the Meneghinis stayed on for four more days, continuing to socialise with Elsa Maxwell and her guests: titled aristocrats, international playboys, society celebrities, famous musicians, stars of stage and screen, and some multimillionaires. Among them was Aristotle Socrates Onassis. He showed the Meneghinis around his luxurious yacht anchored at the mouth of the Grand Canal. A 2200-ton converted frigate, the *Christina* was his pride and joy. He had personally supervised the refitting of the ship down to the smallest detail, causing many headaches in the German shipyard where the work was carried out. No expense was spared in his effort to impress. Flaunting his wealth, he had the public rooms designed with lavish use of gilding, marble and semi-precious stones, and furnished with antiques, valuable *objets d'art* and oil paintings, a large *Madonna and Angel* by El Greco prominent among them. In accord with the overall Greek theme each cabin, no less opulently furnished, was given the name of a Greek island. The swimming pool, filled with thermostatically controlled sea water, was designed so that at the touch of a button the bottom, a mosaic of the mythological bull of Minos, could be raised to the level of the deck and become a dance floor. The running of the ship was controlled by the most up-to-date radar equipment and radio-telephone systems. Nothing must go wrong when his floating palace cruised with guests of the eminence Onassis had in mind. For the daughter of a Manhattan pharmacist the vessel must have been an intoxicating sight. The skipper and his officers who were presented to her could not know that they were meeting a future mistress of their ship.

Snow was falling when Ivor and I arrived for a rehearsal at the Munich Deutsches Museum on 6 November 1973, the day of the concert. Maria, in knee length black leather boots, her long newly washed hair hanging loosely down her back, came directly from a shopping spree, showing off two cashmere jumpers Di Stefano had bought for her, one white the other brown – to match her poodles. She was wearing a fashionable black coat, simple in style, beautifully cut and finished, its popularity proved by the number of office girls wearing mass-market copies as they enjoyed their lunch-time stroll. How modest, I thought. Only when she took it off and threw it across the back of a chair did I see the white mink lining.

During the rehearsal she mentioned casually that Gorlinsky was expected at the hotel. 'Yes, I know,' said Ivor, looking pointedly at me. 'The boss will be in the house tonight.'

In the evening Maria, Di Stefano, Ivor and I were driven to the concert hall by Ferruccio, guided by a local taxi because of the complicated new road system. Maria said little during the journey. I could feel she was upset; the tension was tangible. Collien greeted us at the hall, worried and looking perplexed. 'Mrs Di Stefano has arrived again,' he whispered to me. The strained atmosphere lasted backstage throughout the concert.

Maria was wearing a brand-new dress, tight-fitting, floor-length, midnight–blue velvet, broken at the waist so that it looked like a two-piece, with a loose chiffon scarf. While we talked she stood before the full-length mirror playing with the scarf, trying out its possibilities. During the concert she used it differently for each character. As Queen Elizabeth in *Don Carlo* she wore it as a cloak of sovereign authority; as Santuzza, in the *Cavalleria* duet, it became a village girl's neck-scarf; but for 'O mio babbino caro' she left it off altogether, her shoulders pulled in to give the appearance of a girl thirty-five years her junior.

Di Stefano was given a great reception when he came on to sing his first solo, but as the applause died down we heard some insistent booing. He stepped forward to the edge of the stage, cupped a hand around one ear and said in German, 'Please, am I hearing correctly?' When the boos were repeated others in the audience, many of whom had travelled up from Milan, tried to block out the noise by applauding even more loudly. It was a very tense moment and I felt hurt for him. 'Ladies and gentlemen,' he said, 'I shall sing for you later,' bowed and walked off. Ivor and I followed.

[63]

Backstage everyone felt the insult – he must have sensed our support – but we were apprehensive of his next move. He paced up and down for some time while the audience applauded and called for him. 'They did this when I sang *Bohème* here last time,' he exploded. Mrs Di Stefano claimed the claque was engaged by a mysterious rival tenor whom she would name if she discovered him. When he had found enough courage Di Stefano announced 'Lalo!' to me and walked out to a most moving reception. In his performance of 'Vainement, ma bien-aimée' there were one or two moments of technical uncertainty and he forgot his words (only once), but he sang the aria with an elegance and charm that I had rarely heard from him. With admirable bravery he had shown what a great artist he could be. The audience responded with a roar as vociferous as they had given Callas. He beamed. In a curious, unexpected way I felt proud of him. If only he would work as hard as this in every concert, I thought.

Before the concert Ivor was so pale and withdrawn that Collien quietly suggested to me I had better be ready to play, but once at the piano Ivor played better than he had since Hamburg. 'The Boss', I supposed, was worth the effort. Collien, anxious as ever, spent the evening worrying that the programme would not be long enough.

Afterwards the Di Stefanos went out to dine with some of the supporting team from Milan, Maria remained in her suite with Elena, while Ivor and I were glad of an uncomplicated tranquil dinner in my room, relieved to be free from the Latin exuberance of our Mediterranean colleagues. Gorlinsky passed as the trolley was brought to the door, bright-nosed as though he had taken one too many, but refused our invitation to join us. Perhaps he had his own little rendezvous.

Maria and Di Stefano said they would drive to Frankfurt so Collien called off the press at the airport, but when they discovered how long the journey would take they decided to fly. Collien was abject because of all the unnecessary changes he had to make and now the new job of getting them on a suitable plane and rearranging the press conference.

In the VIP lounge, as I regretted the brevity of our sojourn in one of my favourite cities, Di Stefano said, 'I'll be glad to get away from this bloody town.' He saw Munich only as the place where he had been twice booed. We sat around reading papers and magazines. The American scandal of Watergate was hot news, bringing from Di Stefano, 'I feel sorry for Nixon. He's the biggest crook in a nation of crooks.'

Maria drew my attention to some pictures of Aristotle Onassis in a glossy magazine, telling me with a fond smile how well the photographer had caught some of his typical gestures. Lost in memories, she scanned the pictures for some time before closing the journal with a sigh. Onassis's wife, Jackie, was featured in each photograph, but she might not have been there. Maria never mentioned her. Our plane was announced and we made for the boarding gate.

Di Stefano spent the day of the Frankfurt concert in bed with a cold. When I went to collect the music from the apartment he greeted me with, 'They don't even have a thermometer in this bloody hotel!' He and his wife were sharing the suite with Maria. There was a television set in the sitting-room and one in each bedroom, all switched on, though in Maria's bedroom the sound was turned off. Unaware of my presence, she came out dressed only in a bra and a slip. When she saw me she reacted with the nervousness of a girl of sixteen and jumped back again. 'I'll get you the music,' she called with a giggle.

I joined Ivor in his room where he told me that Gorlinsky had been talking to him of the London concert and saying how important it would be for everyone. He asked me to tell him where he might improve his performance. 'Will you coach me?' I suspected Gorlinsky had been more specific about the situation than Ivor cared to tell me. The news from Madrid and Paris was good, both engagements being confirmed, but Ivor had difficulty getting the dates out of Gorlinsky. 'By the way,' he said, 'Madame has suggested we might try "Suicidio" a whole tone down. Don't talk about it – I don't want to have to work out the new key.'

[65]

During the concert Di Stefano seemed nervous. He began the first duet, 'Io vengo' from *Don Carlo*, in good voice but cracked on his final high note, marring the excitement of the climax. We hoped the critics would recognise this as the result of his cold, as no announcement had been made. After the second duet Maria asked me if she should sing 'Suicidio'. 'To give Pippo a rest,' she said. Ivor looked up in alarm. 'In the usual key,' she said, to his obvious relief. 'Do you think it will be all right?' she asked Di Stefano. He grasped her by the hand and took her to the stage, encouraging her all the way. The audience gave her a clamorous reception when they saw her come out alone, realising she would sing a solo. Di Stefano was waiting for her when we came off, but he himself did not appear inclined to sing so there was the usual situation of Ivor and Collien asking me what would be next, no one daring to approach Di Stefano for fear of being rebuffed.

'They can't have an interval yet – it's too soon,' groaned Collien, but when Di Stefano started out for his dressing-room saying *'Basta'*, no one objected.

Meanwhile Gorlinsky was sitting in the wings reading a programme of the Berlin Opera, apparently unconcerned. 'It doesn't matter, they can do what they like, I don't care any longer about this circus,' he said. Seldom had there been so many people backstage during a concert. Collien had his wife and Gorlinsky supporting him, Di Stefano his wife, and Maria had Elena and her ever faithful butler Ferruccio, who hovered around his mistress at a respectful distance, never taking his eyes off her, ready to spring should she glance in his direction. He was pleased to see 'Madame' so happy and smiling, he told me. 'She is so alone and sad in Paris.'

The second half of the programme started with the *Carmen* duet, which went well, Di Stefano having overcome his cold, and from then on the concert really caught fire, the *L'Elisir* duet being given even after their solo encores. By the end of the evening Collien was beaming.

Most of the following afternoon I spent coaching Ivor in the piano parts of a likely programme for London. His responses were instantaneous, proving how he had once been one of the world's most sought-after accompanists.

Di Stefano did not like the hotel in Mannheim, quite accurately describing it as a sanatorium. In the evening they set out to dine in a local Italian restaurant, Pippo at the wheel of Maria's Mercedes Pulman 600, but on the way he changed his mind and drove all the way back to the hotel in Frankfurt where they took the apartment they had left only that morning. They ordered dinner in the room and watched the American Forces Network television programme till 1 a.m. before returning to Mannheim.

Next evening we rehearsed in one of the conference rooms of the hotel. Both singers were in good form. After working on Maria's vocal technique for about an hour Di Stefano took up the score of *Cavalleria Rusticana*, opening it at the soprano's famous aria 'Voi lo sapete'. I thought perhaps it was chosen as an exercise in the way some songs had been used in our Milan sessions, but Maria was very serious about it and coached Ivor in the piano introduction when Di Stefano was not coaching her in the vocal line. At one point he wanted her to change some musical phrasing, but to my amusement she ignored his suggestion and sang it as she felt the music. Her way was much more effective. Working on the aria brought memories, Maria telling us how, in Athens when she was just thirteen and a half years old, she sang Santuzza in a staged production with full orchestra. She had matured very early, she said, then startled me with, 'You see, I had my first menstruation when I was ten.'

Di Stefano was pleased about the aria. 'Now we have three,' he said, giving me a wink. Maria pursed her lips indignantly at his taunting, then asked me to let her have my score so that she could later study the words. Teasing her again Di Stefano said, 'Yes, no sex for you tonight – you only take that score to bed.' Maria shrugged her shoulders as if to say, 'what else?' We left the hall happy and relaxed, Di Stefano saying, 'Tebaldi sang that aria in London,' with a mischievous glint in his eye.

In the morning, when we arrived at the post-war theatre grandly called the Opera House, we found that most of the house staff had turned out to see Maria. A TV crew appeared and started filming for an evening news programme. Ivor tried the piano, while Maria discussed the lighting with a technician and Di Stefano joked with the TV presenter. Maria declined to sing for the cameras but gave a short interview. That was our rehearsal. Di Stefano showed me a bright yellow tin brooch he had found in a joke shop, about four inches in diameter displaying a picture of an ass with the words 'Kiss my' writ large above it. 'They'll get this if they boo tonight,' he said, grinning.

Maria, wearing her glasses, peered out into the auditorium, with its stark modern shapes and fashionable, committee-approved battleship-grey décor. Teasingly I asked if she felt good being in an opera house again. 'This?' she said, taking me seriously. She opened up the palms of her hands, looked around and said, 'Come on, Robert, this isn't a real opera house.' I thought of the glorious red-plush and gilded splendour of La Scala Milan, where she was reigning queen for so many years, and understood how she was thinking. 'When we were young an opera house was like a place of worship,' she said. 'We went in on tiptoe and we spoke in whispers.'

Mannheim was the last of the German concerts. Perhaps that was the reason for the light-hearted atmosphere backstage which complemented the gala atmosphere out front. As usual, Di Stefano gave no hint of a programme. Between each item he paced up and down, fidgeting with his tie, coughing, clearing his throat and breathing deeply, then just as he was about to step out on to the stage he would announce to me the next item. We had learned by this time not to be impatient. During the recital in Hamburg Ivor asked what would be next. 'Oh, leave me alone. Can't you see I'm breathing,' Di Stefano shouted, puffing up his chest and strutting around like a cocky pigeon. After that we never asked. Before his first solo he gave me a conspiratorial glance, turned back the lapel of his tailcoat and flashed his secret weapon, the yellow ass. Meantime, nearby in the wings, an apparently unconcerned Maria sat chatting with Mrs Di Stefano and sipped at the hot apple juice which Elena had prepared and served. The audience applauded for twenty-seven minutes after what Collien called 'an unreasonably short programme' and they were already changed and ready to leave when he persuaded Maria and Di Stefano to return to the stage. Even Ivor said he was amazed at their nonchalance and lack of respect for the audience. I felt it most ungracious of Di Stefano not to announce another duet. 'We need a stage manager,' Ivor commented. 'I will speak to Sander about it.'

During dinner Maria said to Ivor, 'Next time we meet will be in Madrid,' and to me, 'You'd better come to Paris a little earlier, Robert, perhaps we'll start some new duets.' Ivor said later it was a joke that they should take on fresh work when they had not yet conquered the difficulties of the current repertoire.

13 November

Maria to Paris. Di Stefanos to Milan. Colliens to Hamburg. Ivor and I to London.

5

MADRID – SUTHERLAND AT
THE PIANO

ON 14 November 1973, the day of Princess Anne's wedding to Captain Mark Phillips, Ivor asked if he might watch the ceremony on my new colour television set. He did not own one himself, not even a black and white, and colour had just been introduced. We toasted the newly-weds with champagne, Ivor's silk handkerchief wet with tears before the happy couple left the Abbey, then I served lunch.

He had only just left when Gorlinsky phoned. How could he put Ivor off the London concerts? he asked. He had used the excuse of expenses for Madrid, but could not for home ground. Had I any ideas? I suggested a compromise. Ivor would accompany the solo items – the cream of the concert – and I would play for the duets – the more technically difficult piano parts. Not an ideal or usual situation but it could be a solution if Ivor would agree. He told me he was about to phone Ivor.

I was not at home that evening when Ivor telephoned and left a message asking me to call him no matter how late. I found him in a distressed state, his ideas ill-formed, his sentences incomplete. 'I want you to approve a telegram I'm sending to Callas,' he said. He had a royal appointment on the day of the Madrid concert and would ask if he could send me in his place. The Master of the Queen's Music, Sir Arthur Bliss, was ill and could not attend the St Cecilia's Day Concert, which was to be graced by the presence of the Queen. Ivor was to be his deputy. 'Don't be nervous when you play for them,' he said rather disdainfully. 'I shall be sitting beside the Queen!'

The lift at 39 avenue Georges Mandel, a rickety though charming piece of nineteenth-century engineering, had become mechanically unreliable. A new lift, of polished steel, was being installed when I arrived from London. I looked at the lovely rococo box, a whiff of *fin de siècle* Paris with is bevelled-glass panels in the doors and sides adding a light airiness to the fancifully carved mahogany, and wondered what would become of it. As though my thoughts were being read a voice behind me said, 'We're going to keep it.' Maria, with Di Stefano, was just returning from shopping. She took my arm as we walked up the stairs, once again saying how anxious she had been that Ivor's playing might have thrown or confused Pippo. She could cope, she repeated. 'Anyway now it's quite definite that you're coming to the States, Robert, only we don't know yet about London – Ivor's not taking the hints. He sent me a telegram saying he had obligations to the royal family and that's why he can't do Madrid. Hm, just think, to get you I have to thank the Queen of England.'

As we entered the apartment she took me to see her latest acquisition, a pair of early eighteenth-century sandalwood torchères carved in the shape of Chinese figures. They stood at the entrance to the dining-room. 'Smell,' she said, closing her eyes and holding her face close up to the wood, inhaling deeply to relish the *chypre* fragrance that so amazingly survives the passing years.

Di Stefano was already making noises in the music room. I gave him the typewritten 'suggested' programme which Ivor had requested from Gorlinsky but he did not even glance at it as he laid it on the piano. Maria sang half-heartedly through a couple of arias, but having neither the stamina nor the desire to work she suggested we call it a day. Di Stefano agreed and began to talk about how he would entertain his son and daughter who were visiting Paris. A night out on the town was planned. As I was leaving, Maria invited me to stay to lunch after the session the following morning.

The first thing I noticed when we went into the dining-room next day was a large new colour television set, fortunately not switched on. I asked about their night out. 'Oh, we went to Pigalle,' said Di Stefano. 'The kids and I had a wonderful time, but Maria didn't enjoy herself – nobody recognised her.' Maria straightened the napkin on her lap and asked me about Ivor. Again she was concerned about his health and failing abilities. 'He played well enough for me in March at the Festival Hall,' Di Stefano chipped in, eager to justify his choice of pianist for the tour.

While we were drinking coffee Gorlinsky phoned from London to say we were booked into the new Hilton-style Hotel Melia in Madrid. 'Oh, no,' said Maria. 'We don't want those low ceilings and hot air – find us a nice apartment with some style and high ceilings. There are some lovely hotels in Madrid. What about the Ritz or the Plaza?'

Di Stefano shouted at the telephone, 'I told you about this' and to me, 'The louse is trying to save money.'

'He's calling our tour a circus,' Maria said indignantly as she hung up, 'but he's one of them who persuaded me to do it.'

Our flight to Madrid was booked for the next afternoon. In the morning Di Stefano sang some Italian songs with me but was so unsuccessful with his high notes in an aria ('Non piangero piu') he became angry and frustrated, and stormed off. Maria came in to suggest we meet after lunch. Even then he was still having vocal trouble, blaming his 'German' cold, but we ran through the duet from *Lucia*, Maria already wearing her hat for the journey. Gorlinsky's 'programme' had disappeared from the piano and so far the only talk of Madrid was about where we might stay – nothing of the concert.

We arrived at the airport to find only three first-class seats booked. Someone had forgotten Elena, the maid. The ticket clerk made a polite speech of apology and assumed that was an end to it, but Maria said, 'No, we all fly first or not at all.' So we did. I wondered how the airline compensated first-class passengers who were given the push. In Madrid we were met by Gorlinsky with the Spanish agent and his five assistants, and a horde of newspapermen and photographers. We drove to the Ritz.

'Good,' said Maria when she saw her apartment. 'But it's too hot.' Immediately all the heating was turned off. Later in the dining-room a nine-piece orchestra played selections from Viennese operetta as we took our places for dinner. I looked around at the grandeur of the room, high painted ceilings, ornately panelled walls, soft grey-pink touched with gold leaf, enormous floral arrangements on side tables and an army of commis, waiters and head-waiters continuously on the move and appearing to outnumber the diners, dressed in black and white, the shape, location or dominance of either colour denoting clearly the wearer's position in the pecking order. The *maître* wore a carnation. Gorlinsky noticed my glances and asked if I liked the hotel. 'A change from the YMCA?' he teased. I did not respond to his gratuitous taunt. He had reminded me, on the contrary, of how lucky I had been as a student in London, a Scholar at the Royal College of Music and fortunate enough to find lodgings in the extraordinary home of Felix Aprahamian, deputy music critic to *The Sunday Times*.

In the north of London, the house is an unpretentious turn-of-the-century semi-detached, its red-brick façade, bow-window and tiny front garden giving no hint of the treasures within. Books and music are everywhere, floor to ceiling in the rooms, waist-high in the corridors and landings to leave space for original drawings and paintings. Rare books, first editions, manuscripts – some dedicated to Felix – elaborate leather bindings jostling with paperbacks, subjects ranging through the arts, music, architecture, painting, sculpture, Japanese gardening, they overflow on to the table tops and pile up on the floor. As well as two grand pianos, the sitting-room now houses the pipe-organ Felix inherited from André Marchal, the blind organist of Saint Eustache in Paris. Upstairs, recorded music can be heard in two rooms, one with state-of-the-art hi-fi, another with a 1920s EMG gramophone, complete with gigantic horn, which requires a hand-cut fibre needle to play treasured old 78s. Records, discs and tapes vie for space beside a harpsichord and more books. This was an Aladdin's cave to an enquiring mind from 'North Britain'. As a youth in Glasgow, I looked forward all week to the arrival of *The Sunday Times* with Felix Aprahamian's reviews. He wrote with a sensitivity and perception that left the reader feeling he had been present at the concert. He wrote also with courage. House-bound with chicken-pox, Felix listened to the BBC broadcast of Stravinsky's much-awaited new composition for St Mark's in Venice. While all the other critics pussyfooted around in their respect for the venerable composer, Felix spoke out and argued logically how unreasonably difficult and therefore stillborn Stravinsky's first attempt at atonal music was. Years later, many of his colleagues were brave enough to agree with him.

The respect in which Felix is held can be guessed by the signatures that illuminate his visitors' book: William Walton, Victor de Sabata, Francis Poulenc, Eva Turner, Frederic Ashton, Ernest Ansermet, Maggie Teyte, Pierre Bernac, Gina Bachauer, Olivier Messiaen, a kaleidoscopic section of the effectual artistic life of the day. There was often informal music making. On one occasion distinguished players from American and British orchestras gathered in the house to play Schubert's octet solely for the pleasure of a few friends and themselves. On those occasions they would be sustained by the delicious cooking of Felix's mother, Araxie. His father, Avedis, came to England in 1890 to escape the massacre by the Jeunes Turques of the Greeks and Armenians living in Turkey. Some years later Socrates Onassis, a wealthy Greek citizen of Smyrna, suffered also at the hands of the Turks, losing all his property and most of his money. In five days thousands of Greek, Jews and Armenians died in the burning city, what was left of their treasures and property looted by the Turkish soldiers. Socrates and his family were saved from what seemed a hopeless jeopardy by the guile and charm of his only son. At a time when alcohol was unobtainable the artful sixteen-year-old had managed to find some of the precious liquor for his friend, the American vice-consul. His reward was a bottle of raki, which he took immediately to his other friend, a Turkish lieutenant who was so impressed by the boy's capability that he gave him a pass, which freed him from the restraints of the curfew. Established now in the influential role of middleman, the boy was able to secure travel documents for his family and himself. Within a few weeks they were safe in Athens. The resourceful boy's name was Aristotle. That was in 1922, by which time Felix was a precocious eight-year-old attending an English school and enjoying the best of two cuisines.

In Araxie's kitchen my awakening interest in food was nourished by ingredients and recipes unknown in Scotland in my youth, red and green pimentos, garlic, tarama, aubergines, sesame seeds, green and black olives, rosewater, stuffed vine leaves, pilafs of rice, currants and pine-nuts, chicken in egg and lemon sauce, casserole of lamb and quince, all curious combinations to a northerner and, best of all, fresh yoghurt made from a culture bought after an anxious search from a Greek shop in Soho. Left to grow overnight in an airing cupboard, it soon usurped the place of my porridge in the morning. For the delectation of her son and his friends Araxie worked in the kitchen with a diligence and charm that would outshine most of today's television cooks. No trouble was spared, even the making of her own pastry for the walnut-filled and honey-soaked baklava, or the hand beating of the egg-whites for a less cloying delicacy. It was a busy and a happy house.

My reverie was broken by Maria's voice asking to taste the chocolate mousse she had chosen for my dessert. I had eaten out with her often enough to know that before ordering dessert I should confer with her. Chocolate was not in her diet, but she always made sure some fellow diner ordered something containing it so that she could have 'just a taste'.

Gorlinsky told us he had reserved the hall for our use at any time during the next day. Di Stefano was strangely quiet but when Maria said she was looking forward to our rehearsal I suddenly realised that the Madrid concert would be my first public performance with La Callas. After all the months of studio work, travelling, dressing up to turn pages for Ivor, I would actually be playing as she sang.

I was familiar with all the possible music, but I had played it always with the singers in mind, prompting with words and repeating phrases and sections solely for their benefit. I needed space for myself now, an opportunity to polish up my contribution to my own satisfaction. The time had come for me to care about *my* performance. I was looking forward to an indulgent session alone with a Steinway grand.

I arrived at the hall shortly after ten to find the local agent on stage with five assistants. There was no piano. The hall manager came with four minions, each delegating jobs to the next, but no one able to explain the absence of a piano. After an hour the agent declared that there would be none that day and jocularly told me I could have a day of rest – the day before my first Callas concert! I ignored talk of *mañana* and indicated my determination to find a piano. One of the assistants was sent to make a telephone call and came back after twenty minutes saying one would be available after siesta at five o'clock that evening. I had tackled *mañana* but I couldn't beat that bane of visiting northerners, the sacrosanct siesta. Even the Spanish government had failed when, with an eye to international affairs, they tried to line up the Spanish day with the rest of Europe. I returned to the Ritz, hoping I might find even a little upright in a back room somewhere but was again frustrated. In the foyer I happened upon Di Stefano, who asked what was going on. 'I want to rehearse at six,' he said, 'so Gorlinsky had better find a piano.'

At five in the Piano Hagen showroom I woke up the porter who said everything was impossible, until I showed him 100 pesetas. We found a suitable piano. After a while I left for the six o'clock rehearsal in the Banqueting Hall of the Ritz, only to meet Gorlinsky who told me a doctor was with Di Stefano. He had returned unwell from his luncheon appointment. A pathetic old upright with pedals which did not work had been brought to the hall but was so unserviceable that I went back to the showroom and had another set-to with the porter. More pesetas and the promise that I might work until eight-thirty proved a futile pact. By seven-thirty he was already rattling his keys and showing signs of impatience, so that I was forced to give up an hour of much-needed practice. He then insisted on walking me to the main street, though I would have preferred to do some window shopping on the way back to the hotel. Eventually I had to take a taxi to escape him.

There was no sign of the others so I dined alone, hoping the beguiling sweetness of the violins would assuage my frayed nerves. When I returned to my room Maria rang, asking me to come and talk. She was sitting up in bed playing cards with Elena. She was worried about Pippo, she said. The doctor had given him tablets and a spray, but she thought the trouble was deeper. He had been complaining for some days about getting old, saying she had better get another tenor, but she reminded him that in Hamburg he told the newspapers that if one of them should become ill then there could be no concert, so she would stick by that. Gorlinsky had been unsympathetic and did not hide his annoyance from Di Stefano. 'Sander can be so undiplomatic,' Maria said. 'I don't say very much to Pippo when he is like this. You know we are very intimate – but sometimes I just don't talk to him.' She was not really happy about having to sing in Madrid. 'I would rather sing in Barcelona – they're so snooty here. Don't expect much applause, Robert, and goodness knows when the concert will start. It's due to begin at ten-thirty but they never come in time.'

Gorlinsky had talked with her about the programme and suggested Di Stefano sing some of his charming Italian songs. 'I can't sing those little songs – I'm just a lousy opera singer,' she said, feigning alarm when I said her fans would be appalled should they hear her say that. 'Do you think the duets will be all right tomorrow?' she asked me anxiously. As usual, I left the music with her. Although Elena had told me her mistress never looked at it I understood, as a musician, how Maria could feel better having it there on her bedside table.

For the concert Maria wore a gown I had not seen before, cardinal-red chiffon layers with voluminous arms. On a silver chain around her neck hung a large antique Greek Orthodox cross. She looked spectacular. As usual she spent some time before the full-length mirror, adjusting the dress and trying out some movements of her hands and arms. When I remarked on it she gave me a sardonic glance and said, 'Yes, some dress. If only the voice were as good.' She had an unexpected way of talking about her voice as though it were something physically separate from her persona; an intractable, even hostile, entity which she had spent a lifetime struggling to dominate.

The concert in the Palacio Nacional de Congresos y Exposiciones started at about 11 p.m., before a very grand audience headed by the Greek Princess Sophia, who was soon to become the Queen of Spain. As Maria predicted, the applause was not what I had come to expect, but it was polite, even warm. After the frustrations of the previous day and the possibility of Di Stefano being unable to sing I was relieved to find myself walking out on to the stage with them for the opening duet.

It went well, Di Stefano in such good voice that I thought of suggesting he spend the day in bed before each concert. Maria now had three solo arias in her repertoire, 'Suicidio', 'Voi lo sapete', and 'O mio babbino caro'. Free of nervousness, she sang better than in any recital so far, acknowledging me graciously after each item, which seemed to please the audience.

Sophia came to Maria's dressing-room after the concert, cameras flashing all around. Without any formal curtsying or bowing, Maria greeted her warmly and simply as a familiar friend. '*Ti kanete?*', (How are you? an everyday informal greeting in Greece) they both said at the same moment. If there was any hint of protocol in the meeting it was in the picture of a young princess paying homage to a queen.

Denny Dayviss with Carlos Caballé, brother of Montserrat, drove me to the Ritz, where Gorlinsky had invited them to supper in Maria's apartment. She talked of a dinner party in New York when, to her astonishment, she was placed next to Maria Callas. The first thing Callas said was, 'What birth sign are you?'

'Sagittarius,' answered Denny.

'So am I, isn't it hell!' exclaimed the diva. At that time Denny Dayviss was promoting concert performances of rare and neglected operas in London. Joan Sutherland, Montserrat Caballé, José Carreras, Sherrill Milnes and Placido Domingo were among the stars who sang in performances which, although critically acclaimed, were often box-office disasters. Denny was left to foot the bill.

When we arrived at the Ritz I went straight to my room, made a quick call home and, still elated by the excitement of my first Callas concert, began to regret opting out of the party. I was struggling to release my stiff-starched white tie and collar when Maria called asking why I was not with her. I quickly dressed again and joined the group of about a dozen people already in the full swing of the buffet party. Maria made a fuss, kissing me, sitting me down beside her, calling for the waiter and embarrassing me before the others with talk about my playing. After the tensions and frustrations of the past days her compliments were gratifying, though I knew that if I had played better than usual it was due to her inspiring musicianship.

During supper Di Stefano left to telephone his wife and when he returned asked Maria to do the same. He then took to the floor, walking around the room gesticulating and entertaining us with funny tales. He approached me, bowing in mock deference. 'How are you, Mr Newton?' he said. In response I attempted an expression of exaggerated indignation. 'How can you make such a face – only Italians can do that.' I felt like the famous lieder singer, Elena Gerhardt, when after her début an admirer told her she would become the second Lilli Lehmann, she replied, 'I don't want to become the second anybody. I want to be the first Elena Gerhardt.'

[79]

The party began to break up at about 3 a.m., everyone repeating their compliments and congratulations, eager to convince Maria of their loyalty and devotion. Denny Dayviss, the last to leave, spent an irksomely long time at the door being nice to Maria. Maria closed the door behind her, grimaced and, through tight lips, spat out, 'That slimy woman is the one who put Tebaldi on in London.' Di Stefano then came to the door with Maria to say good-night to me, a new warmth in his manner. I apologised for an incident in the concert when, being so busy playing the piano, I had omitted to give him a cue, but he affably insisted on apologising to me for other incidents, saying, 'Never mind, we get paid anyway.'

I met Maria in the foyer next morning as she returned from shopping with Di Stefano. 'I can't tell you what a relief it was to have you play last night,' she said. 'I couldn't say too much in front of that Dayviss woman, or Gorlinsky, in case it should reach Ivor's ears, for I wouldn't want to hurt him, but it was so nice to get through the programme without all those mistakes – and you were so firm and reliable.' I was surprised. Nothing I had read or heard about Maria Callas and her volatile temperament suggested that she could also show a generous spirit to a colleague. It was not to be the only time on the tour that I saw a perceptive concern and thoughtfulness. There was never any false flattery in her compliments. They were straight to the point, honest, musicianly and practical.

I told her something of Denny Dayviss's activities and stressed the laudable part she had played in London opera, but Maria showed no interest. She was still seething at the thought of what she saw now as the Dayviss–Tebaldi concert. She had been devastated by the news and had not forgotten her distress. Anyone connected with that concert was a target for racy invective. Her comments were bitter.

I was resting in my room after lunch when Maria phoned asking if I was ready to go to the Prado. The feeling of a Sunday outing stirred as the quartet (Elena came also) set off on the short walk to the museum, led by Di Stefano who paid the entrance fees and proceeded to guide us around. Whispers echoed through the gallery as Maria was recognised, Di Stefano strutting beside her, she pretending not to notice. We lingered mostly among the Goyas. Maria was taken by a set of gigantic paintings of *The Seasons*, but was just as puzzled as we were by a baffling painting called *The Dog*. In a wild gorge a dog's head shows above a dark mass resembling a river in spate. Although the head is clearly delineated the remainder of the canvas is painted in an abstract manner, the meaning obscure. A sinister picture. Maria shivered. 'Let's move on, it frightens me,' she said. Two cars, already loaded with our suitcases, were waiting outside to drive us to the airport.

6

LONDON

As soon as I returned to London I visited Ivor to give him my report. He showed no interest in the Madrid concert, but instead chattered on and on about his evening with the Queen. I told him we were to rehearse in Maria's apartment at the Savoy on Saturday and he asked me to leave all the music with him. I knew there were two copies of everything but he insisted on having mine also. I wondered why, but could hardly refuse. 'By the way,' he said as I was leaving, 'it must be too terribly boring for you to dress in tails just to turn pages. I think a dark suit would be in order.' That sounded like a command.

We met in the Savoy lobby before going up together to Maria's apartment. There was a party atmosphere, the television going and all the bedroom doors open. I counted four TVs. Maria and Di Stefano were playing cards with Gorlinsky and Cesare Siepi, the baritone with whom Maria had sung during her early years in Italy. He left shortly afterwards but Gorlinsky stayed for the rehearsal. Maria took Ivor through her arias in great detail, before singing even better than she had in Madrid, which promised well for London. While Ivor was busy with Maria, Gorlinsky told me that after London I was to play all the concerts. He said nothing of the two evenings in the Royal Festival Hall leaving me to assume that

Ivor would play both. Later, when we left, Ivor told me again that he did not care about any concerts after London.

During a break in the music making Ivor told us about his evening with the Queen. When she showed interest in his work he had talked to her about the tour. 'It must be difficult to play for Callas,' she said.

'I had to get a special dispensation to be here tonight with you, Ma'am,' he replied.

'Oh, how jolly decent of her, I didn't think she was that sort of woman.' This brought from Maria a story she told more than once, with some pride. To celebrate the centenary of the Royal Opera House in 1958 a star-studded cast was assembled including Joan Sutherland, who had been a member of the cast when Callas made her début in *Norma* at Covent Garden in 1952, and the internationally acclaimed English prima ballerina Margot Fonteyn. The allocation of accommodation backstage was a delicate problem. Dressing-room number one had been the domain of Fonteyn for every performance she had given in the theatre. What to do with Callas? In a brilliant stroke of diplomacy Lord Harewood solved the dilemma. With some furniture shifting and the addition of a dressing-table, a sofa, flowers and some small cosy details, he transformed his own office into a retiring room fit for a prima donna. Callas was delighted with the arrangement.

This accolade, as she saw it, confirmed the high esteem in which she held Lord Harewood. She had met him first in an interval of *La Gioconda* in Verona in 1947, where he was the guest of the mayor. She was immediately impressed by the tall handsome aristocrat, his enthusiasm and his great knowledge of opera. The mayor had earlier tipped her off about his lineage. George Lascelles, descendant of Queen Victoria and a first cousin to the present Queen Elizabeth II, became the seventh Earl of Harewood in 1947. Since early childhood he had shown a passionate interest in opera, an art-form not usually associated with the British royal family. This led him to play an influential role in the history of opera in modern Britain, at varying times becoming a director of the Royal Opera

House, Artistic Director of the Edinburgh Festival and Managing Director of the English National Opera – as well as, in a totally different field, President of the English Football Association from 1963 until 1972. I rarely heard Maria speak of a friend or colleague with such warmth. She saw him as the perfect English Gentleman, charming, kind and understanding, her knight in shining armour. In 1968 when the BBC asked her to talk on television about her life and career she agreed on condition she was interviewed by George Harewood. Her admiration extended even to his accent. When she spoke of him, or with him, her vowels and consonants were delivered in the characteristic pronunciation of the British upper class. This can be heard clearly at the beginning of the programmes she subsequently made for the BBC: a very proper, ladylike Callas. Later in the interview, when she becomes more involved with expressing her thoughts, she falls back into her normal *mélange* of American, Italian and French sounds.

In 1958 Lord Harewood was largely responsible for her engagement to sing at the Covent Garden Gala. It was a splendid evening but despite the presence of the much-loved Margot Fonteyn, the star of the show, in the 'Mad Scene' from *I Puritani*, was undoubtedly Maria Callas, who had to take eight curtain calls.

After the programme the artists were lined up on-stage to be presented by the General Administrator, David Webster, to Queen Elizabeth and Prince Philip. With each one in turn the Queen chatted graciously for a few moments, but when Callas was presented she simply smiled, said nothing and moved on. Puzzled and worried, Callas asked George Harewood during dinner that evening if he could offer an explanation. He promised to find out and phoned Maria the next day. The Queen had told him, 'I just didn't know what to ask her or say to her.'

The Queen of England was not the only head of state to be at a loss for words when faced with Callas. In May 1962, an extravagant fund-raising event was held at Madison Square Garden to celebrate President John Kennedy's forty-fourth birthday. Among the entertainers were Jimmy Durante, Ella Fitzgerald, Harry Belafonte,

Hamburg, 25 October 1973. After nine years Callas returns to her public.

Pixie's party piece after the concert. *Left*, Ivor Newton, the author,
Edith Gorlinsky. *Right*, Sander Gorlinsky stands behind Maria.

Elizabeth Taylor congratulates Maria. Ivor Newton in the background.

Mario De Maria, Di Stefano and Maria in-flight.

New York, 27 January 1959. After her great success in *Il Pirata*,
Maria is surprised to discover her father had been in the audience.
They had not met for some years. Alan Oxenburg in the background.

Yacinthy and Maria with their mother in wartime Athens.

Verona, 1947. Maria with Lord Harewood and the Mayor.

Before (as Violetta, 1952) . . . and after (as Amina, 1955).

(Above) Royal Festiva[l]
London, 1973. Flower[s]
handshakes at the end [of the]
first concert.

(Left, and previous pag[e])
Paris, 1973, Théâtre d[es]
Champs Elysées. Mari[a]
acknowledges the app[lause]

New York, January 1974. Di Stefano, Maria and Sol Hurok answer the press.

The American tour begins.

Maria, supported by Mario, arrives at the Carnegie Hall
a few hours after hearing of the death of Sol Hurok.

Maria Callas and Marilyn Monroe, who sang without accompaniment her famous teasingly sexy version of 'Happy Birthday, Mr President'. In accordance with the festive nature of the evening Callas gave them nothing too demanding, singing the 'Habanera' and 'Seguidilla' from *Carmen*, with piano accompaniment. But Callas was not used to being upstaged by any other singer, male or female. Perhaps that is why she was not amused when the only comment the President could muster was, 'Say – what a lovely gown you're wearing – wish Jackie were here, she'd love it.' The First Lady had retreated to the country when she heard that Marilyn Monroe was to sing at her husband's birthday party.

On the day before the first London recital, 26 November 1973, Maria invited Ivor and me to stay to lunch after our rehearsal in her suite at the Savoy. Di Stefano ordered the traditional English Sunday roast beef for everyone, but when the waiter returned after half an hour to say it was finished he flew into a temper, pacing in and out of the room saying what a rotten hotel this was, then ordered fillet steak for us and refused anything for himself. We began with smoked salmon, Maria giving him some on her fork, then while we started in on the steaks he poked around at the Melba toast, eventually eating all there was in the basket. At three-thirty in the afternoon he called the waiter again, asking for tagliatelli. 'Sorry, sir, not until six-thirty,' came the reply.

Miffed again, he shouted, 'I'll wait!'

Maria reprimanded him with a maternal, 'Pippo, remember we have guests,' as she cut the weekly TV programme out of the *Sunday Telegraph*. 'I love TV,' she said. 'Last night was a great evening.'

'There's too much talk in the Westerns nowadays – not enough action,' Di Stefano threw in, still on the move. At that time the Saturday evening programmes on British television were generally considered, in artistic and cultural endeavour, to be the weakest. The set in the room where we were eating was switched on, but without sound.

Maria was surprised when Ivor told her he did not possess a

television set. 'You must get one,' she said. Just then, Di Stefano rushed in from the bedroom, shouting 'There's a good fight on!' Maria quickly stretched over to the TV set and turned on the sound.

The telephone rang to announce the arrival of Mrs Di Stefano. Maria leaned across the table to me and whispered, 'She thinks it best always to give us warning.' Mrs Di Stefano and her daughter Luisa arrived in a great flurry of noisy Italian excitement, loaded with an assortment of light luggage, handbags and duty-free packages, greeting and kissing everyone in sight. Orders were given for their lunch, Maria taking the opportunity to make a new order for chicken and a hamburger because her steak had been too well-cooked.

Luisa complimented me on the Madrid concert then, to my alarm, said, 'I hear you're playing all the concerts from now on.' Fortunately Ivor had escaped from the noise around the table and gone to a quieter part of the room, observing the view out of the window to the Royal Festival Hall across the Thames. Di Stefano appeared from a bedroom wearing a new shirt, which his wife had brought from Milan. He enjoyed the general chorus of approval before disappearing back into the bedroom to return, showing off another. When the conversation switched to family affairs Ivor and I took the opportunity to escape. We arranged to meet Maria and Di Stefano at noon next day to rehearse for the concert that evening. In the lift, Ivor appeared apprehensive and again asked me to give him all the music, including the duplicates. As though suspecting a conspiracy, he seemed determined to block any possibility of my practising.

Maria was remarkably contained during our rehearsal in the RFH next day, saying little and taking Di Stefano's comments dutifully like a schoolgirl on best behaviour. Instinctively, I felt I should tell her about Ivor asking me to wear only a dark suit at the concert. 'Oh, no you don't,' she said. 'I want you in your pretty tails.' This was the first indication I had that she had noticed how I was dressed.

My garb was the last thing on my mind when, arrayed in white tie and tails, I arrived at the concert hall that evening. I was anxious to know what kind of state Maria would be in. She was already there with Di Stefano, Elena and Gorlinsky. Outwardly calm, she appeared in control, quietly determined, but I could see the anxiety in her eyes. It was almost tangible. The ordeal of Hamburg could not equal the stress of this first London concert. A similar audience, if not even more star-studded, was expected and, in addition, it was to be recorded by EMI and televised by the BBC. There was no escape. I could feel her tension.

In the past I had often been able to offer comforting words to a nervous singer. It is considered part of the accompanist's job. Expected to have powers of understanding and an ability imaginatively to enter into the other artist's feelings, the pianist must never allow his own sensitivity to show its other face in the form of apprehension in the green-room. We are assumed to be indomitably in control, assured and immune against the ravages of stage fright. Whatever happens, we must never show the slightest sign of nerves. We find ourselves, instead, tactfully bolstering the wavering confidence of the 'artiste'.

Holding her hand firmly, Di Stefano led Maria to the curtain dividing us from the audience, Ivor and I silently falling in behind, unable to cast off the heavy air of anguish in which Maria enveloped us. There was no escaping the power she had of drawing one into her feelings. As we paused behind the curtain, Maria startled me with, 'I'm scared, Robert.' Somehow the usual words of encouragement seemed inadequate. I knew how justified her fear was but I was surprised to hear her express it at this moment, just before she strode out to face her audience. At a loss for words, I gazed warmly into her eyes, hoping she would find some comfort in mine. She smiled.

The curtain was pulled back and once again I witnessed the magic of a trembling frightened girl instantly transformed into a sparkling diva. La Callas was with her public. She was wearing a simple body-fitting white silk dress with a floor-length cobalt-blue cloak fixed on her left shoulder, coming across the front of her neck and floating out behind as she moved. A ring and her favourite outsize pearl-drop ear-rings were the only jewels. The audience came to their feet as one, cheering and calling her name, while Di Stefano led her around the platform. No one saw Ivor or me as we made our way to the piano. I was hoping that Maria would sing at least as well as she had when I played for her in Madrid, but I was disappointed. This was vocally the least successful concert of the tour. Even so, the audience gave her a wonderfully warm reception each time she appeared. Among the celebrities in the audience was one of Maria's most ardent fans, Claudio Arrau, and two sopranos who had recently given recitals in the same hall, Elisabeth Schwarzkopf and Jessye Norman.

After the first duet Maria said to me, 'Go and tell Sander I want you to play.' She knew as well as I did that this was impossible, but just putting the thought into words released a little of her tension. I said nothing. Often enough she had stated she would do nothing to Ivor that might induce another heart attack. To dismiss him now in the course of this concert, which meant so much to him, could easily be fatal. He had engaged a photographer privately to take only shots of him alone with Maria, one of which later featured on his Christmas card.

At the end of the concert the usually reserved English audience, normally shy of displaying their feelings, flocked down to the stage, their arms outstretched to touch Maria or shake her hand, bringing flowers and gifts, some climbing up on to the stage, their eyes brimming with emotion and excitement.

CALLAS WISE TO RETURN? headlined one of the tabloids next day, but critics in the more serious newspapers wrote lucidly of her with respect and affection. After relating her effect on him in past performances – 'A voice that was never quite tamed but whose command of flame and tears, fireworks and tender caress could leave no one unmoved' – Andrew Porter in the *Financial Times* continued with, 'An artist as great as she has been must not be insulted with less than the truth from an admirer. The voice was a shadow of its former self. Perhaps it could be said that the voice has, at last, been in some sense "tamed" – in that the interpretations were kept carefully within the bounds of what it can still do.' Of Di Stefano he wrote, 'There is plenty of good full tone left in his voice, but the mechanism for producing it seemed often to function in slow motion, so the results were sticky.'

Another much respected critic, William Mann in *The Times*, had a similar response to Di Stefano's singing: 'Strong vocalism, plenty of fire and tenderness, and the so-called temperament which consists of unmotivated messing about with note-values and dynamics . . . Four operatic duets and three solos from each artist is not much for an evening,' he wrote, 'but it was stretched to just over two hours with exits and reappearances for applause after every item.' He also had come to hear 'the greatest operatic actress of our time, singing in person for the first time in eight years', noting that 'many in the audience may be too young to have experienced her artistry in the theatre'. His general impression was of 'a monochrome reproduction of a favourite oil-painting', but he hoped 'that she may yet give us her Carmen in the opera house'. Another reviewer wrote that the thirty-minute applause at the end of the concert was pure love. 'That may sound corny,' he said, 'but how else does one describe the depth of emotion that her audience felt for her?'

They were able to express their love even more vociferously at the end of the second London concert, given on the afternoon of Maria's fiftieth birthday, 2 December. During the apparently end-less applause, Ivor sat down at the keyboard and began to play. The audience recognised the tune instantly and sang 'Happy Birthday'. Seldom have I heard such a warm, full-throated chorus. They were demonstrating their love by embracing Maria with the vigour of their singing. This was for her, not Callas, and she knew it. I had seen her elated by a reception, the normal reaction of any artist, but that afternoon she glowed in a kind of euphoria. Her eyes were moist. Backstage she was too aware of the reality of her situation not to recognise it and face up to it. 'They love me more than I deserved for today,' she said later with honest perception. 'They love what I was, not what I am.'

In the evening, Sander and his wife hosted a birthday dinner in a private dining club in Mayfair. It was a lacklustre affair. A dozen people sat around the table, mostly business friends of the Gorlinskys, the conversation stiff, uneasy silences leaving them searching anew for a subject of mutual interest. I sat near Rudy Nureyev, who listened to the others but said nothing. Even though one sensed a strong character, he appeared ill at ease, uncertain of the use of the cutlery, waiting until the others had started before picking up a fork or a knife. Maria was not alone in feeling relieved when the coffee arrived, we toasted her health with liqueurs, champagne or brandy and the party broke up.

7

PARIS AND AMSTERDAM

'Have you seen the posters?' Maria said as I walked into her apartment in Paris some days later. 'Your name is on them.' She smiled broadly. (Edward Greenfield, music critic of the *Guardian* had said, 'I wonder if she will enjoy having that name in smaller print under hers on the bills.')

Di Stefano said, 'Did you get my shirts?' They were being laundered when he left London so the Savoy sent them to me to deliver to him in Paris. I sensed an unusual air of mutual respect between him and Maria, as though they were being careful not to upset one another. Elena had told me of the terrific row they had had in London. The day after the first concert, when Maria wanted to relax and enjoy herself with Di Stefano, his wife had insisted on shopping with them at Harrods. Much of the time their spree was interrupted when Maria was recognised and the promenade was held up as she signed autographs. One fortunate sales assistant, who had spent the morning gushing to his colleagues about Callas, the concert and showing off his programme, could not believe his eyes when Maria walked into his department. She was delighted when he produced his programme for her to autograph, watched by envious colleagues and curious customers. They visited other shops, Mrs Di Stefano clinging on. 'She never leaves us alone,' Maria had said to me in the Savoy that evening.

Now that we were back together again in Paris, our work began on my first day. Maria was still having difficulty in the middle range of the voice, which features so much in the *Cav* duet. Fortunately, Di Stefano was able to restrain his temper so that the work moved faster and more smoothly. It was a short session, though, Maria soon saying she was tired. She was pleased that I had brought a written-out transposition of the *Lucia* duet but suggested we look at it another time. There was little interest from either of them in the repertoire they sang in London and presumably would perform again in Paris. I hoped that would not mean a dull concert, which can sometimes happen after a big emotional success.

Next day I was alone with Maria. She was very concerned about her voice, asking me to help her sing as Di Stefano wanted. She was extremely unsure, since his ideas were not clear to her. 'I don't know what I'm looking for,' she said. We worked in the early afternoon and again in the evening. 'Tu! tu! piccolo iddio' (*Madama Butterfly*) was new to me. Without warming up she plunged into the dramatic little aria as though it were still in her repertoire. When I suggested that she was forcing the voice and she should for the time being forget the drama and take the climaxes more lightly and with less effort, they sounded better. 'It's such a crazy voice I have,' she said. 'When I was singing Lucia I warmed up on "Ritorna vincitor",' the equivalent of a harpsichordist lifting body-builder's hand weights as preparation for a Scarlatti recital or a needlewoman sewing mail-bags for a week in order to perfect her *petit point*. We moved on to Massenet's 'Adieu, notre petite table', the simple but moving farewell of Manon when she believes her love affair with Des Grieux is over. No great dramatic vocal climax here, as a warm-up it would have been a more suitable piece. I was anxious to know what I should be practising for the concert. 'Will there be anything new for Paris?' I asked.

Maria answered simply, 'We'd better ask our tenor, he'll be here soon.' I left just before a television programme she did not want to miss. Di Stefano was due back in time for dinner. The midday session next day was cancelled.

In the evening we worked on the soprano parts of the usual duets and now *Lucia* was added. As I had done, Di Stefano was encouraging her to sing lighter which brought quick improvement, but after a few moments' work on *Lucia* he lost his temper, cried '*Basta*' and made for the door. 'Oh, Pippo, be reasonable,' Maria implored. 'I'm trying.'

'But you're not articulating,' was his answer. After a pause Maria sang parts of the *Lucia* duet with a beauty of sound I knew from her records, but she looked worried and said she was unconvinced. Di Stefano rewarded her with a sweet kiss on the cheek. I thought how strange the world of opera is, how different from the world of lieder and song, where the performers discuss the fine points of interpretation up to the last minute. Tomorrow, I realised, we were to have a recital at the Théâtre des Champs-Elysées and all I could be sure of was that Maria would be wearing a new dress. I could only guess at the programme.

Kurt and Eva Collien came from Hamburg, and Edith and Sander Gorlinsky from London. Ivor phoned the Gorlinsky office for his flight ticket to Paris, only to find an embarrassed Sander fumbling for words and being evasive at the end of the telephone. When, eventually, Sander got the message through that as far as Ivor was concerned the tour was over, the eighty-two-year-old wept and moaned, 'Are you trying to cut off my career?'

Already dressed in my white tie and tails, I arrived at Maria's at 6 p.m. on the evening of the concert, hoping for a constructive rehearsal. Di Stefano sang through the 'Flower Song' from *Carmen* without comment. We were not far into the *Don Carlo* duet before he began to attack Maria, insulting her singing in a way unimaginable at any time, let alone before this concert in her adopted home town, which he certainly knew meant a great deal to her. She retaliated, which meant a shouting match and another period of discomfort for me before their anger was spent.

For some time I had been growing aware of an evolving pattern: there was always a row before a concert. At first I put it down to pre-concert nerves on both their parts, but soon it became clear that these quarrels were no accident. Di Stefano was deliberately provoking Maria. He believed she needed to be fortified by rage in order to give a good account of herself and that by making her angry he was stimulating her, pulling her out of a phlegmatic indolence, encouraging the flow of adrenalin, preparing her for the performance. (Mrs Di Stefano said she was simply lazy, but there was more to it than that. Maria's habit of resting her legs on a nearby chair or stool was not laziness but an attempt to relieve the poor circulation caused by the low blood pressure which dogged her for most of her adult life.)

Di Stefano's method of bringing her to concert pitch – however well-intended – simply caused Maria a great deal of unnecessary distress, which was painful to witness; how unnecessary I saw each time I walked on to the platform with her. She needed only to hear the welcoming applause of her public to be energised, revitalised and braced for the struggle which she experienced each time she sang in public. 'Every performance is a battle,' she said, 'and my only weapon is my voice.'

As we drove to the theatre Maria remarked that she was surprised Ivor had not been in touch with her, asking me if he had sent me a telegram of good wishes. 'Nothing,' I had to tell her.

'That's mean of him,' she said. 'Perhaps I should write him a nice letter.' Once settled in the dressing-room, she asked me to go to the foyer to see what was happening.

Camouflaged in a light-weight raincoat, I found my way to the front of the house, where a glittering, animated throng was gathering, many of the men sporting rosettes of the *Légion d'honneur*, each different colour denoting his position in the rigorously established ranks of members, officers, commanders or grand officers; and the women making an impression with their most ostentatious and extravagant jewellery. The bright lights sparkling in the precious stones were reflected also in the gleaming helmets of the soldiers of the *Garde Républicaine* who lined the splendid marble staircase and stood in their dazzling uniforms at strategic points around the foyer, shining silver swords held upright to attention before their faces. The atmosphere was charged with the heady fragrance of expensive perfumes and the buzz of excited, expectant voices. I loitered a while to enjoy the spectacle before telling myself it was time to get back to work. Maria was examining her make-up in the dressing-room mirror. 'The Garde is out,' I reported.

She tilted her chin a little, correcting a wayward eyelash. 'Hm-hm,' she hummed, as though expecting nothing less.

In the green-room Di Stefano again could only make negative comments when we went through some of Maria's part in the duet from *Don Carlo*, leaving Maria very unsure when we went on at the beginning of the evening. Her first solo aria was 'Suicidio' and as the evening progressed she gradually gained more confidence so that it became as great a success as the second London concert. As an aid to the acoustic the fire curtain had been lowered, cutting off most of the stage and creating a long shallow platform. After her solo 'Voi lo sapete' from *Cavalleria Rusticana* there was such a roar from the audience I found myself swaying on the piano stool as the pressurised current of air created by the clapping hands, unable to dispel up the stage, buffeted off the fire curtain and came at me like an enormous tidal wave. I grasped the knobs of the piano stool to stop myself from falling off.

Di Stefano also was very well received, especially after an elegant performance of 'Vainement ma bien-aimée'. In the interval they vied with each other over who had won the longest applause. 'The fairies are all there,' Di Stefano said to Maria. 'They don't like me, but they just adore you.'

Gorlinsky, wearing an indeterminately coloured rosette of the *Légion d'honneur*, lifted his eyes from his reading, sat up in his armchair, took the cigar out of his mouth and said to him, 'Never mind, you don't have to sleep with them.'

Maria showed her appreciation of my playing frequently during the evening, getting me up to share her reception after each item and complimenting me backstage.

We were a long time in getting away from the theatre. With Maria, Di Stefano, Elena and me obstructing his vision Ferruccio

[95]

had difficulty backing out of the narrow street, hindered by a mass of people clambering around touching the car, applauding, taking pictures and calling 'Diva', 'Maria' and 'Bravo'. Driving very slowly to avoid any injuries, Ferruccio became flummoxed and more and more annoyed as Di Stefano impatiently shouted conflicting instructions at him from the back seat. The police arrived to control the crowd; then, when we reached avenue Montaigne, they stopped the flow of traffic, allowing us a clear passage, the calling of the fans echoing in our ears as we sped off.

We took a day of rest before flying to Amsterdam for the concert on the 11th. A happy and relaxed party, we enjoyed our usual stroll around the shops at the airport. In the duty-free shop Gorlinsky bought Maria a large bottle of expensive perfume, which she accepted as casually and easily as she had my bar of milk chocolate earlier. Reflecting on the concert of the previous evening I mentioned the remarkable audience reaction to her solo appearances.

'That's their way of showing how much they love me . . . and respect me,' she said. 'That's what I've been working all my life for.' During the flight as the steward offered us newspapers, Elena was alarmed when she saw which French paper Di Stefano had chosen. She had already read the review in which the critic had been severe on him, writing, 'He did not sing, he barked.' This was never mentioned but that evening Di Stefano was quick to show me a piece in the TV section of *The Sunday Times* which said that although Callas's voice sometimes let her down Di Stefano did not.

Maria, who said she would like to work as soon as we had settled into the hotel, was disappointed when the manager told us the piano had been booked only from the next day. I set about finding one in a place where we could rehearse in private. After spending some time showing me the possibilities, the management offered to relocate a private function so that we might be accommodated. An hour later, enjoying a sense of achievement, I phoned Maria to ask what time we should meet. 'Just a minute,' she said. 'I'll ask Pippo.'

From somewhere else in the room I heard his voice shouting, 'We are not working tonight.' The management, at least, were pleased to be able to revert to their original schedule.

The pursuit of a piano for practice is a travelling pianist's first concern. Sometimes luck is with him and a suitable venue has been arranged before he arrives, but this is not always possible. The search can be a headache. When I travelled with Maria I was often embarrassed by the flurry that resulted when I quietly asked for a piano. Soon I learned never to make this request before first playing Sherlock Holmes. I discovered that in most modern hotels there would be a restaurant or, better still, a night-club on the top floor. If it were a restaurant waiters would come to set up for lunch, but in the night-club nothing stirred until late afternoon. In either case no one used it before midday, so that I could slip in and enjoy some unbothered piano practice without any rumpus at the reception desk. So it was in the Okura Hotel in Amsterdam. No one ever found me out.

A piano having been delivered to Maria's apartment the next day, we were able to rehearse there in the evening. The quarrelling started early but gradually Di Stefano succeeded in getting Maria to sing as he wanted. 'But I can't sing like that at the concert,' she cried out. 'I haven't the nerve – and it rings so in my ears.'

'But that's the true coloratura sound,' he shouted. 'How you used to sing in the old days.'

Puzzled and exasperated, Maria pursed her lips and sat down in the corner of the sofa. After a few moments she relaxed, changing the subject by asking what I was doing for dinner. I produced a poster of the Paris concert and a photo of Callas, the prima donna, for my mother, asking for autographs. She pondered long over what to write for her, in the end saying, 'Oh, I've just written something very ordinary – I can't think of the English words I want to use.' Perhaps I had chosen the wrong moment. On the poster she wrote, 'To Robert with love – Maria.' Di Stefano saw this when I offered him the poster and cried to her, 'What do you mean "Love"?' He signed 'Ciao, Di Stefano' in his flamboyant hand. He was often warm in his appreciation of my playing but sometimes he gave me the feeling he considered me as he would one of the musicians who scrape away in the back desks of a provincial opera house pit.

On the morning of the concert our visit to the hall in the Concertgebouw was short. Long enough only to learn our whereabouts backstage and discuss the lighting. Even before I sat down at the piano Maria said, so typical of her thoughtfulness, it would be bad for me. She was right: one of the lights shone directly into my eyes.

In the evening Maria was very worried. Di Stefano had been making her sing all afternoon, she told me. She felt tired and hoarse. 'If only he wouldn't lose his temper,' she said. 'It only makes things more difficult for me.' Again there was an argument in the artists' room before the concert began. As we left we were approached by a small, fat, bespectacled Italian who had eluded the security and found his way to the green-room, camera in hand and a bundle of records and photos in his arm asking for autographs. Di Stefano advised him to return after the concert.

Behind the platform in the Concertgebouw, semicircular rows of seats rise up as in a Roman amphitheatre, straddling two floors of the building, offering places for a large choir or, in our case, extra audience. When the doors on the top level opened and we began the long walk down the steps to the platform the audience in those seats stood up as we levelled with them, Di Stefano guiding Maria by the hand on the steep steps, with me behind, carrying my music. It seemed like a royal procession, the successive rows of rising bodies creating waves like the choreographed dancers in a Busby Berkeley film. When we reached the platform the people in the parterre and balconies also rose, and the magnificent concert hall was filled with cheers and bravos. It was all for Maria but she insisted on presenting Di Stefano as they circled around the platform acknowledging the crowd behind them as well as in front.

Neither was in top form in the first duet (*Don Carlo*) though the reception was good. In the green-room afterwards Maria expressed her doubts, while Di Stefano did his best to humour her. He then went on to give a relaxed and beautiful account of 'Vainement', the audience standing to applaud before and after the aria. They did the same for Maria's 'Suicidio', though it was not her best perform- ance by far.

Just before the *Carmen* duet, which Di Stefano introduced in a frivolous, inept manner, a small bunch of three roses was thrown on to the stage. Di Stefano picked it up and gave it to Maria. I saw her at first receive it as a bouquet then, as she felt the stems, realising each was wrapped separately in silver foil. Immediately she gave one to me and one to Di Stefano. The audience liked that very much.

Each time we went on to sing a Callas solo Maria grasped my hand tightly as I led her down the steps, giving me a radiant smile when I told her how much I was relishing the moment. Arrau had wondered how she would handle all those irksome steps each time she came on and off. Now I could tell him what use she made of them, turning a possible difficulty, with her myopia even a danger, into a theatrical asset.

When the end of the programme came, with the *Cavalleria* duet in which Maria found much of her thrilling voice of twenty years earlier, the audience would not let them go, roaring and stamping their feet. Di Stefano asked me to fetch the music for 'O mio babbino caro', my return to the piano provoking another roar from the audience. During the furore Maria said to Di Stefano, 'Let's get off now,' but he made no attempt to move, basking in the tumultuous reception. 'Please,' said Maria, but he took no notice of her. He was holding Maria's hand triumphantly high in the air when suddenly she took a dive into a low bow, pulling the startled Di Stefano down with her. On the way up she was crying to him emphatically, 'Get me off and I'll come back on again.' It was no longer a suggestion or a request, it was a command. Straightening up, he glowered at her, his eyes blackening with anger as she once again begged him, all the while talking through her teeth like a ventriloquist and sustaining a brilliant smile. I knew he was thinking that once off she might not return again. I sat at the piano and waited while the little private drama was enacted before the eyes of the unknowing audience until eventually, accepting defeat, Maria lifted her hand for silence and announced the encore. I had to break into the applause with my introduction before they would stop clapping.

At the beginning of the concert and even while we were performing, the continuous flashing of cameras became so intrusive that Maria, with the voice of a hostess addressing her most intimate friends, affably requested them to stop. She could not see, but clearly visible to me, looking down from the platform, many fans held tape-recorders at the ready.

In the green-room after the concert Di Stefano shook me by the hand, his 'Bravo, Maestro!' a nice reassurance after the poster-signing incident. In the corridor outside a long line of fans had already gathered, records, biographies and autograph albums in hand. At the head waited the Italian who had accosted us earlier. Maria gave him about a dozen autographs before drawing his attention to the waiting line outside. He reluctantly stood aside while others were let in, four or five at a time. When eventually a halt was called there was a commotion at the door. Gorlinsky and a security man were struggling with the Italian who was becoming hysterical, clinging on to the doorknob and insisting that Maria had asked him to wait. Just as they got him beyond the door Di Stefano recognised him and, jumping up from the table, rushed to the three grappling men demanding that the Italian be released. With a comforting hand on his shoulder Di Stefano took the sobbing man to a chair near Maria, who began again the task of autographing his collection. This was not the first time I had seen Di Stefano being kind. At airports and railway stations, even after Gorlinsky or the agent travelling with us had organised the luggage and rewarded the porters, he insisted on tipping them again, whether with his money or mine did not matter. Wide grins expressing their pleasure and surprise at receiving something well beyond their expectations were his reward.

After the concert a relieved and relaxed group returned to Maria's suite, where a magnificent buffet had been arranged in our absence. She was ensconced in one corner of a sofa, I in the other. 'Ah, you like corners too, do you, Robert?' she asked. 'Pippo teases me because I always take the corner seat. Is it a kind of timidity or something?'

CALLAS STILL SHINES headlined one newspaper next day. The critics were kind to Maria, the bulk of their reviews dwelling on the glories of her past before reporting the actual concert. One, uncomfortable with the behaviour of the fans, wrote of a 'Callas-circus' and complained of Di Stefano's light-hearted manner, going for a cheap laugh even when introducing a serious item. The interpreter who read the Dutch newspapers to us diplomatically avoided translating the final comments of the critics asking why Callas should take part in a so-called '*Rentrée* (Comeback)', which at best could only be considered a farewell. He stressed instead how one wrote of the 'warm glow in the duets' and being 'ripped apart by a passion' he had never heard before in the 'Suicidio' aria. With a gesture of wide-eyed bafflement Maria said, 'I get reports like these now and twenty years ago they panned me when I was singing like a *Goddess*.'

In London that evening, my luggage unpacked, I telephoned Ivor. 'Hello, Ivor, it's Robert.'

'Robert? Robert who?'

'Robert Sutherland.'

'Oh, what do you want? We have nothing to say to each other,' he said bitterly. Gorlinsky, during a long conversation, had ultimately told him the true reason why he was not wanted any more. 'Gorlinsky told me that the artists think I'm forgetful and unreliable – I would like to know exactly what "madame" means by that – but of course you wouldn't have the courage to ask her.' He tried to incite me into saying I would, but I withheld comment. I said simply that Gorlinsky had told me he could not afford the expenses for two pianists. I did not say that were I the devious character he was accusing me of being I could have taken over after the first concert. 'I will see to it that you never play in London again,' he threatened and remained belligerent to the end of the telephone call. I was sad that he should react in this manner after all the loyalty I had shown him. (Although I later made several attempts at reconciliation we never met again.)

8

PREPARATIONS FOR

NORTH AMERICA

'I've BROKEN two jackets chewing a hard-centre chocolate,' Maria said when she phoned me on my return to the Hotel Belles Feuilles. 'The most expensive chocolate I've ever eaten.' She was referring to the extravagant cost of having her front teeth capped as part of the preparation for the relaunching of her career. 'Would you like to come round this evening and look through some new stuff or would you rather leave it till tomorrow?' I went round and took with me some letters sent to her in London and the vicuna blankets she had ordered on one of her shopping expeditions. 'Everything is getting so expensive,' she said as we admired them and enjoyed the sensation of the luxurious fabric between our fingers. We arranged to meet next day at noon.

Elena phoned in the morning to say Madame was at the dentist. Maria greeted me with a kiss when I arrived in the afternoon. 'Ah, carnation,' she exclaimed, recognising my after-shave from Floris. 'I like that.' I remembered her obvious delight in the aroma of the sandalwood torchères in the hall, her acute hearing, and wondered if in some way these two heightened senses were compensation for her weak eyesight. She was listening to a radio programme comparing the performances of Beethoven's 'Moonlight Sonata' by different pianists. She did not like the Schnabel, on an old brittle-sounding recording, and was angered by the comments of the presenter on the next. 'How dare he criticise an artist of the standing of Horowitz! I wouldn't dare. Who does he think he is? You work day and night perfecting a performance, trying to reach the composer's meaning and along comes a critic with not enough imagination to understand what you're getting at. He hears you once and thinks that gives him the right to stab you in the heart. But we artists have to suffer, it is our destiny,' she said rather loftily, then scornfully dismissed the subject with, 'Anyway, I know better than they do if I have sung well or not.'

She told me of her early days in Athens when she was being encouraged to become a concert pianist. Even though she worked all day at the theatre and had only a few hours to practise on the day before her piano lesson, they were enthusiastic about her talent. She changed the subject to Di Stefano, telling me that she had telephoned him to say that he must consider singing something between pianissimo and fortissimo, because her admirers did not like it when he drowned her out. 'I'm told even some of the newspapers said so, though I didn't notice them. I'm not that interested,' she said to me. 'He gets angry at me when I don't sing as he wants and then he thinks I'm doing it deliberately. Please tell me, Robert, when I make a wrong sound . . . I told Pippo he must learn to match my volume, otherwise the critics in America will pan him.'

Since their assurances in Milan that I would be playing in America I had been wondering if, in fact, I would be happy there with a life, on and off the platform, that was simply a continuation of the strife-ridden European tour – the bad notices and the frequent rows which their Mediterranean temperaments so easily shrugged off, leaving me with a lingering distress.

In addition, there were faults in Maria's singing, which I believed could be easily remedied but until now had not dared to mention. I decided to risk offering my opinion. My opportunity came one evening when Maria turned to me after singing an aria and asked, 'Was that all right?'

'Yes, I replied, 'but I wonder if you are always doing what you think you're doing.' There was a pause.

Maria took her hand off the piano, pulled herself up to her full five foot nine inches and faced me square on. 'What do you mean?' she challenged me.

'Can we do it again?' I asked, switching on the tape-recorder. While she sang I stopped her now and again to make suggestions.

There was another pause when we finished, I uncertain of my next move and Maria deep in thought. 'Will you stay to dinner?' she asked.

'No,' I answered. 'I suggest you listen quietly to the tape alone and consider what we have done together.' I was glad she agreed and I could escape such an ambiguous atmosphere.

As I walked up the stairs to her apartment the following morning at ten I could hear Maria singing. When I reached the music room she was sitting at the piano. She lowered her head, looking at me over her outsize glasses, and stretched out her arm, pointing a long finger at me. Was this to be the curse of Medea, I thought, and imagined myself packing for London. Instead, to my relief, she called out, 'You were right.' Treading carefully, we launched into a session that proved to be one of our most satisfying and fruitful. She was seldom so enthusiastic.

Another day I produced Mozart's 'Alleluia', suggesting she take it very easy as a warming-up exercise but as usual she broke off after only a few bars, impatient to know how it sounded. Later we worked on parts of *Lucia*, her voice, free from tension and the effort of pleasing Di Stefano, sounding through the uncertain technique like the unmistakable Callas of twenty years earlier. After a break and some coffee, she opened the music cupboard and brought out a copy of Duparc's 'Chanson Triste'. 'Gorlinsky is talking about a record of popular classical songs,' she said. 'Have you any ideas?' My mind raced beyond the merely popular songs to other possibilities. Callas singing *Frauenliebe and Leben*, the Gretchen songs, Hugo Wolf, or even, as two other great female singers of the past, Elena Gerhardt and Lotte Lehmann had done, Schubert's *Winterreise*. I needed only a moment's reflection to realise how unlikely this would be. The language itself was so inextricably tied up with memories of the hardships she and her family had suffered during the German occupation of Greece. It was not a happy time for the Athenians. 'I hate those songs,' Maria said, talking of German lieder. 'I had to learn some to sing to the Germans in the war. It was the only way to earn a loaf of bread, but I've hated them ever since.' Schubert's 'Ave Maria' was given a run-through but discarded when we realised the melody featured some of the weakest notes in her voice. 'Perhaps you will bring me a list of songs in the morning, Robert,' Maria said as I left.

Despite her invective against German lieder, I walked home to the hotel, my mind searching through the repertoire, dreaming of Callas singing the great songs for soprano, Schubert's 'Gretchen am Spinnrad' or 'Die Junge Nonne'; and what she might do with the fiery female songs in Wolf's *Italienisches Liederbuch*. To make them more accessible to her, I might search out the original poems and she could sing the songs in Italian. Poor Hugo Wolf, who set the poet's words with such meticulous genius, might turn in his grave but Callas singing the *Italian Song Book* would be a phenomenal curiosity. Even Dietrich Fischer-Dieskau, the great lieder singer, might forgive her as he had earlier excused what he called 'her very disparaging remark about the German Lied'. And what would be his answer if asked to record the *Italian Song Book* with Callas? (That he respected her 'artistic power' is evident from his autobiography, *Reverberations*, where he mentions her five times. On a visit to New York in the spring of 1974 he and his wife stayed at the Stanhope, a quiet, discreet, hotel favoured by the famous seeking escape from the public eye. We were there also. 'Usually Julia and I do not listen at hotel-room walls,' he writes. 'Once, however, we could not prevent ourselves.' They were staying next to Maria's suite and could hear us working. 'Julia [Varady] pressed her ear to the wall so as to be sure not to miss a note. Callas's voice was strained and no longer beautiful in every register, but we admired her way of repeating, improving and instructing Di

Stefano.' Such was the power of the media image of Callas as a domineering woman that even a man of Fischer-Dieskau's intelligence could mistakenly assume that Maria was instructing Di Stefano and not the other way around.)

In our very first session Maria had shown me the vivid use of words I knew from her recordings, but surprised me with a feeling of ensemble and response to the piano part not usually associated with opera singers. This is the basis of all good song singing. My imagination was racing ahead to the overwhelming repertoire of great songs not in the German language. Maggie Teyte and Jennie Tourel famously sang the French repertoire. Duparc, Debussy and Ravel lead on to de Falla, Barber, Copland and Britten, and the list goes on. Perhaps the recital platform would be the answer to her search for a new career. Andrew Porter, in his *Financial Times* review, had suggested that hers was 'a voice that should now be turned to romanze, melodie and lieder'. I realised, though, I would need to move carefully.

Next morning at ten I began my usual practice, knowing that Maria could hear me in her bedroom next door. 'I like to hear you working,' she often said. I opened up my Schubert volume at 'An die Musik', his setting of Franz von Schober's paean of thanks to the art of music. One of the best-known and best-loved songs in the recitalist's repertoire, the sentiments of the poem so near the hearts of musicians and music lovers that it has the status of an anthem in the world of song recitals. It is music for a special occasion.

On 20 February 1967, when Gerald Moore played his farewell recital in the Royal Festival Hall, the pages of his music turned by a young Scottish accompanist at the foothills of his own career, his partners were three of the greatest luminaries of the singing world: Elisabeth Schwarzkopf, Victoria de los Angeles and Dietrich Fischer-Dieskau. At the end of the evening, left alone on the platform before an adoring audience, Gerald sat down at the piano and with trembling hands played his own solo-piano arrangement of 'An die Musik'. He came off to dry his eyes before returning to the platform and another standing ovation from the nearly five thousand who had come to honour him.

Over the hour of my practising that morning in Maria's apartment I played the famous song several times, the vocal melody as well as the accompaniment, taking it up again as the time approached when I expected her to join me. 'That's a lovely tune,' she said as she entered the room. 'What is it?'

Maria was very talkative next day as we walked arm in arm, window shopping around the Sixteenth Arrondissement, her neighbourhood. Her thoughts were flitting from one idea to another. If she studied again, she said, the subject would be psychology or psychiatry. 'You know, Robert, there are so many people in the world – and what things we invent in our minds! – what fantasies!' she said. 'What responsibilities parents have in bringing up a child.' I asked her if she would like her child to be an opera singer. 'That would be her decision.' I had not asked if she would want a boy or a girl. 'I wouldn't hound her, as I was – oh, I got enough spankings! – but I would try to make her a strong healthy mind. Integrity, that's what matters really, integrity. To know what is right and to keep going till you get it. Sometimes that can make you unpopular with the people around you though,' she added with a wry smile. 'I never had a childhood,' she went on. 'My mother didn't understand me and my father couldn't help me. I was made to sing already when I was four and I hated it. That's why I have always had this love–hate relationship with singing. I think that's why I find it hard to get going now. I was so unhappy as a child. She kept demanding too much from me – too much responsibility for a young girl. Childhood should be a time of wonderful happiness. It should be illegal for mothers to force their child like that. It's just too much for a young mind.'

Pottering around in an antique shop, we became separated in our search for a rare discovery. The dealer approached me and asked in an awestruck whisper, 'Monsieur, is it really Madame Ca . . .' He did not finish the sentence before an acquiescent voice from the other room called with a high-pitched sigh, '*Oui, c'est moi.*' As we left the shop Maria talked about her fame. 'I still don't know, you know, what it is I've got – I mean on the stage. They just go wild for me, but I'm quite ordinary off-stage, in real life. I don't know what happens to me on stage – something else seems to take over.'

Several Christmas shoppers showed surprised recognition as we made our way back to avenue Georges Mandel. 'I don't like traditional holidays like Christmas,' Maria said. 'You're forced to buy presents and be happy and merry when maybe you don't feel like it. I'm asked out all over Christmas but I won't go anywhere. I'll just stay at home and listen to some music.' We stopped to look into the window of an antique furniture shop. I asked her if she had brought the furniture in her Paris apartment from Italy.

'Yes, most of it, though my boy-friend of the time [Onassis] didn't want me to. He wanted me to make a clean break from all that part of my life. So I said, will you furnish the apartment for me then? So I brought most of it from Italy. But I had to leave things behind and I had to get rid of a lot of stuff.' I saw an opportunity and asked if that was when she destroyed her costumes. I was hoping for an answer to a rumour which had teased and puzzled Callas fans for years. That she had burned her collection of stage costumes was known, but not the reason why. Speculation had run high. Was this a signal to the world, an ostentatious act of renunciation of the past, or the melodramatic gesture of a neurotic woman? The reality was more mundane. Maria was moving from a large villa in Milan, where the dresses filled a whole room, to a much smaller apartment in Paris. There was no space for a voluminous collection of costumes, which would never be worn again. In those days the great auction houses, Christie's and Sotheby's, had not yet discovered the rich profits to be made by selling off the private possessions of the famous. The spectacular Windsor, Jackie Kennedy, Princess Diana, and Joan Sutherland stage costume sales lay in the future. Ever practical, Maria decided to burn the dresses, but where? The fountain in the garden was drained, a fire lit, and for three days curious passers-by watched as the colourful garments were carried through the greenery and added to the smouldering remains of the previous lot. Smoke filled the air and the stench of the various fabrics, some impregnated with the stale perspiration of an overweight prima donna, was ' . . . *terribile, bruttissimo!*'

Ferruccio served us tea in the music room while we listened to a tape of a previous session with Di Stefano, apish jokes and all. Maria was bristling. 'That's him and his so-called humour. I hate his jokes! I'm beginning to get fed up with that man. He's got to give up his so-called "lessons". I've tried now for two years to sing his way but I still can't find it. Perhaps it isn't in my voice. If he doesn't stop I'll just call the whole thing off.'

We had started to work on *Lucia* when Maria had the idea of listening to one of her recordings of the first aria, 'Regnava nel silenzio'. A problem which often confronts the singing coach is how to deal with a pupil who has learned an aria from the recording of a famous singer. A student with the sensitivity one hopes for in a budding artist will inevitably repeat more than just the notes from the recording. Personal idiosyncrasies, mannerisms, even individual sound qualities of the recorded artist will be replicated parrot-fashion by the student. They are usually surprised, and sometimes annoyed, when I ask them if they have been listening to a specific recording. One very famous present-day soprano was angry when, after she proudly proclaimed to me that the critics had drawn attention to the similarity of her recording of Richard Strauss's 'Four Last Songs' to one of Elisabeth Schwarzkopf's I teased her by reminding her that she had first learned them by listening to the German soprano's recording. Individual performances are best achieved by studying the music one to one with the notes as written by the composer. Only when they are completely mastered can concentrated listening to as many other interpretations as possible be helpful. It was with some surprise and amusement when, after we had listened to her recording, I heard Maria, with a completely fabricated sound, impersonating the Callas of twenty years earlier. She saw me smiling and quietly giggling. 'What are you laughing at?' was her puzzled response, but after a few moments' reflection she agreed with my explanation and laughed it off.

Our session ended with Grieg's 'Ich liebe dich', most of the time working on a German pronunciation which came out sounding like a very odd Italian dialect. I suggested that if she did not sing the song in Hans Andersen's original Danish it would make more sense to sing it in English, rather than a German translation. 'I don't sing in English,' was the answer. With only half-hearted attempts at a few songs, I found it difficult to believe that a recording would be completed by the end of January.

For three days our noontime session was cancelled. A dental appointment or some other 'urgent' business were the excuses. One was a visit to a couture house. 'I saw some lovely things for our concerts – but what money!' She had a plate of steak tartare in one hand and a fork in the other, telling me between mouthfuls how beautiful but astronomically expensive the dresses were. 'You have to ask the prices and they whisper them at you. I'll just describe what I want and Biki will make it up for me.' As a hint that I could not go on working indefinitely that evening I told her of a dinner appointment, but my precaution was hardly necessary. She was not inclined to work, finding all sorts of excuses to distract us. 'Let's watch the telly and see if there's anything new on the hijacking.' Palestinian extremists had taken to attacking travelling Jews, hi-jacking planes and cruise ships, in an effort to bring their cause to the attention of the world. Maria thought the solution would be to deny the use of the airlines to all Jews and Arabs.

'Then that would prevent Sander Gorlinsky travelling with us,' I said.

'But they can't do that,' she exclaimed indignantly. 'He's a British subject.'

When at last we started to work she did not give the voice a chance to warm up before complaining of hoarseness and repeating bad notes over and over again. We listened to a recording of Rach-maninov conducting his orchestral arrangement of his wordless 'Vocalise' for solo voice, a possible number for the record, then worked on it a little. She sang the long, sinuous melody with a smooth legato line, the colour of her single 'Ah' vowel changing chameleon-like with the rich harmonies I was playing underneath.

Our work was interrupted by a telephone call from Luisa Di Stefano telling Maria that her parents were in San Remo inspecting their apartment after it had been burgled. Maria phoned them immediately and commiserated for forty-five minutes, while I sat impatiently waiting for the call to end. Eventually she hung up, told me of some treasures they had lost, then said, 'Well, I suppose you want to get off to your dinner appointment now, and I have a TV programme I don't want to miss. Let's meet again early tomorrow – around midday – and really get down to some good work.'

I spent the next morning searching various music shops for duplicates of some arias, rushing back to my hotel only to find a message asking if we could meet in the evening. I puzzled over these frequent cancellations. Were they a sign of distress, a despondency ensuing from the struggle with her voice, was her inertia and listlessness related to her low blood pressure, or was it simply unalloyed laziness as Mrs Di Stefano so often asserted?

I was faced with a different Callas when I arrived at six in the evening. 'I couldn't sleep at all last night,' she said. 'I have been so depressed by my singing these past few days I've decided to do something about it.' She certainly had! I could hear the difference in her attitude as soon as we swung into action. For an hour and a half we worked, concentrating, recording everything on the tape machine, listening and improving. 'Pippo had better watch out. I can't take much more of that stuff from him. I've got the bit between my teeth now and I'm determined to get it without him,' she said. She was annoyed by his insensitive singing in the duets, so loud that he drowned out her lower range. 'And we do it in those keys for his sake,' she said, referring to the transpositions into lower keys. 'My admirers don't like it – nor do I. He'd better do something about it for the USA or I'll just give up.'

The morning session was not cancelled next day. I went at noon as arranged and noticed at once the gift-wrapped parcel on the piano addressed to me. I waited for Maria before opening it. She came in immediately and thanked me for my flowers, which had just been delivered. My Christmas present was a cashmere scarf, which she said I would need when we got to New York. We kissed affectionately. 'Oh,' she said, 'they are arranging a giant party for me in Chicago, but I will write and tell them I couldn't possibly attend because that would mean the same all over the States and I could never stand up to that ... I don't feel like working today, Robert, let's listen to some records and I have arranged a nice lunch for just the two of us.' I was happy to comply since I felt rather end-of-termish.

We listened to a recording of a rehearsal in Dallas of Mozart's 'Martern aller Arten', Constanza's great taxing aria from the second act of *Die Entführung aus dem Serail* (*The Abduction from the Seraglio*). Maria begins with a kind of easy half-voice, known in the profession as 'marking', but is soon swept up by the emotion of the music into singing in full voice, showing such a complete mastery of all the technical difficulties that the hard-headed, blasé orchestral players break into applause at the end. When I complimented her on this truly astonishing singing she replied, 'Yes, it is marvellous, isn't it. I only wish I could do that now.' She was impatient to hear the tapes of our Amsterdam concert. 'The pirates have probably already started selling them, you know.'

We went into the dining-room, where a large painting of the *Adoration* dominated one wall. It was an attractive picture, painted in rich, warm colours and featuring foreground figures with their backs to the viewer so typical of a famous eighteenth-century Italian artist. 'A Bassano?' I asked.

'Yes.' I was not convinced, but it would have been churlish of me to add 'more likely to be School of'.

Ferruccio, impeccable in his white starched jacket and white gloves, served lunch, standing by the kitchen door almost to attention while we ate, seldom taking his eyes off Maria, watching her every move and anticipating her every wish.

First came a fragile pink-coloured soufflé. It was delicious and I was curious. 'Brain soufflé,' Maria said. Sorry I had asked, I gulped down half a glass of the red wine. Illogically, particularly for a lifetime eater of such a mysterious dish as the Scottish haggis, to me the brain seems too near the soul of the animal to be consigned to the knife of a gourmet chef. Roast guinea-fowl followed and with that and the cheese and fruit I savoured the comfort of the mellow Lafitte. During the whole meal Maria ate with the finesse of a gourmet, but hardly tasted the wine.

In a relaxed mood, she reminisced about her early career and how she found the opportunity to sing the coloratura roles which were to make her name – the famous occasion when she created a sensation at the Teatro La Fenice in Venice. She was singing the role of Brünnhilde in Wagner's *Die Walküre* under the baton of Tullio Serafin. He was also conducting the other new production of the season, Bellini's *I Puritani*, in which the principal role of Elvira was to be sung by one of Italy's leading sopranos, Margherita Carosio. A few days before the opening night the unfortunate lady became ill and had to cancel all her performances, leaving Serafin with the fruitless task of searching Italy for a substitute. 'The weather was rotten and we were housebound,' Maria told me. 'A flu was around and Serafin insisted we avoid public places, so on our nights off we made our own entertainment – no TV in those days. One evening, just for fun, I sight-read Elvira's aria, which surprised Mrs Serafin and she suggested I sing it for her husband when he returned home. Next day I had to sing it before the director of the theatre. After a short discussion Serafin told me they wanted me to sing Elvira. I told him I didn't know the role, but he insisted. I thought, if that man, with all his experience, believes I can do it, then I have nothing to lose.'

I wondered about 'sight-read'. After all, her teacher, Elvira de Hidalgo, who made her career singing the heroines of Donizetti and Rossini operas, must have passed on her knowledge of other bel canto roles to her omnivorous pupil. Perhaps Maria meant she did not know the aria from memory and was obliged to read it from the music. The other numbers, duets, trios and ensembles might be new to her, but sight-read the principal aria? At a distance a little embellishment made for a better story.

As a poor student in wartime Athens she had borrowed music from her teacher, de Hidalgo, learning her parts quickly so that she could return the scores in a week. Perceptive and astute, she developed a technique of quick study. Secure in this ability, she needed only the greatly esteemed Serafin's confirmation to convince her she could do it. He was the man who had coached her great idol, Rosa Ponselle, in *Norma*, the role that Callas was to make a corner-stone of her future repertoire. At that time Maria was a single-minded, ambitious young artist who must have seen in the situation an opportunity not to be missed. She was eager to show her abilities, to prove she was no ordinary soprano. Her début in Italy, at the Arena of Verona the previous year, had not been the earth-shattering success she had dreamed of. The reviews were good but not exceptional, nor was she overwhelmed by offers of future engagements. If she could win this new challenge it might be the beginning of her real career. Maria embarked on a period of intense study. During the day, Serafin sat at the piano, coaching her in the part of Elvira in *I Puritani* and in the evening stood before the opera house orchestra conducting as she sang Wagner's Brünnhilde.

When people buying tickets at the box-office were told of the change of cast for *I Puritani*, with Callas singing the role of Elvira, they were amazed and indignant. 'It's not possible, you're mad, Callas sings Brünnhilde.' In a world where every fan considered him- or herself an expert it is easy to understand their confusion. There were many squabbles and much angry shouting. 'That voice can't sing Elvira,' they objected, their disbelief understandable. In the opera repertoire two roles more completely divergent than Brünnhilde and Elvira would be difficult to find. The heroic voice of Wagner's dramatic, declamatory heroine is worlds apart from the agile coloratura and delicately graceful ornaments of Bellini. No wonder the fans were incredulous. News of their doubts spurred Callas on more than almost anything else. As she was to show again and again in her career, it was the public in the stalls, the banquettes, boxes and galleries who mattered to her, a volatile audience versed in the art and history of singing who did not hesitate to show their displeasure. She sang for her public and they were the people she strove to contact and win over. Her communication and rapport with them was paramount. More than the newspapermen, the critics, the agents, or even the opera house administrators who engaged her, Callas needed the response of the people sitting in the theatre.

'By that time I was already learning the role and I was determined to prove them wrong,' Maria said. Callas scored a spectacular success as Elvira and next day the whole of opera-loving Italy was agog with the news. It was not just that she had overcome the difficulties of a role thought to be outside her abilities, but to an audience accustomed to hearing it sung by light coloratura sopranos who were content with flexibility and beauty of tone, Callas had opened up a new world, imbuing the music with an intensity and emotional meaning they had never imagined. Up and down the country the newspapers acclaimed her. She became famous – not because of a diet, a divorce, a scandal created out of illness, or a millionaire lover, but because she had shown herself to be a great musician and a unique artist.

'I always like a challenge and would sing anything I was asked if it was rewarding or difficult. In those days I had no nerves – that came when I became famous. Then people expected so much of me it was frightening.'

After lunch we returned to the sitting-room. Maria opened one of the Chinoiserie lacquered eighteenth-century armoires which stood either side of the door, threw up her arms, partly in indication, partly exasperation, and exclaimed, 'Look, all pirates. They get all the money – I don't get a penny.' The cupboard held a large number of LPs and boxed sets of records illegally pressed from unauthorised recordings made either in the opera house during live performances or, better still from the point of view of the sound quality, copied from broadcasts. She knew her way around, reaching straight for the record she wanted, a concert with orchestra which included 'O mio babbino caro'. The piano tuner arrived while we were listening to it so we retired to her bedroom where there was another hi-fi set-up. She asked me to compare the recorded performance with those she was singing now. 'Did I sing as well as that in our concerts?' Then, almost as though she was thinking aloud, 'It was about that time that my boy-friend started to influence me away from music and I gave it up. I was so tired of all the fuss and problems in opera houses, and intrigues between sopranos and tenors. But in the end I learned it wasn't worth giving up everything for him. He was only interested in his family. After all, music is the only thing I have in my life, and he took it away from me.'

The time had come for me to leave for the airport to catch my plane for London. We stood talking at the open door for some time, Maria thanking me for being helpful and particularly for my loyalty during the Gorlinsky–Tebaldi concert crisis. She seemed reluctant to let me go, stepping out on to the landing as I edged my way towards the lift, skipping from one subject to another and stretching out the goodbyes so that I began to despair of getting to the airport on time. She suddenly looked desperately lonely. Her favourite maid, Bruna, was at home in Italy caring for her ailing mother, but her second, Elena, was kind and devoted, and she was lucky in Ferruccio, who manifestly idolised her. I was sad to leave.

'Music is the only thing in my life and he took it away from me.' As a casual remark made while sipping after-lunch coffee it was an interesting, if simplistic, summary of a major part in Callas's life that in reality was much more complicated.

In the late Fifties her voice was beginning to show signs of overwork, of the wear and tear of the improbable demands she had made on it. There was a perceptible decline in the ease of production and even tonal beauty of her singing. She was approaching forty, a time when the human body begins to show changes. It is not uncommon for artists who were child prodigies to stumble on a difficult period at this age. In youth, while the child's flexible young body grows, the technique of playing or singing is developing, the two becoming indivisible, the muscles of breathing in particular. Unlike artists who learn their technique as adults and have a clear idea of the place it takes in their general physique, the prodigy knows no such distinction. The body *is* the technique. Later, when the musculature changes noticeably in ageing, an artist begins to question not what they or she is doing but *how*. In 1973, after a period of eight years when she had not sung in public, her muscles weak from lack of use, I had to show Maria she was breathing only with the top of her lungs. I found myself reminding her how a singer uses the diaphragm and intercostal muscles.

This predicament is not unusual in the music world, even the late great violinist Yehudi Menuhin experienced it. He made the wise decision of taking time off from performance and spent a year restudying his technique. Callas had come to this crossroads in the late Fifties. With such a wide range of operatic roles, where she daringly ignored the conventional boundaries between the differing types of soprano voice, and the famed intensity of her performances, the strain on her voice was beginning to tell. Her performance record shows a falling-off in frequency of stage appearances. She had reached a peak in her career that became increasingly difficult to sustain. To be a prima donna was a burden, each performance a battle with her voice which she came to accept as the cross she must bear for her art. (Even in better times she was never content with her interpretations, being the first to see the imperfections. On the night of one of her greatest successes as Lucia, 29 September 1955, she cried herself to sleep, unhappy in the belief that she had let herself down – and failed to reach the standards she held in her imagination. Ironically, a recording of the broadcast of that performance at the Berlin Festival under Karajan, originally available only from a pirate company, is now one of the treasures of the EMI CD list.)

As a teenager Maria had lived in the fantasy world of the romantic heroines of opera. Callas the artist had shown she was mistress of that world and, in doing so, was now rich and famous. While striving for that goal she had not only lost weight but become a woman famous also for her beauty. At this time she was tiring of the dull bourgeois domestic life with her Italian businessman husband, Giovanni Battista Meneghini, whom she had married in 1949. The fledgling woman who had grown up in the nourishing care and protection of her father-figure husband had now grown her own wings. In glossy magazines she read of the glamorous, exciting lives of the rich and famous, the so-called Jet Set. Self-confident and proud of her beauty, she was ready to join them in a world where she would shine as a woman. Instead of truthfully facing her difficult situation, reassessing her technique and possibly narrowing down the range of her roles, she turned her back on her artistic problems and took the easy way out. She allowed Aristotle Onassis to court her.

A rough-hewn, vibrant personality, Ari moved in, full steam ahead, overwhelming her with his vigour, humour and insidious charm, gifts of precious jewels, flowers, often thirty red roses three times a day and the style which his limitless wealth allowed him. Largely self-made, he had proved himself a daring entrepreneur who could flummox rivals, national institutions and governments with a combination of business flair and the wiles of the bazaar, dealing in tobacco, whaling and oil-tankers, and proud to claim he was the only man in the world to own a national airline, Olympic Airways. Women of standing in their own right were always important to Onassis, if only to be shown off, like trophies, as a measure of his success. As his fortune grew so did the importance of his women. In his early days they were actresses or ballerinas, followed by women of social distinction who, with their connections, could further his business ventures. When it came to marriage and respectability he targeted and won his greatest catch so far, Athina, the seventeen-year-old daughter of Stavros Livanos, one of the wealthiest of Greek shipowners. They had a son, Alexander, and a daughter, Christina, after whom he named his yacht. It was a successful marriage, despite his philanderings, until he met Maria Callas. Tina could turn a blind eye to his occasional affairs with an unknown model or starlet, but not a woman of the international status of the diva.

Attracted at first by his wealth and the glamour of his life-style, Callas soon discovered they had much in common. Each had been born in a foreign country, spent only a few years in Greece while growing up, suffered wartime privations, family discontent, and both had reached the pinnacle of success in their chosen fields by force of character and passionate determination. No Greek man was as famous as Onassis, nor any Greek woman more famous than Callas. Their Greekness and mutual love of the homeland was one of their lasting bonds.

Maria's life now revolved around Onassis and his beloved yacht *Christina*, where captain and crew were instructed to treat her as 'La Padrone', and she became hostess to film stars, ex-kings, the Rainiers, the Begum Aga Khan, rich bankers, aristocrats, society beauties and others whose talents or inheritance had given them reputations. Among her guests on the *Christina*, or mixing with the beau monde in night-clubs ashore, no star shone brighter than Maria.

'She is the only woman I can talk to about business,' Onassis told a friend and Maria, intrigued by the machinations of high finance, relished the late-night exchanges with him and his cronies. For the first time she was being loved as a woman, not a singer feeding her mother's ego or Meneghini's bank account. But as their relationship developed Maria learned a darker side to Onassis's character. He was given to extreme reactions, prone to fits of temper. If frustrated in a deal, or by an imagined social slight, his pent-up rage easily turned to uncontrolled violence and Maria's outspokenness could trigger off an aggression that seemed an intrinsic element of his character. (She was luckier, though, than a former girl-friend whose bruises were bad enough to need the attention of a doctor.) Maria looked on it as behaviour that confirmed the depth of their intimacy and the price she must pay to have a man worthy of Callas's eminence.

Intensely proud of being Greek, Onassis and Maria would often eschew the glitter and glamour of the Mediterranean night-spots for the unsophisticated pleasures of a simple taverna on a Greek island where they could enjoy the directness of the Greek character, drinking Metaxa, dancing and smashing plates with the locals until the early hours.

Through all this Maria's mind was on marriage. She desperately wanted to have children, preferably twins, but though it was a constant subject in their conversations and plans were often drawn up, Onassis always found some reason to defer the ceremony. Nothing came of Maria's hopes, not even a pregnancy could get him to the altar. Angry that she had not taken precautions, he told her that if she had the child she would never see him again. Maria had an abortion.

At no time had Onassis ever been interested in opera, only in the fact that Callas was the superstar of that world. Insensitive to her creative nature and her needs as an artist, he could never understand why she should want to continue singing. As he saw her off one morning on his private plane to sing at Covent Garden, where tickets for her performances were being sold at enormously inflated prices and lines of opera lovers in sleeping bags waited overnight outside the box-office, he said to her, 'Why do you bother to sing? I've got plenty of money.'

'He was a very oriental man,' Maria told me.

With the assassination in 1963 of John F. Kennedy, President of the United States, Onassis saw in his sights an even greater trophy than the queen of opera; the queen of the United States of America. After nearly nine years of living together as man and wife, the yacht their home, he abandoned Maria to marry Jackie Kennedy in October 1968. A few days after the wedding he was back in Paris whistling under Maria's bedroom window. 'I've made a big mistake,' he told her.

After Christmas Maria went to stay with the Di Stefanos in Milan. Whenever I telephoned he was reluctant to let me speak to her, making feeble excuses to put me off. 'Madame Callas is in bed,' he would say, which seemed a lame excuse because I knew that the telephone was the first thing Maria reached for after drinking her coffee in the morning. It was a favourite time to gossip. His attitude continued even after I got to Milan. It seemed to me that he was afraid of me speaking alone with Maria.

He was in his dressing-gown when I arrived at noon for my first session with him since Amsterdam. He took the keys to open the studio which, although on the same landing, was not directly connected to the apartment. I asked Mrs Di Stefano as she came out of Maria's bedroom if I might go in to say hello, but to my surprise she said she must ask her husband. He came along just then and flared up at the idea. 'She's in bed,' he cried as though outraged. Some time later, as I practised while waiting for the session to begin, he came into the studio, making unusually polite small talk and asked me to come back in the afternoon.

They were playing cards when I was shown in and greeted me quite casually. Maria looked up from her hand. 'You were to be in Paris on the 4th – where were you?' she asked rather peevishly.

'Gorlinsky said you wouldn't need me,' I replied.

'Oh, didn't he tell you all about the record being off? Those little songs are not for me. But what about our concerts?' she asked. I had hardly time to register my disappointment before Di Stefano started moving from the table, a signal that we all assumed meant we should go to the studio to work. Again he was inordinately polite, surprising me by asking me for the first time ever that I correct him should he make any mistakes.

We worked our way through all of the finale of Puccini's *Manon Lescaut*, including the soprano aria 'Sola, perduta, abbandonata', before listening to their 1957 recording with Serafin. Little by little through the session I became aware of a new Di Stefano as coach. Very polite, suppressing any impatient anger, he treated Maria in a most respectful manner, moving unconvincingly away from his former brash treatment into a pattern of continuous flattery. Maria was dubious about her singing, repeatedly asking for reassurance and never convinced. She stamped her foot. 'I must get it,' she said quietly, as much to herself as to him. 'If we're going to do this in New York I've got to get it right.'

'You'll be brilliant,' Di Stefano said encouragingly.

We broke up early so that Maria could visit her dressmaker. After she left, Di Stefano lingered a while in the studio asking how things were in London. I told him of Ivor's regrettable reaction to the new situation. 'Oh, so you have lost a friend,' he said. 'Never mind he's just another old prima donna' – chuckling carelessly. 'Maria and I are giving a little concert for the hospital where Luisa is being treated,' he added. 'I've been promising for some time and now seems a good opportunity.' Having Callas as a partner was certainly a feather in his cap. 'By the way,' he went on, 'it's a private concert. Keep it quiet – we don't want the press there.' As he made no mention of any part I might take in it, I surmised that in the city of La Scala he must know innumerable experienced pianists, one of whom had perhaps agreed at an earlier time to play. Nevertheless, I wanted to be sure. 'Of course we need a pianist,' he answered. 'You'll play.'

A situation was arising which left me feeling uneasy. Di Stefano was so unusually formal and Maria so inaccessible that I began to feel very alone, more and more like a stranger with each visit to the studio. I was missing the warm, homely hospitality of Georges Mandel, which always enhanced my sojourns in Paris.

They did not appear at a session arranged for twelve noon. At two-fifteen I ventured into the apartment to find them at the closing stages of lunch. They had forgotten. Maria was full of apologies. Di Stefano said, 'Let's meet at seven this evening.' I worried all afternoon. Could this be a beginning to Ivor's warning? Before we started work I spoke with Di Stefano, telling him of my misgivings and Ivor's threat of revenge. I hinted that we were not working in the usual friendly way. 'It's because *we* are worried about *our* singing,' he said impatiently. '*You* have nothing to worry about. All you've got to do is *play*.' Perhaps I am fortunate not to be a singer, I thought, relieved by his explanation.

They sang through some of the usual duets, both sounding as though they needed the practice. I was glad to hear them at work again. Afterwards he was warmer to me, even jocular, while I dressed to leave, Maria still asking him for advice. He sat down at the piano ready to continue the work. 'Roberto, don't worry about anything. You're coming to America . . . and don't think evil thoughts.'

Maria joined him in his reassuring remarks: 'We like you, and that's what matters.' I left, feeling much happier and once again wishing I could do more to help them. Our thickly dated American tour appeared difficult enough for singers at the height of their powers.

On the afternoon of the concert at the Istituto Nationale per lo Studio alla Cura dei Tumori we started the session with Di Stefano's solos. He sang the Lalo aria in the original key but it did not go well. He noticed the *Bohème* aria, 'Che gelida manina', in my music case and said he would sing that instead, and turned away from the piano. I reminded him that we had never done it together. 'OK, do the last page.' That was all the rehearsal I got. Maria asked to go through the *Cavalleria* duet. 'Just for the sake of the words,' she said. As we arrived at the hospital we met some of the children being led along a corridor to the lecture-room where the concert was to take place, looking like shop-window mannequins, with hairless heads and puzzled, expectant eyes. 'Don't let me take my glasses,' Maria said. 'If I see them in there I will be too upset to sing. I really won't be able to sing.'

Despite the informality of the occasion both singers were surprisingly nervous during the concert; in fact, I had seldom seen them so uncertain. They stood very close to the tinny upright piano, which I played with the lid open to give more support. Maria's memory failed her in the *Cavalleria* duet so often that even in such a small hall I was obliged to prompt her. Geoffrey Land, a cultured English friend living in Milan, later told me he was surprised by their behaviour. 'The whole thing was decidedly amateurish,' he said. Despite the intended privacy the next day's edition of the London *Telegraph* carried a small piece reporting that Callas had sung in the hospital. Not many lines, but it was on the front page.

A thick fog was covering the broad Lombardy plain that evening, so instead of flying we travelled by rail to Stuttgart. Hoping to board the train and retire as early as possible, I asked Di Stefano for my ticket. 'Oh, just go to your hotel and wait. I'll ring you when we are ready to leave.' He did not think that I might have something better to do – eating dinner, for instance. Quite firmly I told him it would be easier all round if I had my ticket and found my own way to the station. That the train might not be starting from Milan had not occurred to me, so I found myself sitting on the platform guarding my luggage for two hours before they arrived, accompanied only by Elena, both looking rather grim, he clinging close to Maria as he usually did when they walked together. As ever, he had no change for tipping. When I brought out all the money I had in my pocket, notes and coins, he grasped everything and without giving it a glance passed it to the porter. There was one happy man on the station that evening.

Next day a Maria I had not seen for some time met me in the hotel foyer. Relaxed and glowing, she gave an interview to the press. Di Stefano sat her down alone to be photographed, taking part only when asked about their joint activities. He said they were planning to produce and sing in a production of *Carmen* the following year in Dallas. 'Why Dallas?'

'Because Maria is on the Board of Directors there and they've got enough money to have sufficient rehearsals.'

'I want four or five weeks of musical study with the conductor and principals before even the first production call,' Maria said. 'It has got to be a concerted effort – we build together.'

We drove to the Liederhalle where we found, instead of a piano on the platform a table and some chairs had been set up, with a noisy crowd of young people settling into their stall seats. Maria was quite unconcerned by the mistake in our booking. She chatted in a relaxed way with a few of the students, showing no hint of annoyance. 'We're having a seminar on Meditation,' she was told.

'Meditation,' she said to me as we left the hall. 'Meditation! When we were young we didn't meditate, *we worked*.' She was still

[125]

talking about it when we were settled in the car. 'Dates or not, I always worked. Then, when the chances came I was ready.'

We had left the hotel early, at 6 p.m, with the intention of rehearsing on stage to get the feeling of the acoustic of the hall, which we had been denied the previous day.

Everything was happy at the beginning – even some clowning from both in the *L'Elisir* duet. I put the transposition of *Don Carlo* up on my music stand but Di Stefano said, '*No, in tono.*' It went very badly for him, which was embarrassing because Frau Collien, who was looking after us in the absence of her husband or Gorlinsky, was sitting in the stalls with Herr Hofmeister, the local agent, and some others. Di Stefano began to pace about restlessly, directing his singing to the back of the stage, then suddenly broke off mid-phrase protesting loudly enough for all to hear, 'It's that awful air-conditioning in the hotel.' He turned to me. 'Come on, let's go,' he said brusquely.

In my dressing-room I was grappling with my stiff white tie when, at seven-thirty, Eva Collien came to tell me the concert, due to start at eight o'clock, was off. There was general consternation, the puzzled house staff asking for instructions, Hofmeister arguing with Eva about the best course of action, then making a loudspeaker announcement to the public in the foyer, but not to those already finding their seats. More confusion resulted when the half-baked information filtered through the foyer doors into the auditorium. I went to see Maria and Di Stefano. He was packing his evening suit, she still in the long black dress she had travelled in, the red gown worn in Madrid unpacked. Hofmeister came to ask if they would at least show themselves on-stage while he made the official announcement that Di Stefano was too ill to sing. Most of the audience, some seated others still moving around, applauded warmly when they saw Maria. Some booed. 'Let Callas sing then,' someone shouted. I grabbed my music. Di Stefano stepped down into the auditorium while Maria sang 'O mio babbino caro'. During the applause he made to climb back up again but his way was barred by a uniformed guard who refused to believe he was the tenor. A shouting match ensued until someone in the crowd convinced the guard that indeed he was Herr Di Stefano. A piqued tenor returned to his dressing-room via the stage.

The audience was calling for more from Maria. We went on-stage again to a great reception but as Maria announced 'Suicidio' a man, still in overcoat and scarf and, curiously, smoking a pipe cried out 'Boo'. Maria listened to him as he complained of the cancellation and how many kilometres he had travelled, then she apologised to him as she would do a guest in her own living-room. 'I'm sorry,' she said, 'but I can do nothing about it.' At this the man turned his back on her and walked away. 'Do you want me to sing?' she cried after him. There was an outburst from the audience, some upbraiding the heckler for his rudeness others applauding and encouraging Maria. But now she was annoyed. She walked off indignantly. I waited at the piano, the audience still applauding, till Hofmeister appeared, indicating with a gesture that it was all over. 'If only she had sung four arias,' he said later. 'We could have kept a percentage of the takings.'

Only the Italian and Greek consuls were to be allowed backstage, but a determined female fan got as far as speaking with Maria before one of the security guards, a German in uniform, pulled her away. In the corridor he was outraged when she called him an idiot. The argument was getting near to being physical when I interrupted and in my best German told the guard I would be responsible for the young lady. She was still weeping when I took her to Maria, who consoled her with soft words and two autographs.

At the hotel, while Di Stefano was waylaid by old friends, I took Maria to her apartment. She offered me a drink. 'Take a whisky,' she said while Elena unpacked the unworn red evening gown. She appeared quite calm, insouciant and not inclined to talk about the fiasco of the evening, except to say that Di Stefano had had the first signs of a sore throat already in Milan. Instead, we talked about her work in the studio. I mentioned that despite Di Stefano's changed manner the tension in the air had left me feeling uncomfortable. 'Yes,' she said, 'things were a bit nervy. I told him he must stop bullying me and if I didn't make quick progress I would just stop singing.' Suddenly the reason for Di Stefano's changed attitude in the studio became clear to me. He knew that his diary would be much thinner without Maria. 'Come up and have something to eat when you are ready,' she said as I left to change.

When I returned the two TV sets were on, one in the open-doored bedroom and the other in the sitting-room. She and Di Stefano were watching John Wayne and Henry Fonda in a film about Custer's last stand, a tempting cold collation on the table. While we were eating a doctor came to examine the patient for the sake of the insurance claim. 'What else could he do but agree that the throat was bad,' Eva said to me later.

Two American reporters sent a message to Maria pleading for three minutes and a photograph. She asked me to phone them and say she was already in bed. When I told her how the two intrepid adventurers had faced the hazards of modern travel, at their own expense, to search her out, hoping to interview her for the sake of promoting opera in Detroit and writing about her glorious art for the poor students at home her response was 'Oh yeah?' and a cynical chuckle. 'They always say it will be a cover picture and then the three minutes becomes thirty before I can get away. You can never trust them. They even print so-called interviews I've never given. They write things I've never said – it's unfair.'

Di Stefano came out of the bedroom dressed in his beautiful new dress-suit. 'Made in Milano,' he boasted, 'and they [the Stuttgart public] didn't even get a chance to see it.'

A documentary on the television prompted Maria to talk of Marlon Brando's support of the American Indian. 'He made a film about them,' she said. 'If he objects so much to their treatment why doesn't he give them the money he made on the film?'

Later, before I left, it was agreed that we should all go to New York at the same time. 'We have work to do,' Maria said.

*   *   *

In London a few days later, I received a call from Maria in Paris: 'We must work on repertoire, Robert, I mean, if anything like Stuttgart happens again we must be prepared.' That was the first inkling I had that she was considering a concert without a partner.

9

ON THE ROAD AGAIN – THE USA
AND CANADA

'Mario! Mario! Mario!' crooned the voice on the telephone. '*Son qui*,' came the response, evoking Cavaradossi's answer when Floria Tosca makes her first entry in Puccini's opera *Tosca*.

Maria Callas had arrived in New York. She was a week earlier than expected because rain had cut short her pre-tour holiday with Di Stefano in Puerto Rico. The first thing she did was to contact the man who was to be the tour manager for our time in the USA, Mario De Maria. Mario was chosen by Sol Hurok, the Ukrainian-born American impresario, because of his myriad talents and abilities. He was Italian-born, an opera lover, spoke five languages, had worked with the Italian Shipping Line before establishing his own travel business, was an International Systems Analyst for Olivetti, taught computing, worked as a road builder when he landed in New York, then quickly became involved in the theatre and music world, managing the visits of the Bolshoi Ballet, Bolshoi Opera, international orchestras, the Royal Shakespeare Company and new productions of various musicals including *Most Happy Fella* and *Porgy and Bess*. He first met Callas in 1959 when he was assistant to Alan Oxenburg, founder of the American Opera Society. During rehearsals she was amused by the felicity of the name when she was introduced to Mario De Maria.

Oxenburg, who had heard Callas singing *Il Pirata* some months earlier at La Scala, read in the newspapers of her spectacular sacking from the New York Metropolitan Opera by Rudolf Bing, saw an opportunity and invited her to sing a concert version of *Il Pirata* in the Carnegie Hall. (The dispute with Bing centred ostensibly around the choice of operas Maria was to sing at the Met but, in fact, was instigated and manoeuvred by the wily Meneghini to get her out of the strenuous seven-week tour which was part of the deal. Bing lost his patience and cancelled the contract.) That Oxenburg offered her a much bigger fee than the Met was not the only attraction. Callas relished the idea of putting Bing's nose out of joint by singing for her New York public in spite of being banned from the Met.

While negotiating with Sol Hurok, Mario was on the West Coast touring with *Godspell*. In a break he and some of the crew visited nearby Las Vegas. After a night of carousing in clubs and gambling palaces, Mario returned to his hotel at 6 a.m. to make the pre-arranged telephone call to Hurok in New York where the time was 9 a.m. They were to discuss details of his forthcoming tour with Callas and Di Stefano. 'You know, Mario,' Sol Hurok said to him, 'Maria is not a difficult person, but Di Stefano is a tenor. Be careful. They are in a certain tax bracket, they are not allowed to spend any money, you have to pay for everything – *but*, you must be watchful of Di Stefano because he's a *gambler*. Where are you now, by the way?'

Mario bit the tip of his tongue and said, 'Oh, I'm half-way between San Diego and LA.' Geographically not far from the truth. In the next few months his mental agility and diplomatic alacrity was to stand him in good stead.

Mario's first assignment as treasurer was to accompany Maria to Madison Avenue, a place synonymous with advertising, where artists, marketing psychologists and sales people contrive to manipulate the buying habits of America. Their offices are on the upper floors, above the unbroken street-level façades of art galleries, expensive boutiques and fashion showrooms. Maria's luggage had not yet arrived from Paris and she needed a dress to wear at the dinner Sol Hurok was giving in her honour. Mario dutifully paid out the $4000. During the meal that evening, after telling Maria how well she looked, Sol said, 'I must tell you, Maria, I do like that beautiful gown you're wearing.'

Maria put her hand on his and said, 'Oh, I'm so glad you like it, Sol. You paid for it.'

'Would you like to come up and see my new place?' Maria asked when she rang me on the morning after I arrived in New York. I gathered all my music together and took the elevator up to her apartment on the tenth floor. I was glad to see a piano already installed. A splendid Persian carpet, which the management had rented to enhance the décor of her sitting-room, spread luxuriously across most of the floor and under the piano. 'It's nice of them,' she said. 'But I only asked for two things, a piano and windows that can be opened.' Mario had chosen the Stanhope Hotel on 5th Avenue opposite the Metropolitan Museum and a few blocks from his own home around the corner from the Guggenheim.

I enjoyed some time alone with Maria, catching up with our news, before Di Stefano arrived. We started work on the tenor aria from *Adriana Lecouvreur*, only to be interrupted by Maria saying something was wrong. I was hesitant about making any such comment myself, especially if Maria were present, since the damage to his Sicilian macho image might lead to a fit of temper. He sang the passage again, Maria stopping him when she heard the wrong note. 'Ah, it's my ear again,' she said. 'I just knew it wasn't right!'

In the *Faust* duet Di Stefano's voice cracked again as it had in Stuttgart, frustrating and angering him with each repeat. 'It's too dry here,' he cried, as he moved into the bathroom and turned on the hot water full blast. When the steam billowed out of the bath he used his two hands to waft it in the direction of the sitting-room. 'Instant humidification,' he said. The next object of his ire was the Persian carpet. In his opinion it was too thick and should be removed.

Maria said, 'Come on, Robert, let's lift this carpet,' so as our tenor strutted about, coughing and clearing his throat, I lifted the corners of the grand piano while Maria pulled out the carpet from under each leg and attempted to roll it up. We looked at the forest of furniture standing on it – tables, chairs, sofas – and called the manager. While we waited Maria apologised to Di Stefano for being so troublesome. Eventually two janitors came, took the carpet away, hoovered the fitted carpet and left. I put up the transposition of the *Don Carlo* duet as at last we gathered round the piano again. '*No, in tono, Roberto*,' Maria said. It went very well for her, less so for him. 'It suits me better in the original key,' Maria said casually afterwards. Di Stefano said nothing. He telephoned a doctor who had already 'Dropped some oil in his larynx', put on a record of Gershwin hits and sat down to drink coffee with us. 'You could stay longer and practise if you like, Robert,' Maria said. 'Couldn't he, Pippo?' turning to Di Stefano, always thoughtful as a musician but ever needing to defer to him. I realised the impracticality of the idea, however kind the gesture appeared, made my excuses and left.

A press conference had been called for the next day at two-thirty, but before it Di Stefano wanted to sing through a possible addition to our programmes, a duet from *Andrea Chenier*. A single run-through seemed to satisfy his curiosity before asking for the transposed version of the *Forza* duet. After a few bars Maria stopped and said we should do it '*in tono*'. In the confusion of fingering I fluffed the introduction in the new key.

Di Stefano swung around to Maria crying, 'Did you hear that?'

'Oh, it's only a little accident,' she answered. 'Hearing Ivor's playing has spoiled it for him.' I made a mental note to ask her again not to defend me. Our work was interrupted by the arrival at the door of Sol Hurok, come to take them down to the press conference. They were very nervous.

A fuss was made of the seating arrangements, Maria eventually settling down between the two men. Questions came thick and fast – about her reaction to the adverse reviews in Europe: 'I happen to be the best critic of myself'; about other present-day singers: 'I don't know them because I don't go to hear them, I'm not curious'; about her own singing: 'Nobody can sing as well as in the old days. Now,' with a touch of the grandiose prima donna, 'one is more mature. Some things I can do better, the feeling, the line and atmosphere stays on. If you're born an artist you stay an artist. Your materials are always there. If I feel my voice is losing its possibilities I would not sing any more. This tour will be good practice for next season.' She repeatedly deferred to Di Stefano but the newspapermen were interested only in what she had to say. All their questions were addressed to the star of the occasion. Asked if she considered herself to be a temperamental person, she began hesitatingly with, 'I do have a temperament . . .' and was saved by Hurok who chirped in merrily with, 'I wouldn't have an artist who didn't have it.'

Would she sing and produce at the Met if invited? 'Oh yes,' was the enthusiastic reply, though she was not happy with the growing powers of producers and directors: 'There's too much going on on the stage. It makes it difficult for the singers to concentrate. In our day the public came to hear the singers.' Neither was she happy with the additions of the 'cadenza man', meaning Richard Bonynge, husband and coach of Joan Sutherland: 'There's too much concentration nowadays on decoration.' Later she told me that she was angry that our concert in New York was a benefit for the Metropolitan Opera Guild. 'What did they ever do for me?' she complained. 'I had to sing in tired old sets with a cast I didn't know from one night to another.' As the interview drew to a close I kidded myself I would not be needed and escaped to my favourite New York museum, the nearby Frick, a haven of civilised beauty and tranquillity in the noisy metropolis.

'Oh, he's playing the tourist, is he,' Di Stefano said to Mario when he discovered I was not in the hotel.

'Let him enjoy himself,' Maria said.

Later in the afternoon, hearing him singing in his bedroom, I went in to pick up the *Andrea Chenier* score so that I could practise our new piece. 'What do you want that for?' he asked. 'We're not going to sing *that*. Why don't you spend your precious time practising the duets we *are* going to sing?' Exactly what they were I would have been glad to know, but that snap of sarcasm seemed to relieve his feelings, leaving him quite affable and friendly. Despite all the difficulties and scenes, the result often of his frustration with his own singing, he had a boyish charm which could quickly resolve any discord he had created.

In the evening Mario brought Maria a pirate recording of her Berlin 1955 *Lucia*, a record she had never heard. Excited, 'I can't believe I sang so well,' she said. 'That's always what I aimed at but felt I never achieved . . . and to think I was so unhappy after that performance.'

Life with a person of fame needs care. Informality is acceptable so long as it suits the mood of the celebrity, but woe betide anyone who steps beyond the unknown boundary or assumes intimacy at the wrong moment. They can be jolly and friendly, encouraging you to make jokes and treat them as though they are ordinary human beings, then suddenly the barricades are up and the fangs bared. Maria's maid, Consuelo, was not on guard when Di Stefano came into the kitchen at 36 Georges Mandel one morning while she was preparing lunch. Like a little boy he impishly began to nibble at the food and, just as playfully, as a mother would reprove a naughty son, Consuelo gently slapped his wrist. He flew into a rage. 'Do you know who I am?' he shouted at her and stalked out, demanding that she be sacked. Maria knew that Consuelo was a fiery spirit, but with that went an alert mind and super-efficiency in her job. She had no intention of losing one of her best maids to a whim of Di Stefano. Consuelo was confronted and though at first refusing to apologise, eventually, after three days and a hint that she might be taken to America, agreed. 'But I do it for you, Madame,' she said, 'not for him.' She never really did forgive him.

This is why I was surprised to find that Maria had chosen Con-suelo to accompany her on the American tour. Elena, who had been with us in Europe, was gentle and attentive but could be forgetful. Bruna, her favourite maid since the early days in Milan, was still nursing her ailing mother at home in Italy. Maria missed her sorely. 'Why doesn't the old woman just die,' was her exasperated comment.

We drove in two limousines to Philadelphia for the opening concert of our American tour. In the first car I sat with the chauffeur, Maria and Di Stefano in the spacious seats behind. Mrs Di Stefano looked annoyed at being ushered into the second limousine beside Consuelo and Mario.

The programme at the Academy of Music that evening consisted entirely of items we had performed in Europe. We had a capacity house.

'Whether one has heard her before or not,' wrote Louis Snyder in the *Christian Science Monitor*, 'Callas displayed all the qualities of the superstar. A majestic figure, the impeccable taste of Callas's platform manner could, in itself, be an etiquette lesson for aspiring performers. Taste, unfortunately, was not the outstanding characteristic of Callas's singing partner Giuseppe Di Stefano. In what was undoubtedly well-intentioned exuberance, he committed all the sins of vocal excess that self-confident favorites are heir to, and offered a strangely florid contrast to the dignified carriage and projection of Callas. The accompanist, Robert Sutherland, might be said to have complemented Callas and coped with Di Stefano. A certain kittenish deference was acted out by the two principals – the soprano protesting being left alone on-stage for a solo bow by the grinning tenor who skipped into the wings. In this carnival ambience one could hardly be surprised at anything.' He ended his astute review with 'Callas, even with the blinding brilliance of her powers undeniably dimmed, belongs to the operatic stage where she can logically dominate the scene. Her appearance in concert only hints at what the excitement has been about all these years.'

Maria was indignant when she heard that another critic wrote she was no longer a tigress but a lamb. 'I resent that,' she said.

'They called me a tigress because I knew what I wanted and I was firm. But I'm certainly not a lamb. Who wants a lamb? I couldn't be an artist if I was a lamb.'

The morning after the concert we returned to New York to face our next big hurdle, the first concert in Carnegie Hall on 17 February. As the day approached Maria became increasingly nervous. She could not tolerate anyone being present when we worked at the hall, complaining about the electrician busy around us and even asking her old friend Dario Soria, Executive Director of the Opera Guild, to leave while we rehearsed. Without allowing her voice some time to warm up she complained after one short phrase, calling 'Basta, Roberto', but I remained seated at the piano. Despite her protestations the voice was as good as it had ever been on the tour.

We had planned a drive through Central Park after the rehearsal but Mrs Di Stefano and a companion appeared at the stage door and climbed into the car with us, much to the chagrin of Maria. No one could agree where we should go, so Di Stefano flared up in anger and told the driver to take us back to the hotel. Maria immediately went up to her apartment. She was in bed when I visited her before going out to dinner, furious that her outing had been spoiled. 'Can't she ever respect my privacy?' she shouted.

At about 2 a.m. I was woken by the ring of the telephone. Maria could not sleep, bedevilled by thoughts of the concert next day. Puzzled that she was ringing me, when I knew Di Stefano usually comforted her before a concert, I asked, 'Are you alone?'

'Yes. He's gone to the other woman,' she replied. I assumed she meant his wife. She had already taken two sleeping tablets but they were ineffective. 'Will I be all right tomorrow?' she asked, searching for reassurance. 'Will you pray for me Robert? Please pray for me,' she begged as we said good-night after half an hour on the phone.

In the morning I slipped out of the hotel without telling anyone, determined to have an untroubled period alone with the Steinway on the platform of the hall. I returned to the hotel feeling invigorated and ready for the concert that evening, phoned Maria's apartment and spoke with Consuelo. She sounded flustered and hesitant, uncertain what to say, then I heard Di Stefano shout that he would ring me later. About five in the afternoon Mario telephoned me to say he was coming to my room and would I fix him a large, strong whisky. There was trouble. In the night, after speaking with me, Maria had rung Mario but thinking Di Stefano was with her he did nothing. Now he regretted that he had quashed his impulse to go to her room.

The note which Consuelo found pushed under her door was from Maria asking not to be disturbed in the morning, but when she had not appeared by midday Consuelo became anxious and went into the bedroom. Maria lay in a deep sleep, her deathly pallor a shock to Consuelo and when Maria did not respond to her calling and shaking she rushed to phone Di Stefano. He rang Mario, who called Dr Louis Parrish, who arrived to find Maria unconscious and Di Stefano in tears. She had taken more of the sleeping tablets after ringing Mario and me. Blabbering and incoherent, she could not say how many tablets she had swallowed. The doctor gave her an emetic to clear anything that remained of the drugs, lifted her out of bed, slapping her face while walking her around the room and forcing her to drink strong coffee. 'Don't let her sleep,' he instructed Consuelo and Di Stefano. 'Keep her active.' Meanwhile Mario was rushing about fetching medicines from the pharmacist, contacting the Hurok office and telephoning anyone who might be involved with the concert. By mid-afternoon Maria was regaining her power of speech and managed to say to Di Stefano, 'There's something I must tell you but can't say it. Consuelo will tell you.'

'Madame can't have Mrs Di Stefano around any longer,' the maid told him nervously. He made no reply. Whatever his thoughts he was too distressed by the situation on hand to think clearly.

Dr Parrish tried everything he could, but Maria's nasal and throat cavities were dry and inflamed. After some hours he had to admit that she would be incapable of singing that evening. He gave Mario the signed certificate to take to Sol Hurok. Mario, who had not smoked tobacco for fourteen years, cadged a cigarette from the taxi

[138]

driver who took him to the hall. When he arrived he went straight to the bar, where the press waited for an explanation. Sol Hurok waved the doctor's certificate in the air before reading it out aloud. 'Incipient influenza and acute inflammation of the respiratory tract,' it said. A yell from the reporters as they rushed off to the telephones.

Earlier, Maria had given me a weary smile when I went into her bedroom. I sat with her for some time before she asked me to go downtown to see what was happening at the hall. 'And bring me back some of the flowers,' she said in a low monotone.

Shortly before the inner doors were due to be opened the manager of the concert hall received a call from a friend of Di Stefano warning him to stand by for bad news. He never opened the doors that evening even though the foyer was already packed and more people were gathering on the sidewalk, spilling out on to the road, puzzled at not being admitted. Mounted police on agitated horses attempted to keep some control while at either end of the short section of West 57th Street, between 6th and 7th Avenues, more mounted police were checking the chauffeur-driven limousines carrying the rich and famous. A flashed concert ticket was the pass. The clamorous mob on the sidewalk were agog with excitement and gleefully shouting advice to the arriving notables: 'Go home. She's done it again'; 'She's cancelled'; or 'She's not singing tonight, Hermione Gingold is singing instead'. While a souvenir hunter tried to pull a poster off the wall, a young shaven-headed clone in black leather and chains cried out, 'It may be a cancellation but this is the biggest event of the season.' The diamond- and fur-bedecked glitterati did not even bother to get out of their cars before being driven off to make way for another unsuspecting group.

Devereux Danna and I fought our way into the foyer where we were recognised by the manager and taken to a room stacked up with flowers. Only an open coffin was needed to complete the impression of a funeral parlour. We disregarded the names on the cards, choosing only the blooms in Maria's favourite colours.

The melancholy scene we found on our return was something

of a shock. Maria, wearing a dull-blue caftan, was sitting hunched up in the corner of a sofa, without make-up, ashen, sapped and lifeless. Around her, friends, among them the parents-in-law of Di Stefano, sat in groups speaking in whispers like mourners at a wake. He himself looked emotionally exhausted and to my astonishment his wife sat beside him, apparently unaware of the part she had played in this débâcle. I stayed just long enough to show Maria my concern and support.

Next day the *New York Post* headlined CALLAS: THE FLU OR A CASE OF NERVES. 'Miss Callas, now fifty and renowned during her early career for cancelling performances at whim, cancelled the first concert of the come-back tour,' the writer said, quoting the director of Carnegie Hall as stating, 'Well, if its psychosomatic, she's still sick. That's the worst kind.'

Maria spent most of the day in bed receiving telephone calls from many friends at the far ends of the earth. A local New York call lasting nearly two hours was from Renata Tebaldi.

Rivalry between singers is not uncommon in the history of opera, though usually only between artists with similar voices. In the early Fifties Renata Tebaldi was the reigning queen of La Scala Milan. She had a beautiful, pure and smooth voice, and a sweet personality, though she could be firm in rehearsal if asked to do anything other than what she had always done. (Rudolf Bing, of the New York Metropolitan Opera, said she had dimples of iron.) She was the darling of the Milan public. Callas, who was soon to take her place at La Scala, had a fiery temperament and a voice that could not be called beautiful in the traditional sense, but she had a command of all the technical challenges of the bel canto operas. 'It's not enough to have a beautiful voice,' Callas said and showed she was not afraid of singing harshly if the dramatic interpretation of a role demanded it. With two such different voices one wonders why anyone could have been irrational enough to set one against the other. It was a matter of taste: one voice easy on the ear, a beautiful vocal quality at the expense of dramatic truth, the other an instrument capable

of a theatrical intensity that might mean unevenness in the singing
but which impels the listener to sit up and take notice. There was
room for both.

When Callas arrived in Rio de Janeiro in September 1951, she
found its opera world buzzing with acclaim for Tebaldi's *Traviata*.
Her performance of a week earlier was still being talked about. But
if Tebaldi's *Traviata* had completely won the Brazilian public, they
were bowled over by Callas's *Norma* and gave her a standing ovation
– a unique tribute in those days. Inevitably a feeling of professional
jealousy developed, quickly taken up by volatile aficionados on rival
sides. The one-time cordial friendship of the two prima donnas
was in jeopardy.

Things came to a head during a Red Cross benefit concert given
by the stars from the Teatro Municipal: the two sopranos, Giuseppe
Di Stefano, Boris Christoff, Tito Gobbi among others. Although
Tebaldi's suggested policy of 'no encores' had been agreed, she
sang the 'Ave Maria' from *Otello*, then followed it with not one but
two encores, 'La mamma morta' from *Andrea Chenier* and 'Vissi
d'arte' from *Tosca*, to the delight of the audience but the anger and
chagrin of the other singers and Callas. However, Callas's chosen
solo was 'Ah, fors' è lui . . . Sempre libera', Verdi's testing show-
piece from the first act of *Traviata*, the vehicle of Tebaldi's great
success less than two weeks earlier. It is hard to believe this was
an entirely innocent choice. It was certainly provocative, if not
confrontational. On the other hand, what about Tebaldi's encores?
These could not have been spur-of-the-moment reactions to the
demands of an excited audience. With a piano, yes, but an orchestra
needs more preparation; the parts must have been on the musicians'
desks before she sang her first piece. So neither appears entirely
blameless.

Afterwards there was a pre-arranged dinner, Callas and Meneghini, Tebaldi with her mother and another singer, Elena Nicolai,
with her husband. At first there were only a few sly little remarks
between Tebaldi and Callas, Meneghini nudging Maria with his
elbow in an effort to quieten her. Then the gibes grew louder and

more acrimonious, until eventually the situation developed into an affray which was seen and heard by everyone in the restaurant. Maria claimed that Tebaldi started the fracas by making the comment that some arias are not suitable for concert performance. 'What did she mean?' she asked me in 1974. '"Sempre libera" is sung all over by sopranos in concert!' Perhaps Tebaldi meant it was unsuitable on that particular evening – or had perceived a challenge in Callas's choice of aria.

The feud became world-famous, delighting the media, opera buffs and box-office managers alike. At every opportunity the progress of the rivalry was relished as news. When asked by a newspaperman to explain the difference in their singing Callas is reported to have said, 'Hers is Coca-Cola to my champagne.' Coca-Cola, as everyone knows, is a drink of the masses, popular with all ages. It is a good thirst quencher, has a high sugar level and is commonly drunk in everyday life. Champagne is a wine of character and strength reserved for special occasions. Its effervescent bubbles give it a miraculous liveliness and it has a heady energising kick, which leaves the imbiber elated for some time afterwards. Once again, with an instinctive *bon mot* Callas had hit the mark.

The feud was kept alive for years by the press and rival partisans, until 1968 when, on a Tebaldi opening night at the Met, friendly relations were re-established by the intercessions of Rudolf Bing. As a guest in the General Manager's box, Callas agreed to go backstage with him after the performance. Bing knocked on Tebaldi's dressing-room door. 'Renata, I have an old friend here to see you,' he called. Tebaldi and Callas fell weeping into each other's arms. Renata remained a supportive friend until Maria died.

Six years after the reconciliation, in 1974, I asked Maria who she thought had the most beautiful voice of her time. Without hesitation her answer shot through the air as though from a pistol: 'Tebaldi.'

We left for Toronto a day before the scheduled date, not to be there earlier, but to get away from New York and anyone who might upset Maria in her need for some peace. On the plane she and Di Stefano ordered gin and tonics, the first time I saw them drink alcohol without eating.

My heart was with Di Stefano during the concert in the Massey Hall on the 21st. From his first phrases in the opening duet from *I Vespri Siciliani* I could hear he was in great vocal difficulty, the voice hoarse throughout its range. After announcing that he was unwell but would sing to avoid disappointing the audience, he added that he had '. . . caught the cold [!!!] that Miss Callas had left in New York'. Had it not been for the disaster in New York he certainly would not have sung, but he knew the consequences of another cancellation would have been catastrophic in box-offices around the country. He sang only one solo, one of the less taxing in his repertoire, Lalo's 'Vainement, ma bien-aimée' but to sing at all through his affliction took bravery and deserved admiration. The atmosphere backstage was heavy and things looked decidedly black in the interval. In quiet moments Maria spoke to me again about the necessity of extending her solo repertoire. The audience could have guessed nothing of her concern when she was on-stage, a scintillating figure in billowing flame chiffon, moving with the grace of a ballet dancer. She was a delight to the eye even when not singing.

When we had settled back in the hotel, Mario accompanied the waiter to Maria's rooms with caviar, champagne and a richly laden dinner trolley. 'What do you think this is,' cried Di Stefano, 'a honeymoon party?'

On the plane next day I contrived to sit far enough away from the stars to have seclusion while I read a newspaper. I was glad to see that the critics' comments on Di Stefano were sympathetic, admiring his 'expressive interpretation' of the Lalo aria, though noting that in the duets 'he gave the impression of being in competition with the soprano, outshouting her in a manner decidedly not reminiscent of this singer at his best'.

Mrs Di Stefano was still at the Stanhope when we returned, but the accommodation had been changed. She had a room on the seventh floor and Di Stefano had one on the sixteenth near Maria. He seemed pleased and was in a good mood as he saw his wife off to spend the weekend with her family in the Bronx.

We flew to Washington for our concert in Constitution Hall on the 25th. There was tension when Di Stefano sang in Maria's apartment before the concert. In his solos the high notes were out of reach, and when Maria joined us and he was just as unsuccessful in the duets, he stomped out of the room calling '*Buona notte*'. Maria followed him into the bedroom to offer some consolation, coming out after a few minutes to greet Dr Parrish, just arrived from New York, who gave her the intravenous boost which had now become regular before each concert, 10cc calcium glucomate with 1000mg ascorbic acid. She then went back to Di Stefano and asked him very sweetly to come and listen while she sang: 'It would just be nice to have you there, you don't have to sing.' But when she was singing her part in the *Faust* duet he began to mark and was soon singing in full voice without any strain. If only he could always have such patience, I thought. As Maria warmed up, continuously asking his opinion, he fell into his role as coach and the work went well.

The concert turned out to be the longest we had yet given. Once he got going Di Stefano seemed determined to show us what he could do, even as far as singing, for the first time, the *Don Carlo* duet in the original key. Just before we went out to sing the *Faust* duet he whispered that I should bring also the music for the *Carmen* duet, giving me the impression he might change his mind once in front of the public. He did announce the *Faust*, as he had instructed Maria, but the surprise came when immediately after we had ended, the audience still applauding, he announced the *Carmen*, with no break and without leaving the stage. Maria was furious when we came off. 'They didn't like the *Faust*,' he said, 'so I had to do something to get them going.' He seemed determined to make us work. 'We don't have enough material,' he said in the interval, Maria responding with a black glare.

An idea Maria had in Philadelphia was tried out in this concert. A strip of white canvas leading from the wings to the front of the piano like a carpet would have the dual purpose of guiding her steps when she appeared alone and providing protection for the hem of her dress. It did not work because both singers, especially in the duets, moving around on the platform as freely as they would on the operatic stage, were often in danger of tripping.

In the hotel after the concert a row erupted, which Mario tried to calm by reminding them how well they had been received. 'If that's how you sing when you are angry with each other I will try to start a row before each concert,' he said.

Simultaneously they cried out, 'You don't need to help us to do that – we manage too easily ourselves.'

But next morning when we were all together they were still at it, Di Stefano now turning his anger on Mario. 'Mind your own business,' he shouted.

Maria cut in with, 'Mario has loved us both since he was fourteen and now he is our tour manager and has to take all the knocks, please don't be rude to him.' Mario stood by, the innocent schoolboy. When we were alone he told me that Onassis had phoned him to ask how things were going. Every day he was speaking to Maria and Mario was afraid that he might hear of the trouble with Di Stefano and persuade her to give it all up. Mario's mandate from the Hurok office in New York was no longer simply to be tour manager, but now to be tour rescuer.

I, too, had spoken to Onassis. He telephoned one afternoon when I was practising in Maria's apartment while she was out shopping. In a gentle, velvety and engrossingly charming voice he made a few expertly placed enquiries, soon knowing exactly where I fitted into the picture. He asked me if Madame Callas was happy 'doing this'. My first reaction was to say, 'No, come and take her away,' but I side-tracked his question by telling him of the extraordinary reaction of the audiences and how radiant she was on stage. We left it at that and he asked me to tell Maria he would phone later. She told me he was concerned about the 'Entertainer', as he called Di

Stefano. He didn't want her to be treated badly. 'If he doesn't turn up to sing, just give me a call and I'll come over and appear with you. The audience will be just as pleased,' he reassured her.

His opinion of Di Stefano might have been titillated by the comment of one critic: 'His solo items must have been a nightmare for accompanist Robert Sutherland.' But he surely must have been pleased by another who wrote, 'When the crowd of 3800 caught their first glimpse of Maria Callas on-stage a great noise like a natural force went up, as if an army through the desert had sighted the sea. It was not at all the usual screaming assortment of bravos, but something much deeper than that.'

Back in our familiar quarters at the Stanhope, Di Stefano took to his bed, not well enough to travel as planned to Boston on the 26th. I took advantage of Dr Parrish's frequent visits, suspecting the first warnings of a flu. He treated me with the same intravenous injection he had been giving Maria before each concert. Almost immediately I felt much less lethargic and asked about Di Stefano. 'It's a case of anything she can do I can do better,' he said and felt sure he would be fit to sing the concert. I pulled myself together and went up to Maria's apartment where Mario, Sheldon Gold from the Hurok office and some others were having tea. Despite their presence Maria and I worked on on 'Casta Diva', 'Vissi d'arte' and 'Tu che le vanità', half a tone down at Maria's suggestion. The conversation hovered around the consequences of Di Stefano not singing in Boston and whether Maria should, could, or would sing alone. We agreed to wait before a decision was made. The answer came when Di Stefano woke in the morning hardly able to speak, obviously not in any shape to sing a recital. He took a plane to Italy that afternoon. It was decided that Maria would sing alone, the burden of her programme lightened by interludes played by a guest pianist.

Maria came to my room about midday to tell me the limousines were waiting outside. She was wearing an unglamorous but smart brown two-piece, with shoes to match and a fur hat, an outfit which reflected her look of quiet determination. As we drove to the airport, Mario, Elena and the jewel box in the second car, she let off some steam about Mrs Di Stefano. 'I'm tired of her being around wherever we go,' she said. 'She's stupid and insensitive – we artists need understanding around us. Unless she goes home to Italy I'll cancel the rest of the tour.' Later it was Mario who had the unpleasant job of facing Mrs Di Stefano with this ultimatum.

The décor of Maria's apartment in Boston was typical of most prestigious hotels of the day, luxurious and expensive but not idiosyncratic or individual enough to offend. The colour scheme of the sitting-room was soft cream and browns. Blinds came half-way down the windows, inner curtains covered by heavy elaborate drapes, not permitting much of the brilliant sunshine outside. The room was lit by low-voltage wall lights and numerous lamps on tables against the walls and at the ends of the sofas. The general impression was of bland elegance, an excellent venue for an intimate tête-à-tête or a chic cocktail party but, unfortunately, not for a myopic prima donna who needed to read her fan mail, her horoscope, the local TV programme – or even a vocal score. Only a few moments after Maria asked for more light, two electricians arrived, scurrying around changing the bulbs, their expressions almost crying out, 'Yes, we've heard she is a trouble-maker.' There was another small problem. In the uncertainty of whether we would arrive at all, the management had opened up the Presidential Suite and already let out one room. This had an interconnecting door with Maria's sitting-room. The manager apologised to Maria who, with her usual quick grasp of a situation and practical sense, suggested, 'Why don't you just put a mattress up against it. Then I can sing if I want.' A maintenance man and a decorator, rather disdainful of such an inelegant idea, arrived and after much murmuring and coming and going announced their decision. A mattress would be used. It was a large one, double-bed sized, fixed up to cover the door completely, with a piece of fabric draped over and around it to blend agreeably with the décor. Now both sides would have privacy.

When I went up again later, dressed in tails for the concert, my stiff collar and tie still in a laundry box, a hairdresser was in Maria's bedroom fixing her coiffure. 'Let's run through "Tu che le vanità",' said Maria.

'Which key?' I asked.

'Oh, it doesn't matter,' she replied, 'it's only for the words.' With the bedroom door wide open I played the aria pianissimo and half a tone down for my own practice, while she sat at the dressing-table turning her head now and again for the hairdresser while marking the words. Her hair finished, she came into the sitting-room and sang half of 'Casta Diva' as a warm-up, sounding in good form, which boded well for the concert. But thoughts of Di Stefano still bothered her. 'He's let me down again,' she said angrily, 'and just when I need him most – in Kennedy country.'

At the hall I met Sheila Porter, the English girl who was press officer for Hurok, with the pianist Vasso Devetzi, another Greek living in Paris and known to Maria. She had been preparing to fly home that day after a tour in the States. 'I'm nervous. I haven't practised for a few days,' she told me. As one pianist to another I wanted to tell her she was lucky that at least she knew which key she would be playing in.

She had to look after herself during the evening, Elena, Mario, Sheila and I being much too concerned in giving Maria all the support we could, trying to ease her anxiety and tension. Throughout the day she had moved in an air of self-contained fortitude, giving only a hint of her feelings and thoughts with 'My life has been full of challenges'. She did not ask for help. She assumed that those around her had a sensitivity and perception as sharp as her own, and would give her any support she needed. This was the little girl who, while walking with her father in Manhattan, would never ask for ice-cream but slow down as they approached the ice-cream van. This was the prima donna who in gentle tones told me one day in Paris that she had a friend who could arrange a visit for us to Louis XIV's palace at Versailles on a day when it was closed to the public. I was expected to recognise that as an invitation. Having issued no invitation she could not be hurt by a refusal.

The only request she had in Boston's Symphony Hall was for Sheila to write out the lyrics of her arias in over-large letters in a spiral notebook. But once involved in the performance she hardly glanced in the direction of the book. Till the last moment before her entrances on to the stage she could not decide what to sing next, or in what key. I thought I could get away with a shortened version of the long introduction to 'Tu che le vanità', but she read my thoughts and said, 'You will play all the intro, Robert, won't you? I need it for the character.' She always encouraged me to spend plenty of time over introductions and interludes, so that she could take advantage of the extra moments' rest. I should have remembered that she was famous in this piece for the way in which she enacted Elisabeth's emotions through the orchestral intro-duction.

'This is a great test for me,' she told the audience when she announced the aria, treating them, as she had done all through the evening, with the candour of an intimate domestic gathering. Without Di Stefano's presence she sang with greater technical con-trol than in any other concert, high notes still giving trouble, but finding impromptu ways of disguising the weaknesses. This was a voice that was within reach of a return to the operatic stage. She had never been so elated after a recital. The challenge had been overcome. She knew now that, if necessary, she could dispense with a singing partner and perform alone.

At the dinner-table afterwards Maria surprised me with generous remarks on my playing, which took me aback. 'I'm proud of you,' she said. During the long day and evening everything had been concentrated on her singing. I never expected her to bother about my playing, let alone compliment me on it.

Vasso Devetzi played groups of Schumann and Chopin, but in her first spot was unkind enough to subject the audience of Italian opera lovers to seventeen minutes of keyboard music by Handel. Months later, in Paris, I watched as she began a campaign of flattery and deviousness clever enough to overcome Maria's natural aversion and won herself such a place in the household that on Maria's death in 1977 she was able to take charge without contention. She delivered all Maria's papers to Athens and persuaded Mrs Kalogeropoulos that she, Devetzi, was the person who should have the *droit moral* (moral rights), a French legality, over the memory of her daughter. Her first moral act was to cheat Mrs Kalogeropoulos out of a sizeable portion of the $15,000,000 estate.

In the reviews of the Boston concert new words now appeared, the critics impressed by Maria's attitude to her audience. 'Frankness, openness, warmth', were 'unexpected'. Richard Dyer, in the *Nation*, wrote what remain today the most touching words on Maria: 'The evening . . . moved me mostly because it was such a human triumph, the triumph of an artistic personality, the triumph of a will, still daring and risking much when it sets out to dominate ever more refractory means. Callas has long commanded our attention, our respect, our gratitude, our awe. Now in her struggle and in her exhaustion she asks and earns, at cost to herself and to us, what she never before seemed to need, our love.' Without knowing it, he had precisely and beautifully summed up the feelings of all of us backstage before and during the concert.

A few days later someone else, writing for the same newspaper, reported that 'the people in the next suite [to Callas] complained about the noise and the hotel manager had large mattresses put up against the walls to muffle the sounds'.

In 1951 Rudolf Bing, General Manager of the Metropolitan Opera in New York, began a series of lengthy negotiations with Callas's husband Meneghini, who had given up his part in a family business to look after her affairs. Bing resisted for so long his unrealistic demands for a fee greater than that paid to any other artist performing at the Met that it was 1956 before Callas sang there. In the meantime Carol Fox and Laurence Kelly, founders of the new Chicago Lyric Theatre, moved in and secured Callas for $2000 per performance – twice the fee offered by Bing. She sang two seasons,

always with Di Stefano as tenor, becoming the darling of the city
and firmly establishing the new Lyric Theatre on the international
circuit. It is difficult to imagine who was more pleased, Fox and
Kelly who had managed to steal the world's most talked-about
soprano from the Met to make her American début in Chicago, or
Meneghini who twisted out of them his biggest fee so far. Everyone
agreed that Callas was a triumph and the Chicago public claimed
her as their own. In 1954 New York newspapers had also claimed
her as their own but with an acidic, cutting edge to the headlines.
DAUGHTER OF THE CITY TOO GREEDY TO SING AT THE MET
was typical.

Travelling from Italy to Chicago in those days meant a change
of aeroplanes in New York. When Callas stepped off the plane the
usual posse of cameramen and newspaper reporters faced her, one
asking, 'Madame Callas, you were born in New York, grew up in
Athens and now you are queen of the Italian Opera, which language
do you consider your mother tongue?' Without hesitation Callas
answered, 'I count in English.' Callas may often have been accused
of lacking humour, but she was never at a loss for the *mot juste*.
Another Callas headline hit New York.

After her second season at the Lyric Theatre she sang twice again
in Chicago, a recital with orchestra in January 1957 and another
in January 1958.

Now it was March 1974 and the city was expectant. In a tremendous
build-up the newspapers wrote possessively of her in Christian-
name terms: 'Maria the Magnificent', 'A prodigal daughter comes
home', 'She was ours first', 'La Diva returns to sing more history'.

Maria chose a grey fox fur coat and matching hat for her return
to the 'Windy City'. We went straight to the Drake Hotel where
we hoped to meet up with Di Stefano. He was not to be found.
On his arrival from New York he had attempted to sign in, the
receptionist made a mistake and wrongly told him there was no
booking in his name, asking him to take a place in a long line at
the desk. Not knowing what to think and wondering if this might

be part of a plot, he marched out and booked into another hotel, leaving no message. Mario, tired from being kept awake until 4 a.m. listening to Maria ('She was talking like the prima donna of ten years ago,' he said), had to give up a siesta and go in search of his tenor.

Di Stefano had retreated to a decidedly down-grade hotel in the suburbs. Maria was angry when she heard the news, disdainfully scornful of what she saw as childish behaviour. 'It's unmanly,' she said. 'He's just jealous of my success in Boston,' crying out imperiously, '*I am the prima donna!*' and later displaying some of her alleged temperament as she was leaving the hotel.

At the reception desk she put her poodle, Gedda, on the floor, while examining her mail. Mario discreetly attempted to fit the dog into a travelling bag. 'What are you doing with her?' Maria asked sharply.

'Maria,' he answered, 'there are no dogs allowed in the hotel, don't you remember we had to sneak them in? It's against the rules.'

'Rules? Rules?' exclaimed Maria. 'What do you mean "rules"? Wherever I stay *I* make the rules. Let them talk to me about the rules and then we'll see what Callas is.' The people standing around in the lobby, startled by this outburst, watched in bewilderment as Maria picked up Gedda shoulder-high and strode forward towards the exit, at the same time as a large group of tourists, just arriving, were climbing the broad stairway from the street level. Whether they recognised her or not, they saw before them an unstoppable force and parted like the sea in the biblical story.

On the sidewalk a well-dressed man stood waiting for his wife by an open-doored limousine. Maria made to go straight into the car. 'But Maria,' Mario objected, 'this is not our car,' whereupon the man, recognising the irate prima donna and gesticulating with both hands, yelled to Mario, 'Take her, take her wherever she wants to go.' Mario clambered in after her, wondering what would happen next as the car drove towards Di Stefano's hotel.

Maria, furious when he refused to open the door of his room, called the manager. They found the bathroom door wide open, the hot water tap running full blast, and the entire room as full of steam as a Turkish bath. He was 'treating the voice'. Maria stayed with him for more than two hours and came out exhausted and still angry, her pleas that he come to the Drake with us rejected.

That evening, having identified the carless couple, Mario sent them champagne and a letter of thanks. The perceptive man responded with a warm sense of humour. In the morning Maria received red roses with a card: 'A pleasure to be of service'.

On the day of the concert she was in fighting mood. 'Get ready with the Boston arias,' she commanded. 'I'm going to sing, whatever happens.'

At about 5 p.m. Di Stefano arrived and we began a rehearsal. It lasted only a few moments before he started coughing. 'You can go and undress,' he shouted to me. 'There's no concert tonight.' Ignoring this outburst, I finished dressing and we all left together for the opera house, where Mario was relieved to see Devereux Danna, who had come from New York at the expense of the Hurok office to be company and support for Di Stefano.

The usual standing ovation greeted Maria when she appeared. After leading her around, presenting her to the audience, Di Stefano announced that he had a cold. A groan of disappointment was followed by an encouraging round of applause as he and Maria moved towards the piano. Their cheeks were wet with tears.

The programme started with the *Vespri* duet 'Voi lo sapete' and the Lalo aria but trouble began in the *Don Carlo* duet. When I heard him give up in the high passage I hammered out his melody in octaves but as Maria sailed in, on time and perfectly in tune as always, he held up his hand to me, grasped her arm and stopped her mid-phrase. In an emotionally charged voice he told the audience his cold made it impossible to go on. 'I tried it for Maria,' he said, the inflection in his voice sounding almost as though he were blaming her. There was an embarrassed silence while the bewildered audience wondered how to react. Suddenly, and with great charm, Maria took over the situation. She threw open her arms, one to Di Stefano and the other to the audience saying, 'No, not for me, let's say we are doing it for our Chicago public. We are among friends here and I'm sure they will understand.' Pandemonium broke out, as people made every conceivable noise to show how much they supported her. When they had quietened down Maria addressed Di Stefano with the utmost tenderness: 'You go and rest and I will sing a song.' Thunderous applause accompanied us as we left the stage. Di Stefano and Dev disappeared to his dressing-room, Maria sat down for a moment to gather her thoughts, I found the music for the aria and we returned to her public. During the interval and the awful uncertainty of whether or not Di Stefano would sing again, Maria said she would go ahead with the Boston arias. I could see she was prepared for the challenge when suddenly Di Stefano reappeared, declaring he would sing. During the ovation at the end of the concert Maria left him alone on the stage to acknowledge the applause, but despite her gesture of friendship he returned to his own hotel when we left the opera house.

The after-concert dinner which seven months earlier, well before the tour began, Maria had decided to decline was set up in the ballroom of our hotel and once again there was pressure on her to put in an appearance. 'All of Chicago society is there including five governors,' she was told. I was shown one of the handbills for the event. 'Have dinner with Maria Callas' was the heading above the prices of the tickets. In a friendly gesture Maria invited the governor of Illinois, Dan Walker, and his wife up to her apartment for champagne. He tried to persuade her to join the diners, offering even to carry her in his arms into the dining-room. When he left, unsuccessful, Maria said scathingly, 'They always want to use me.'

Our food had arrived on trolleys but Maria pleaded tiredness and had just gone into her bedroom when Di Stefano appeared with Dev. He went to join her and after about ten minutes she came out and apologetically asked us to leave. Dev stayed on, and told me next day that they had argued and shouted at each other about Mrs Di Stefano's presence in Maria's life until nearly five o'clock in the morning.

The following day a newspaper headlined CALLAS DISAPPOINTS WAITING DINERS.

After Chicago we returned to New York to prepare for the replacement concert on 5 March. With bronchitis and now a burst blood vessel in the trachea we never knew from one hour to the next whether Di Stefano would sing or Maria would need to continue the tour alone. The conflicts between them went on in hot spurts, every change watched carefully by the Hurok office. Sheldon Gold, a senior executive, was exasperated. 'This is it,' he exclaimed. 'If they don't perform on the 5th I give up the whole tour – my entire work is affected – other artists getting neglected, and I'm fed up with it.' Everyone in the office was aware of the situation, gossiping among themselves, eager to hear the latest news coming out of the Stanhope. Gorlinsky was no help when, with staggering insensitivity, he told Di Stefano he could no longer offer him work. 'Nobody wants you,' he said.

Everything around us was moving as though there would be a concert but of what kind no one could guess, soprano and tenor or soprano with supporting solo pianist? Nothing could be decided, one move depending on another and changing by the hour. Without an inkling what it might turn out to be, we were waiting for something to resolve the situation. No one could have known, or wished, the tragic solution.

After sending Maria thirty of her favourite red roses, the eighty-five-year-old Sol Hurok went to lunch with his old friend Andrés Segovia, the doyen of Spanish guitar players, just turned eighty. They talked about life and death, heaven and hell, Hurok saying, 'I don't intend to go anywhere.' His next appointment was with his banker, but he never made it. While announcing himself at the reception desk he suddenly slumped unconscious to the floor, struck down by a massive heart attack.

Maria was distraught when she heard the news. Always quick to recognise the hand of fate, she saw in the passing of one of her dearest father-figures a bad omen for the tour, a warning signal from her god. In religion she was like her mother and many other Greeks, their beliefs encompassing ancient myths, the evil eye, soothsayers and fortune tellers as well as the Orthodox Church, the indiscernible point where one leaves off and the other takes over shrouded in mystery. Maria prayed in churches without fuss, often alone, seldom during an official service. She had no need of a ministry to intercede on her behalf. Hers was a direct line. 'I never ask for favours from God,' she had said to me as we passed by the Greek Orthodox Church one day in Paris. 'He can send me what He will, but I ask Him only to give me the strength to deal with it.' Today she needed that strength. The rows with Di Stefano, superseded by this new shock, were of secondary importance. The show must go on, if only to avoid a second cancellation for the same audience, but now it would be dedicated to the memory of Sol Hurok. The lovable and flamboyant impresario would have relished the idea that only by dying was his concert saved.

Two hours before the start Dr Parrish came to give Maria her regular injection. 'You've got to give me a big strength tonight,' Maria said. 'I need a boost.' Dr Parrish obliged by adding vitamin B to his cocktail and 'a little something else'.

Another row erupted when Di Stefano came to Maria's apartment before we were due to leave, Maria claiming that it was she who was responsible for getting him work when he needed the money, he insisting that without him she could not ever contemplate singing again. When things quietened down and they were sitting together on the sofa, she caressed his head saying, 'Don't worry Pippo, I'm here to help you.'

He sprang up. 'Help *me*?! You are the one who needs help,' he yelled and stormed out, slamming the door.

'Go after him, Roberto,' Maria said anxiously. I went into the hallway, where he was waiting by the elevator, and spoke gently to him. When I returned with nothing positive to tell Maria, she said, 'Thank you, Roberto, but even so you may have saved the concert.'

Never in any of our appearances was there less certainty about the order of the programme. 'What next?' – 'Will you sing a solo?'

– and at one point, when all three of us were ready to appear, Di Stefano changed his mind and told Maria to sing alone. It would be easy to say that I was relieved when the evening was over, but despite her grief and the backstage turmoil there were the rewarding moments when Maria worked her personal magic and I could feel the growing elation of the audience welling up to an emotional explosion on her last note.

The resentment which had been bugging Maria since she had heard that her concert was to be a benefit for the Met burst out in a long, incoherent speech with which she astonished the audience at the end. The celebrity-filled hall, including everyone of importance from the New York Metropolitan Opera, sat stunned while she attacked the administration of opera houses, their meanness at the expense of art and the lack of proper working conditions for singers. A voice from the balcony interrupted her with, 'You are opera.' Another voice, perhaps expressing the embarrassment of the listeners, shouted 'Sing – don't talk', but she went on. Unrestrained, she ended up admitting that to sing in opera was easy compared with what she had been compelled to do that evening. The whole confused speech so lacked any shape, sense, or rational argument that I wondered about the 'little something else' Dr Parrish had put in his cocktail.

It was a long time before we left the hall, Maria receiving celebrities who waited in an informal line like ordinary fans while she saw them in small groups. Di Stefano appeared, having changed out of his tails, asking to speak to Maria alone. He told her he and his wife had moved that afternoon to the Elysée Hotel and left. 'Stay close, Robert,' Mario hinted. 'She will be needing company tonight.' It was two hours after the end of the concert before we could set off for the Stanhope.

Three steps led from the sidewalk up to the stage door of Carnegie Hall, so that when the door opened Maria appeared to be standing on a pedestal. The people who crowded the street roared when they saw her, their solid mass blocking any possibility of us reaching the waiting limousine. Clutching the enormous bunch of red roses, her head held high, hair a mass of trailing curls, she appeared a living classical goddess. Not Phidias's *Pallas* Athene who, the scholars assure us, was enshrined in her temple on the Acropolis in Athens. Her fans saw a *Callas* Athene. With tears rolling down her cheeks, Maria fumbled into the bouquet and released a single rose. 'These are the flowers Sol sent me before he died,' she cried, throwing it into the crowd. The screaming swarm of bodies fighting for the single rose seemed to give her an idea. She opened up the bouquet, separating it into two bunches and threw them left and right into the crowd. In the mad scramble that followed we were able to squeeze our way through the two packs of fans to reach the limousine.

Dr Parrish (now known intimately as Louis), Mario, her maid and I accompanied Maria to her apartment, but while she was changing in her bedroom Mario and I discreetly departed, leaving Louis to give her the sleeping injection. 'Not yet,' said Maria, sitting up, relaxed, in a peignoir and supported by fluffed-up pillows.

He expressed his annoyance with us when we saw him again. 'Y'all abandoned me,' he said in the Louisiana accent which surfaced when he was tired or irritated. After Maria was ensconced in her bed she offered him some whisky while Consuelo brought in a tray with six family-sized tubs of different flavoured ice-creams and two spoons. 'Maria laid into them,' he said, 'passing the tubs back and forth, keeping our own spoons, and telling me the story of her life – according to Maria.'

The sun was coming up when Louis, intoxicated by whisky and ice-cream, could take no more of Maria's outpourings, gave her an injection to send her to sleep ('tablets are not good enough for a prima donna') and prepared to leave. Maria kept on talking as he made for the door: 'What shall I do, Louis?'

'Git a life,' he answered in his southern drawl, 'an' staap watchin' Westerns.'

Next day Maria visited a throat specialist, Dr Reckford, who told her the pharynx and soft palate were inflamed and she should avoid talking, but she paid no attention to his advice when I visited her later in the day. She was furious with Di Stefano, had not forgiven him for announcing the *Carmen* duet immediately after the *Faust* at the Washington concert and complained that he was not being firm enough with his wife, sang badly, would not be sensible about his singing and was rude to everyone. 'How can I love a man I don't respect?' she asked with an indignant shrug of her shoulders.

A visit to the lying-in of Sol Hurok had been planned but she announced she would stay in bed. 'He was a friend,' she said. 'I do not want to view a dead body.'

Hurok was such a big, bounteous personality that he made friends with most of the great artists he promoted. He became famous for bringing the cream of the artistic world to America and discovering also the most exciting local talent – he built an international career for the violinist Isaac Stern and at a time of racist oppression and segregation he made the great mezzo, Marian Anderson, a symbol for the black community. With his logo, 'S. Hurok Presents', he contrived that no name would be more prominent on posters and programmes than his, however famous, great or illustrious the artist named underneath, though he did admit to some modesty with 'of all the great people in the world, I have the smallest ego'.

I went with Sheldon Gold and his wife to the funeral parlour, where we met Mario and Di Stefano. He looked washed-out – a broken man. After leaving the Stanhope his wife had stayed only one more night in New York, then flown back to Italy in the morning and left her husband to assert his independence in the Elysée.

Two and a half thousand people, including opera stars, ballerinas, conductors and screen personalities, attended Sol Hurok's funeral in Carnegie Hall. Like the opening of a theatrical performance, the casket was wheeled on to the stage draped in what appeared to be a rich crimson cloth. The pall proved to be a patchwork of red roses, entwined in an unbroken quilt. The Jewish tenor Jan Peerce sang, Isaac Stern played a movement from a Bach suite and, most touchingly, Marian Anderson delivered the Eulogy. The service over, eight pallbearers wheeled the coffin away as the stage curtains slowly closed. Pure Hollywood, but one of the most moving events seen in New York that season.

In the green-room afterwards Montserrat Caballé chatted with me, then moved off to speak with a very elegant figure in a body-fitting leopard-skin coat and a wide-brimmed black hat. The face looked familiar and as she approached with, 'Hi, how are you' in a trenchant Manhattan accent, I recognised Renata Tebaldi. That the great rival should introduce herself to me brought to mind the forewarning of a Callas friend that being with Callas would change my life. I met up with Maria and Mario, and we drove home, heavy rain teeming down from a gloomy sky. Di Stefano had not been seen at the funeral so I telephoned him and was soon driving in the rain again on my way to the Elysée.

He was sitting on an unmade single bed, doubled up, weeping like a little boy unable to understand how the world could treat him so badly. Abject, alone, without his wife, without Maria, without a voice, his daughter dying in Milan and hurtful reviews in New York, his despair stirred my compassion. Whatever my thoughts had been in the past weeks, today I knew I was faced by a shattered soul, a man desperate for a sympathetic ear. If ever I felt like calling him Pippo, the diminutive, endearing form of Giuseppe, it was now and I probably did, but never once in our association did he invite me to do so and I was too British to take the liberty.

I held him as, through his tears, he poured out his side of the story, trying to explain his feelings, his sorrow and also his anger, much of which stemmed from his deep-seated Italian attitude to the opposite sex. In traditional Sicilian manner he had promised two years of fidelity to his new wife, then claimed what he considered his rightful freedom, most of his affairs known to her. In his way he was faithful. His success as a tenor enabled him to create a world in which he was a demigod. Now, more and more, Maria was taking command and he found his diminishing role hard to bear – not because she was a prima donna or the famous Maria Callas, but because she was a woman. Resentment broke through his despondency as he began to attack her. He claimed she had made herself ill on the day of the first Carnegie Hall concert because he was in such good voice in the rehearsal she hated to think that he might sing better than she and that on the night before the second she had kept him awake until 4.30 a.m. for the same reason.

'She thinks she's strong after Boston – she's nothing without me. WE HAVE AWAKENED A MONSTER, we are all going to end up in the mad-house,' he cried. He turned on Gorlinsky: 'He's no good any more, he gets me no work'; then Harold Schonberg, music critic of the *New York Times*: 'He never mentioned my cold. I'll sue him.' To add to his depression a call from Milan told him that the *Corriere della Sera* had reprinted the *Times* review verbatim.

Suddenly he sprang up off the bed, his eyes black with rage, thumped his puffed-up chest and cried, 'She thinks she's a prima donna – I AM A PRIMO DONNO!' Meraviglioso! Machossissimo! Magnificent!

A knock at the door gave me the opportunity of bringing my visit to an end. Gorlinsky came into the room to find Di Stefano kissing me goodbye. '*Caro Roberto*,' he was saying through tears. Gorlinsky glanced at the unmade bed and back to us, Di Stefano still kissing me. He looked puzzled. I grabbed my raincoat, leaving Di Stefano to explain the situation if he felt it necessary.

We left New York for Detroit on a crisp, bright morning without knowing if out tenor would be with us. Maria was already in the limousine when I came down, sitting in the corner of the back seat, the brilliant sun illuminating her face better than any glossy magazine's photographer with a battery of spots, diffusers and reflectors. One foot on the step of the car I hesitated, startled by her beauty. 'What?' she asked.

'You look really beautiful this morning,' I replied. She beamed as the car carried us off to the airport.

We reached our hotel in Detroit after a particularly tiring journey. 'Go and get settled, Robert,' Maria said. 'Then come up and see me.' I returned to find her sitting on top of the bed, still dressed, some pillows behind her, the red cashmere Hermès travelling rug from Onassis pulled up to the neck: a statuesque figure, but drained and weary. As we talked I was examining her features, the ears, the prominent nose, the big mouth, high cheek-bones and the wide dark eyes, all larger than life as though designed specifically for the stage. Even in her tiredness she looked magnificent. 'Do I look awful, Robert?' she asked. 'Tell me what you said this morning.'

'What do you mean?'

'When you got in the car.' I said I remembered how beautiful she had looked. 'No, no, tell me, Robert, tell me the words – say it.' I had to repeat my compliment verbatim. Satisfied, she returned to the subject foremost in her mind, Di Stefano, asking what he had had to say when I visited him. Sticking as close to the truth as possible, I told her only that he had talked about his experiences with Hurok and how sorry he was about his death. She seemed disappointed but I was determined not to become embroiled in their personal entanglement.

In the Masonic Auditorium of Detroit we gave a repeat of the Boston programme, solo piano groups of Debussy, Brahms, Mozart and Ravel played by Ralph Votapek. Di Stefano turned up at the hotel accompanied by a burly-looking fellow and sat listening as Maria warmed up, ever ready to exercise his belief that she was at her best when angry. 'You can't sing a concert like that,' he snarled. 'You're singing like a pig.' I turned the subject to the weather and suggested that in his state of health he should stay in his hotel, hoping he would not come to the hall, but I was unsuccessful. He came, accompanied by his buddy, made comments all through the concert, then pointedly left before the final solo. I was not surprised when things did not always go well on stage. As we approached the penultimate climax in 'Sola, perduta, abbandonata' I could feel Maria tightening up, not a healthy gathering of forces as one could expect at such a point but a body tension that was not going to help her long high note. It is only an A, not particularly high in the soprano voice, but it was a weak note in her voice and she was always afraid of it. The sound was worse than I had expected. I hammered out Puccini's fortissimo theme with the greatest volume the Steinway could give me. Had I been playing for another singer I might have cringed in embarrassment, but somehow I felt confident in Maria; if anyone could, she would find a way out. She held the note long enough to realise that she was not going to improve on it, then, over the remaining four beats, began a long portamento down through an octave to the end of the phrase '*tutto è finito*'; a great heart-rending wail of despair that would not have been out of place in a performance of a tragedy by Euripides. She had taken advantage of a bad situation and turned it into marvellously effective theatre. I shivered and when we came to the end of the aria the audience exploded.

At lunch-time the following day, bright but cold, Maria, Elena, Gorlinsky, Mario and I were eating in an ordinary main-street coffee shop when Di Stefano appeared, his friend still in tow. Despite the weather and his 'indisposition' he was wearing slacks, a casual jacket, an open-necked shirt and *smoking*. As we ate our hamburgers and French fries, Gorlinsky managed to persuade him to come to Dallas, if only for the sake of publicity for the concert.

In Dallas, Maria was very happy to be with Larry Kelly again, her old friend from the early Chicago days. His welcome at the hotel included an underdone baron of roast beef, which stood on a sideboard, for nibbling at between meals.

Our solo pianist was Earl Wild, famed for his phenomenal technique and romantic interpretations. He delighted the audience, and Maria also, by playing Chopin, Liszt and other pieces that blended well with her arias, but after his first group I returned to the piano to find that he had lowered the stool to a level which for me was uncomfortable. I accepted it but before Maria's next aria asked the assistant, who was changing the opening of the lid for us, to return the stool to its fullest height before I appeared with Maria. It seemed a simple piece of stage management. Earl chose to make his own adjustment each time he played. After the concert his only comment was to express his amazement at seeing Maria standing over the long table where, as usual, I had set out all my music separately, each item instantly recognisable and ready to be snatched at the last moment, and hearing her ask me, 'What shall I sing next?'

She sounded tired in 'Vissi d'arte' and when she talked of not singing 'Tu che le vanità' I asked Larry Kelly to give her some encouragement. His methods, so different from Di Stefano's, spurred one of her best performances, turning a concert threatening to be uninspired into another triumph. Paying the customary homage to Maria, a critic next day was impressed enough by the stage management to report that 'Callas's accompanist had an assistant to adjust the height of his stool'.

Our next concert was to be on 21 March in Miami Beach, giving us a longer respite than usual between engagements. Thoughtfully, Mario had arranged that I would spend a week in Key West as guest of his friend the playwright Tennessee Williams, some sun and intellectual stimulation sounding like a welcome break in my current life-style. We had not taken Di Stefano's movements into account. He left for Italy. Maria began to work her charm on me. 'Would it not be nice to have a quiet week together in New York? We could take some nice walks, and when we feel like it do some work together ... otherwise I'll be alone.' She directed a sad, appealing glance at me. Seduced, I knew I was trapped. I persuaded myself that I was tired of flying around the United States of America and gave up my much-anticipated visit to Key West. I would spend the week with Maria in the Big Apple.

Moving up Madison Avenue, the grand international galleries and couture houses give way to smaller, more specialist shops, still elegant and certainly just as expensive, but less intimidating and a little more personal. Between East 87th and 88th Streets they even become domestic: a row of little shops tightly lined up in unlikely consort – fine linens and crochet, shoe repairs, dry-cleaning, a modern art gallery, a florist, another gallery selling Miró and Picasso prints, a kosher butcher, an antique dealer just making the grade above junk shop, an interior decorator and a stationer's selling children's toys. But for Maria the most attractive of all was the corner shop which displayed household wares, everything from a hammer to a Hoover and gadgets of all sorts. She loved to gaze into the windows and, if we went into the small crammed interior, trying hard not to knock something off the overstocked shelves, she would examine a gadget that was new to her and ask how it worked. On the opposite side of the road was a large supermarket and a wine supplier, completing a village atmosphere enjoyed by the well-heeled local residents. On Fridays the wives, in their ankle-length minks, could be seen completing their shopping, picking up the kosher chicken from the butcher, and perhaps even leaving the gallery with that Matisse signed print which had been seen in the window and coveted for a week. This was our stamping ground, all window shopping, except on the day I bought from the antique dealer a small rose-patterned dish. It cost only $3, but when I gave it to her Maria was delighted. 'I have an idea.' She giggled, heading straight for the treasure-trove on the corner to buy me an electrical device for making a single cup of tea. 'Here,' she said. 'Now you can have your tea any time you like when we're travelling.'

The time passed easily, life something like normal, and each day when Maria asked what I was doing for dinner I knew I would be dining in her apartment. The only consolation for my loss of free-dom was the thought of all the men in New York who would willingly give a fortune to be dining alone with Maria Callas.

I went into the apartment one afternoon, calling to announce myself.

'I'm in here,' Maria shouted from the bathroom, 'Come in.' She was sitting on the floor, leaning tight against the side of the bath, head back and her long hair falling into the tub, being rinsed by Consuelo.

'You don't look much like a prima donna down there,' I joked.

'I'm not a prima donna,' she answered. 'I'm Maria having her hair washed.' It was still heavy with water and I was curiously touched to see that at the parting the first centimetre or so of her natural hair was grey. On the floor beside her was her preferred hair dye, a rich chestnut colour, brought with her from Paris in case it should not be available locally.

[165]

Some days, as a change from window shopping, we strolled arm in arm across 5th Avenue into Central Park. Higher up the Avenue, as far away as 105th Street, was the hospital where Maria was born.

In the early days of December 1923, when Mrs Evangelia (Litza to her friends) Kalogeropoulos was admitted to be delivered of her son it was known as the Flower Hospital. She knew her baby would, could only, be a son for she had made every provision. Nothing had been left to chance. To be absolutely sure she had sent her husband to the most renowned astrologer in Meligala, their home town in the Peloponnese, to divine the exact time when they should make love so that she would conceive a male child. Bolstering her belief, the signs evident in the dregs of her coffee-cups and the *phatoe*, a Greek version of the ouija board, had always confirmed the astrologer's prediction.

Against her father's wishes she had married George Kalogero-poulos in 1916 even though she believed him to come from a less socially acceptable background than her own well-to-do army family. Nevertheless, in Meligala he built up a prosperous pharmacy business, which afforded them a comfortable home, a cook, a house-maid and a highly respected place in local society. Their first child, Yacinthy, was followed by a boy, Vasily, who died of meningitis when only in his third year. This was more than a personal tragedy for by now she had realised that George, a quiet man with good looks and charm, and not averse to the attentions of other women, lacked her own snobbish ambition for riches and fame. She had dreamed of being an actress, a career out of the question for the daughter of a Greek army officer. With the death of her first son she needed a replacement to give her something to live for and possibly save the by now crumbling marriage. When she was five months pregnant George sold his business in Meligala and moved his family to America, to New York. Should he be as successful there he could be really rich, which might pacify his discontented, nagging wife.

They arrived in the New World in August 1923 and on 2

December Evangelia gave birth. When told her new baby was a girl she turned her head away from the infant and wept, refusing for four days even to take her in her arms. George was stumped when the nurse attending the birth asked what name she should write on the identity bracelet. They had never considered a girl's name. On the birth certificate the child's name is given as 'Sophie Cecelia Kalos', the mother's 'Litsa Kalos' and the address of the father '87 Sixth Avenue, Astoria, Long Island'. Soon afterwards George changed the family name to the less foreign-looking 'Callas' and moved them to Manhattan. By the time of the christening the new baby had two more names: Anna and Maria.

Mary, as she was called, grew up a shy child, instinctively aware that she had not been wanted and that she was a disappointment to her parents, a sense of rejection which remained with her throughout her life. 'They wanted a boy,' Maria told me defiantly in 1974, 'but I worked like a boy and *made* something of my life.'

As Mary grew up and her strong musical instincts were becoming evident, so did Evangelia's ambition, seeing in her daughter an answer to her own frustrated theatrical ambitions. She set out to prepare Mary for the life of a star. Despite her husband's protests at what he saw as unnecessary extravagance, Mary was sent for piano lessons, as was Yacinthy. Both girls could sing but Evangelia sensed in Mary a streak of independence and determination that echoed her own. Mary would be the singer and when necessary her sister would accompany her on the piano. Yacinthy was on the threshold of a life of servitude to her mother; manipulated, nagged, denied a happy marriage, she fulfilled a role of filial devotion which few would have tolerated. The children had to endure a life that was not normal, every move calculated and monitored by Evangelia, allowed to make friends only with the children of families equal to Evangelia's imagined social status. Whenever there were visitors to the house the often reluctant Mary was paraded to sing, accompanied by Yacinthy. Newspapers were scanned for announcements of competitions in which her daughter might shine. Were she under-age what harm was there in a little white lie; the truth was only another obstacle to be brushed aside, easily overlooked on the way to stardom. Evangelia was suppressing her daughter's normal human reactions, teaching her the value of self-centred, aggressive ambition in reaching the top, but Mary, denied the happy, carefree pleasures of growing up, was beginning to resent her mother's domination. George Kalogeropoulos could only look on as his children became more and more isolated from normal childhood, any effort he made to ease the situation met by angry protestations and threats. If he played a record of Greek folk dances he was accused of being common and brushed aside while the offending music was replaced by an operatic aria. The sisters began to accept the quarrels and shouting of their parents as the routine mode of communication in the house. Peace reigned only when Evangelia was satisfied. A man of quiet nature, the long-suffering George was increasingly uneasy in his own home and, tired of the virago his wife had become, found consolation elsewhere. Only years later did the two girls discover how lovable was the man their mother had taught them to despise.

('I never had a childhood,' Maria said to me as we walked up 5th Avenue in 1974. 'My mother didn't understand me and my father couldn't help me. She kept demanding too much from me. Too much responsibility for a young mind. It should be illegal for mothers to force their child like that. If you haven't got confidence in your mother, if you can't trust her, who can you trust?')

In 1937 Mrs Kalogeropoulos took her two daughters back to Athens where she believed she could find a musical education for Maria cheaper than in New York. Maria was already showing she had inherited her mother's obstinacy, declaring that she would study singing only if she were awarded a scholarship, that is, if people other than her mother believed she had sufficient talent to make a successful career. There was a minimum age limit for entry to the National Conservatory, but even so Evangelia, never one to let such a minor technicality impede her ambition, presented her daughter for a place; at thirteen Maria was a big girl and passed easily for seventeen. Evangelia no longer needed to goad Maria to practise, she had made her own decision. With the scholarship she had been awarded she would study to be a singer, but no ordinary soprano, not just a prima donna. She declared she would become the greatest singer of all time. After a year of lessons with Maria Trivella at the Conservatory, Maria moved to the Odeon Athenon to study with Elvira de Hidalgo, a coloratura soprano with a distinguished career in international opera houses behind her. She became one of the greatest influences in Maria's development. At the Odeon, with de Hidalgo, Maria found the encouragement, admiration and excitement, a kind of love, which was lacking at home. She spent most of her day there, singing and listening to the lessons of other pupils, and to de Hidalgo's tales of work in grand opera houses. The relationship between mother and daughter began to change as Maria discovered the exciting world of opera and a growing self-confidence. In the trustworthy hands of de Hidalgo she became less tolerant of the continuous bossing and criticising of her mother. Resentment set in.

The fact that at thirteen her general education had come to an end was overlooked at the time, but in later years Maria saw this gap in a normal adolescence as yet another injustice inflicted by her mother's voracious and restless ambition.

By 1945, the end of the war in Athens, Maria had established herself as prima donna of the National Lyric Theatre. Evangelia watched as her daughter grew into the star of her dreams, while Maria rejoiced that she had found her true world and with it the approval and love of a public.

In the meantime all contact with George Kalogeropoulos had been lost, the most recent news being that he had taken a job as travelling salesman with a pharmaceutical company and, conveniently for him, could give them no fixed address. In September 1945 Maria, intent on a bigger career than Athens could offer, sailed alone for America, with not much money but a lot of determination and hope. Expecting no one, she was astonished to find her father awaiting her on the dockside. One day while reading a Greek-language newspaper he had casually glanced down the passenger list of a ship arriving from Greece and was just as astonished to find his daughter's name on it. Soon Maria was safely ensconced in his New York West Side apartment enjoying, in the absence of her mother, the unhindered love and attention of her new-found father and a life only dreamed about in war-torn Athens. She could not believe how much food was available, a hot-dog stand or ice-cream van at every street corner to fill the empty gaps between meals, and she tucked in and inevitably soon grew fat.

Once settled, she set out to make herself known to the operatic world of New York: agents, directors and anyone else she thought could help her on the way up. Nothing much happened until the now famous occasion when she sang to Edward Johnson, General Manager of the Metropolitan Opera, was offered a contract on the spot and, to the amazement of those present, refused it. Maria Callas was a prima donna, she had proved that in Athens and, in her eyes, they were offering her a beginner's contract. She did not want to sing Beethoven's *Fidelio* in English and she considered herself too fat for the wisp of a girl that was Puccini's Cio-Cio-San in *Madama Butterfly*.

She had to wait eighteen more months, until the early summer of 1947, to be offered the title role in Amilcare Ponchielli's opera *La Gioconda* at the Verona Arena in Italy. It was the beginning of her real career and she was set on the road to international stardom.

In 1950 Maria invited her mother to join her in Mexico, where she was singing her first season at the Palacio de Belles Artes (Opera Nacional). Evangelia, to her great delight, was treated as a celebrity. Showered with flowers in her hotel, she basked in Maria's triumphs in the theatre, accompanied her everywhere – parties, official functions, embassy receptions – and was treated like a queen. Maria bought her an expensive mink coat, settled her New York bills and gave her enough cash to live on for a year. Evangelia's dreams had come true. But behind the public façade of proud mother and loving daughter trouble was brewing. Maria was angry when Evangelia told her she intended to divorce her husband. At that time, still a devoted wife to Meneghini, Maria, through her puritanical eyes, saw marriage as a sacred institution. This was yet another assault on her image of the perfect loving family. Somewhere deep inside there still lodged the young child longing for her mother's love. Now that she had achieved Evangelia's ambition, she hoped she might be rewarded by the warmth and affection so absent from her joyless childhood. Instead, she found the familiar old demanding martinet who treated her as a fractious child and thrust unwelcome, annoyingly intrusive advice on her. By the end of the six-week season she could take no more. She left her mother to enjoy a few more days of long-anticipated and long-deferred fame, and returned to Italy. They never met again.

The Mexican trip, however, had only whetted Evangelia's appetite. Within a few weeks, instead of showing gratitude, she was writing to Maria asking for more money, not just another gift but a regular allowance. Maria refused. Their letters became acrimonious, Evangelia bitterly reminding Maria of her duties as a daughter and of how she, a successful singer and the wife of a millionaire, could easily afford to support her. The stubborn, self-obsessive determination she had so assiduously inculcated in her daughter was now turned against her. Unfortunately, Maria improvidently gave vent to her anger in the highly coloured, intemperate language she had heard around her as a child. She told her mother she was still young enough to work and if she did not find a job she could throw herself out of the window. Evangelia's response was to show the letters to a newspaper – sensational fodder for an ever hungry public.

The matter of the allowance was resolved years later, in 1962, by the intervention of an unexpected source, the New York Welfare Department. According to the law, Maria was responsible for the support of her ageing mother. If it was not forthcoming, her entry into the United States would be blocked. Maria settled for $200 a month and cut her mother out of her life.

'She showed my letters to the press,' Maria told me as we walked in Central Park in 1974, 'but I never told them anything about her – she *is* my mother after all. They always try to drag something out of me about that – why do they never ask me about my father? But it's no one's business but mine. It's *my* family and she's *my* mother. I'm *stuck* with her.'

We drove one day with Mario to pick up Gedda from a grooming salon on the west side of town, Maria carrying a large photograph, already signed and dedicated. In the shop a thrilled young assistant rushed to fetch Gedda and, grinning with pride, returned with the dog, washed, clipped and looking pretty, a large coloured ribbon around her neck. Maria jerked backwards, her enormous eyes wide, when she saw Gedda. 'Take it off . . . off!' she cried. The ribbon was lavender, an omen of bad luck in Italian opera houses. The crestfallen assistant disappeared with Gedda, returning this time with a bill. 'But I've autographed the photo for you,' Maria exclaimed, assuming that to be of more value than any amount of cash and remonstrating with the girl, her basic Manhattan accent revealing that, after all, her mother tongue was American, not English. Mario interjected and paid as usual.

In the evening Maria wanted to watch Marlene Dietrich in one of her old classics. I looked at the TV programme and wondered how such a film could last so long, unaware of the constant interruption of advertising on American TV. These breaks gave us an opportunity to talk about Dietrich. 'She certainly knows how to put a song over – she uses the words,' Maria enthused, but she was less devoted to the real woman, whose bisexual proclivities were the subject of international gossip. Dietrich repeatedly urged Callas to stay with her in New York, particularly when she was singing at the Met in 1956, but Callas just as fervently refused. 'Oh no, I wasn't going to get involved with that set-up,' she said. 'I didn't want my name associated with that lady-lover.'

In one of her several attempts to nourish a closer friendship Dietrich, who enjoyed cooking for her lovers, made a soup to take to Callas when she had a cold. Several pounds of the best Texan beef were simmered with onions, carrots, leeks, celery, bay-leaves, parsley and other herbs for several hours, then reduced to a rich broth. Callas was sitting up in bed, a cashmere rug around her shoulders, when Dietrich arrived with the thermos flask. With an extravagant show of maternal concern she poured some of the laboriously prepared elixir into a cup and offered it to the patient. After a few sips, Callas said, 'Mm, it's good, it's delicious. Which stock cubes do you use?'

I asked Maria if the story were true. 'Well, yes . . . how was I to know she was such a *hausfrau*?'

The good time in New York ended when we left for Miami Beach. Maria was loath to travel before being assured that Di Stefano would be there, but Mario persuaded her to go, reminding her that a press conference and the TV publicity would enliven a slow box-office.

It is curious how some prudish people, brought up with a strict code of morality however superficial and hypocritical, can sometimes startle with a comment that freer-minded souls would hesitate to put into words. As we waited at the airport for the departure announcement, Maria broke off reading her glossy magazine to draw my attention to an article on body-building, well illustrated with grinning hunks. 'It's so unnatural,' she scoffed, then, to my amazement she said, pointing in the direction of my trousers, 'They only do it because they don't have much down there.'

I stood up. 'We haven't done our rounds yet,' I said, knowing how much she enjoyed the duty-free shops. In a confectionery shop she examined closely all the various sweets, recognising some from her childhood days with juvenile squeaks of delight – 'How nice that they still make them!' – before returning to a counter which displayed a bar called 'The Three Musketeers'. Without speaking, she stood long enough for me to get the message and buy her one. If I had given her a necklace from Cartier she could not have shown more innocent delight. Often on the tour, surrounded in her hotel apartment by decorated and beribboned boxes of expensive hand-made chocolates, homage offerings, she would ask Mario to pick up for her a bag of sweets from the street-corner vendor, 'News-stand candies', reminders of her childhood. The inclusion of a few bars of 'The Three Musketeers', a chocolate and toffee bar bought as a special treat by her father on a Sunday stroll, was imperative. She preferred the miniature version, which spared her any qualms of conscience were she unable to finish a large one, a relic of wartime Athens when it was considered wicked and unpatriotic to waste food.

She was on good form when surrounded by the press in her suite, the reporters impatient with their questions, one asking, 'What is a diva?'

'A diva is a diva,' she replied. 'A great personality. Her achievement depends on the strength of her will when she knows what she must do. I am a diva. My audiences love me but they would not want me as the girl next door. I don't care about the response of the critics. What matters is the feeling you receive from the people who are paying a high dollar to hear you sing.' Asked about her temperament, she replied, 'I don't like being bullied. I appreciate good manners and I don't like yelling or being yelled at' – a dead-pan glance in my direction – 'you may find some contradiction in that because it is not all the way I have been represented. But let me tell you something, your patience runs out sometimes when you are being told what to do and you know it's wrong. Maybe it has something to do with my mother, I don't know, so dominating and insistent that I do things her way. She was very taken with Deanna Durbin and Shirley Temple, and she wanted me to be like that, to make the money they had. Of course I have temperament, thank God. That is what makes me an artist. But it is not temperament to know what is right for you and to insist on it. None of this is temper. It is self-protection. If other people wish to twist my words and intentions, that is their business, I don't have to be concerned with it.'

'Have you mellowed?' came from the back of the room.

'Mellowed, what is that? To mellow is to decay. But I'm more calm than I used to be. That is something you learn. You learn self-analysis, which takes a lot of courage and much time, but it eliminates the need for psychiatrists and keeps a person from becoming deranged, as so many people are without even knowing it.' Another meaningful look in my direction.

A young lady asked if she would like a family of her own. 'I would like to have had children, but my husband . . .' she hesitated, 'oh, there is no point in blaming anyone. There have been two great loves in my life, my husband and another man, but I believe I must be just a little American kid at the back of my mind because I wanted someone, a Prince Charming, to come and take me away. After all, I am only human.' Some time later that day the current contender for the role of Prince Charming was picked up at the airport by Mario.

At the beginning of the tour Di Stefano must have known that the real draw would be the Callas name. Now he was learning that the reality could be hurtful. Although the agents were instructed by Mario to give each artist equal billing, there was little chance before our arrival of controlling this at a local level. In interviews with the press and TV Maria did her best to include her 'colleague', repeatedly encouraging him to confirm her views, but the pressmen were interested only in what Callas had to say.

On the way from the airport where he had picked up Di Stefano arriving from Mexico, Mario was shocked to see, spelled out in naked electric bulbs, as the car passed the theatre, TONIGHT – MARIA CALLAS. He immediately had it changed but the damage was done.

I was with Maria when Di Stefano arrived. He looked splendid, a Mexican tan, slimmer and very smartly dressed, but he frowned when Mario agreed with us that he looked so well. 'I'm ill,' he shouted to him. 'It's my liver.' A decorated cake which Maria had ordered for his Saint's Day was in the fridge, and when not stressing his illness Di Stefano was jovial and friendly. Since all seemed set for a pleasant reunion, Mario and I made the excuse of trying out a highly recommended Italian restaurant and left them alone.

We met Di Stefano in the foyer when we returned. 'You don't seem to understand,' he said to Mario. 'I'm ill. I can't sing on Thursday.' He wanted Maria to sing with a supporting soloist in

Miami and in the following concert in Columbus, then to join her in New York for the Carnegie Hall concert on 2 April. Without mentioning how his evening with Maria had gone, he left for the second-rate hotel which had been his own choice.

I had only been in my room a few moments when Maria rang to tell me the party had not been a success. After Mario and I had left, Di Stefano admitted his liver was not the trouble. 'He told me his nerves were giving out,' Maria said. 'He wants to go to a psychiatrist but I don't believe in those. I had my crisis before the Carnegie Hall, and I saw the doctor and took his vitamin B injections and so on, and I got over it. I told him he should do the same.' Unfortunately Maria mentioned his wife, which brought an indignant, 'How dare you demand that she returns to Italy!' For two hours they bickered over the familiar arguments until he left, banging the door. Maria repeated all the petty details of their row before I hinted that 2 a.m. was way beyond my bedtime and she reluctantly let me hang up, but not before: 'He's trying to show – and I know his wife's behind all this – that I can't do without him. Well, I'm going to show him.'

An agitated prima donna spent all next day waiting for an apology which never came. Exasperated, she phoned Sheldon Gold in New York and told him very sweetly but firmly that he must come down to Miami to 'do something' about Di Stefano. He protested that he had visitors arriving from Europe but when she hinted at cancelling the rest of the tour he was obliged to give way to her demand.

No one knew anything of Di Stefano's movements but eventually he was caught on the phone and agreed to a meeting. Sheldon persuaded him to sing the concert but he made the condition that the warm-up on stage before would be the only contact with 'the soprano'. Mario cancelled the solo pianist who was on stand-by.

With Sheldon Gold on one side and me on the other, Maria looked radiant in a flowing summer dress as we descended the sweeping staircase of our hotel. We had decided to change in the theatre, but Maria had dressed to be seen along the way. Guests and visitors stopped to admire her.

[176]

We were already on-stage when Di Stefano arrived, wearing an orange T-shirt emblazoned with 'Miami Beach'. His greeting was cold and formal, and Maria stiffened as he strutted around, then left the stage. I began the opening duet but he stayed away until Maria had finished singing. She was very nervous. The charismatic beauty who had turned heads earlier in the hotel foyer had become a worn, middle-aged woman and when eventually they sang together, the voice I knew from our time in New York and a short session that afternoon had disappeared. We had performed only one duet before the house manager announced he must open the doors to the public and we went into the green-room, where I took my place at a small upright.

Di Stefano leaned his elbow on the lid of the piano. 'I'm only on holiday here,' he gibed, as Maria settled into the corner of a sofa on my other side and we began again. The atmosphere was tense. Randomly and without enthusiasm we went through the possible duets, Maria commenting at one point that 'the tenor' had made a wrong entry. He went for me: 'You must tell me when I make a mistake. I'm not a musician, you know!' His revenge came when Maria, distressed and unable to concentrate, forgot her words. Again he targeted me. 'Why don't you tell the lady when she makes mistakes?'

Maria leaped up. 'OK, if you're going to point out my mistake, what about this note here which you never sing right?' she said, sticking a finger into my score with such force that it fell off the music stand on to my lap. At that moment Mario, opening the door to come in, was pushed out by Di Stefano and the door slammed in his face. 'Typical Sicilian,' Mario griped later, 'bitter and sweet at the same time.' The rehearsal over, we separated to our dressing-rooms. 'I will not be singing solos tonight,' he called to me, knowing Maria could hear. I was alarmed because this would mean he would be denying her a rest while he sang his solos.

During the first half I did manage to persuade him to sing his Lalo serenade and was relieved to hear the audience receive him so well, but after Maria sang the 'Habanero' from *Carmen* he came out of his dressing-room in a rage crying, 'But that's an encore piece! . . . Right, that's the end of the concert then.' Mario managed to calm him down and persuade him to continue, but he sang no more solos. At the end of the concert, while Maria sang 'O mio babbino caro' as an encore, he changed back into his orange T-shirt and refused to appear again. Maria took her bows with me or alone.

'I'll never sing with that man again,' Maria cried at me when I went into her room next morning. 'He's finished – I did this for him – I don't need the money, I'm rich. He does, though. Now they will try to persuade me to have him again, but you musn't let them, Robert.'

Sheldon Gold spent most of the day as mediator, struggling to find some solution which might save the tour. He did a good job. Later that evening, while Mario and I were in Maria's apartment, they appeared, Sheldon washed-out, Maria and Di Stefano hand in hand, bright-eyed and youthful like spring lovers, as though nothing of the past days had been real.

It was agreed that, before we returned to the winter of New York, we would stay on in Miami Beach to enjoy a few days of sun and swimming. With great enthusiasm Maria taught me how to swim with a mask and flippers, and reminisced about the time when, secure in her role as the Captain's Lady, she swam with Onassis off the *Christina*. After a morning dip together Maria, long since tired of playing hostess to his business associates, was reluctant to follow him when he went aboard to prepare for luncheon guests. 'There are sharks in beside you,' he called. Maria disappeared under the water. 'Come out, we have to get ready,' he insisted. Maria was not always willing to entertain people who did not interest her. She dived again. When she surfaced she was alarmed to see some sailors wheeling the grand piano, the only thing on the boat that represented her music, out of the salon on to the open deck. 'Come out, or this goes in with you,' Onassis threatened. Maria came out. 'He would have done it.' She laughed.

In the morning Di Stefano telephoned me. 'Maria does not like to work in this heat,' he said. 'We're going back to New York.' A little later Maria called me. 'We'll have to give up our swimming – the Sicilian wants to go back to New York.'

On 27 March, after Maria had given a press interview in the Stanhope Hotel to boost sales for the forthcoming Carnegie Hall recital, Consuelo, Mario and I drove with her to the airport to take a plane to Montreal for our next concert. 'See any signs of our tenor?' was Maria's sardonic query at the airport.

'Need you be so negative?' I asked.

She answered, 'Oh, I don't know, I've had a feeling all day.' We went into the VIP lounge while Mario began a search for Di Stefano. He returned with the news that 'our tenor' had gone home to Italy. 'Right, let's go,' Maria said. 'Back to the hotel.' This presented Mario with the problem of our luggage, already loaded on to the plane.

Mario thrived in a crisis. He would withdraw into a trance-like state, shutting himself off, impossible to reach while he concentrated. A tentative enquiry might be met with silence or a snappy reply. But when he had overcome the seemingly impossible challenge his boyish grin more than compensated for any rudeness. It was difficult not to enjoy the restless energy of his gregarious personality, so full of fun, so obviously relishing his work. In the airline office he used his knowledge of the travel business and his Italian charm to cajole the airline staff into allowing him to climb into the belly of the plane and identify the pieces to be unloaded. They included twenty-odd suitcases, two fridge-sized humidifiers and the gadget case containing all the equipment necessary in the nomadic life of our prima donna: a remote control for the TV on a cord long enough to be used from the bed, a tape-recording machine, dimmers to be fitted on lamps, an electric cooker for pasta, and a selection of adaptors and extensions fit to answer any predicament, all gleefully masterminded on arrival in a new hotel by Mario.

Despite her earlier misgivings, Maria was visibly shocked by Di Stefano's abandonment. 'I knew something was up when I got the roses today with that note,' she said, fumbling in her handbag and producing a florist's card on which was written '*Felicità! Pippo*'. 'Just the same as he sent me when I was doing the masterclasses and he started all of this.' During the drive back to the hotel she talked incessantly. 'I've put up with this behaviour for two years but now I've come to the end. I've had to be one of his family but I can't take it any more. It isn't my way of life. I can take a man's love, but he can't dominate me. I gave up Onassis because of that. He can't expect to have his wife here all the time while we're working. I've done all this for him and now this will finish him. All these cancellations – if the papers won't believe that it's his fault, then I will make a personal statement.' In the hotel, Mario busy with the luggage, I offered to accompany her in the elevator. 'No, there's no tragedy – I'm all right. Come up later when you're sorted out.' Despite the harangue in the car I could see she was deeply wounded and took her to her apartment. She thanked me with a kiss.

Mario and I were having dinner with Maria in her room when the Montreal agent phoned. 'Tell him I'm distressed. I'm in my bedroom weeping,' she instructed Mario. The agent told Mario that the Prime Minister of Canada was coming with a party to the concert, could he not persuade Maria to travel to Montreal, if only to sing for one hour? Mario promised him another date. 'Sheldon Gold is coming later,' Maria said to me. 'I want you to tell him how well we've been working together. I'm doing my job. I'm not responsible for the tenor. If only there was one more day, I might have felt strong enough to do Montreal alone.'

Sheldon Gold arrived with some constructive suggestions for saving the tour. She could continue with a supportive pianist, have an orchestra which would play interludes and overtures, or stick to the original format and take another tenor. Maria immediately dismissed the last idea and concentrated on the second. 'He's a fabulous pianist,' she said, pointing at me. 'He can play like an orchestra' (an apposite compliment after all the hours I had spent studying orchestral scores). 'But it's not my style, this recital with piano. Pippo said it would be easier – we could transpose and so on – but it's not right for me.' We then had to consider possible conductors. Rescigno, one of her favourites, was not available and she did not like most of the others.

'What does it matter,' I said. 'He will simply have to do as you say.'

'That's nothing new,' she replied. 'They all have had to do as I say since Serafin. Onassis said I should have been a conductor and he was right. In any case I want my Robert to be with me whatever happens.' I liked the musical compliment but was uncertain about the implication in the possessive 'my'.

In December 1951 Callas was preparing *I Vespri Siciliani* for the opening of the new season in Milan. Her conductor was Victor de Sabata, the Artistic Director of La Scala, a highly respected musician and a magisterial figure before an orchestra. He had been told Callas was as much a perfectionist as he was, but as the ultimate success of the performance was his responsibility he was ready to assert his authority. At one point during the dress rehearsal, Callas up at the back of the stage, he tapped the desk with his baton to stop the orchestra. 'Callas is not with the orchestra,' he called.

For a moment Callas steadied herself, took some long strides down to the front of the stage, peered over the proscenium at de Sabata and said quietly, 'No, Maestro, the orchestra is not with Callas.' They became firm friends.

For some time, when Di Stefano was not around, we had been working on 'Addio del passato' from *La Traviata*, the aria in which the dying Violetta sings farewell to her happy dreams of the past, ending with '*ora tutto finì*', now all is finished. Violetta was one of her most acclaimed characterisations and the beautiful elegaic aria would have evoked significant memories, but the lyric was too pertinent. 'I would love to sing it,' Maria said, 'but what about those words? Just think what the critics would make of that. I would be giving it to them on a plate.' The aria was never included in our programmes.

[181]

Sheldon Gold was with us again next day with news of Di Stefano. He had phoned from Milan to explain that his wife was threatening to divorce him, but now he was ready to return to work. Gold told him it was not as easy as that: he had walked out on his job and broken his contract, and he should talk to Gorlinsky in London. 'I don't care what happens to him, I'm finished with that man,' Maria told Sheldon. 'He's not reliable and I can't go on with all these ups and downs. It's your duty to tell him.' She talked of nothing else for the rest of the day; about the presents she had given his family and the financial help. 'You were there, Robert, when they were refurnishing and I paid for everything, and he was to repay me out of his fees. How many concerts have we done?' We counted. 'Yes, that just about figures. He's clear of his debt to me now.' We took a walk, returned and learned he had telephoned. 'I don't want to talk to him if he rings again,' Maria said. When the phone rang a little later we looked at one another. 'You take it,' she said to Mario.

'You take it,' Mario said to me. I lifted the phone and was told that Mr Di Stefano was calling from Milan.

'You've got to take it sooner or later,' Mario said to Maria, 'so it might as well be now.' She went into her bedroom and talked for forty-five minutes, while Mario unburdened his troubles to me, saying how lucky I was to be able to step aside from their squabbles, but he had no escape and the stress was getting him down. He had decided to leave, he said, if Di Stefano should return. This was unwelcome news for me. He may have been the butt of their mutual ire, but he was also the kingpin who for weeks had held us together. I told him he was needed and begged him not to abandon the job.

He was putting on his coat when Maria returned to the sitting-room. 'Oh, no you don't!' she cried, aiming a long commanding finger at him. 'I've got twenty minutes to unload before you go.' We laughed and she launched into her news. Di Stefano claimed everything was all right and he would be in New York next day. When she told him not to bother he accused her of throwing him into the gutter, scheming to get rid of him so that she could keep all the money. He would take legal action. She was a splendid sight, sitting on the sofa raging in English and Italian, her eyes afire and arms flying in the air. At last Mario was released and when we were alone the conversation turned to Onassis, who was in touch nearly every day. 'We're close friends,' she said. 'I can discuss his business problems with him, but I can't tell him anything of this or he'll make me go home.'

He thought her only problem was with her singing. 'Why do you live like a gipsy when Paris is so beautiful and you have your lovely apartment?' he asked. His marriage to Jackie Kennedy was breaking up, but Maria was more concerned by the strange disease which was affecting his eyelids. He was using adhesive tape to keep one eye open.

It was getting late. She took a sleeping pill and within a few moments was drowsy with sleep and asked me to help her into bed.

Mario arranged that Di Stefano would have dinner with Maria in her apartment on the first evening of his return. She was nervous and, although she knew that I had another appointment, asked me to stay with her. 'I'm scared of what he'll do,' she said, reminding me that in Miami, even with Gold present, he had taken her by the throat. She grew ever more agitated and apprehensive as the time of his arrival approached. 'Am I looking pale?' she asked. 'I think I'll do my eyes as I used to in the last act of *Traviata*, with a thick dark line.' Just then we heard Mario calling as he came into the apartment. She jumped up, her eyes suddenly aglow, thinking Di Stefano was with him, then fell back into the chair, disappointed. Mario was alone.

When at last he arrived, stating, 'I have come to sing,' Di Stefano was accompanied by a friend. In Italian Maria asked if he wanted me to leave. 'Of course not,' he replied.

There was an uncomfortable moment when recriminations began to fly each way, prompting Mario to intercede. 'We must behave now,' he said. 'We must forget everything that has happened in the past.' We sat down to dinner, Di Stefano resigned and submissive, Maria becoming almost a parody of the doting mother, billing and cooing, fussing with his chair, his napkin and feeding him from her own plate.

While in Montreal newspapers headlined CALLAS CANCELS AGAIN, peace reigned in the Stanhope Hotel for two days. Di Stefano was gentle in his coaching, his calls of '*Aperta, la gola!*' less aggressive, and Maria responded like a lamb. He was never more forthcoming with me in the presence of Maria, telling me how much more nervous he was than formerly and, when Maria was out of earshot, how much he worried for her also. 'If only she had worked like this in Milan.' He presented her with a new set of expensive luggage.

'What can one do with a man like that,' Maria said to me.

Consuelo was waiting on the pavement with the two dogs when I went down next morning. We were leaving for Columbus. 'Madame says she is not coming out of her apartment unless Mr Di Stefano is here,' she told me. 'Last night they made another row.' A car pulled up with Di Stefano and Mario, who went up to collect Maria. In the street Di Stefano gave her an extravagantly formal kiss and we set off for the airport. Outside the new hotel, as Mario sorted out the luggage, Di Stefano called, 'The small ones are mine – I'm only the tenor.'

He disappeared for the rest of the day, leaving Maria offended and Mario very worried, but in the evening when, after dinner, Mario and I took Maria some ice-cream, we found him with her. He was annoyed at our intrusion and Maria's jolly welcome, but before we had time to excuse ourselves he jumped up and walked out, leaving us bewildered. Maria opened her arms in a gesture of puzzled exasperation. 'He's a mental case now,' she said with a sigh.

Mario walked me to my room, where he suggested we go out on the town. He showed some surprise and asked for an explanation when I refused. He was wrong, I told him, in thinking I was able to step aside from the emotional turbulence around me. On the contrary, ever since August in Paris, Maria had drawn me into the turmoil of her affair. Like him, I was feeling the strain of the night-time telephone calls, listening to Maria abuse Di Stefano or, when I was alone with him, Di Stefano reviling her, or the embarrassing brawls when they were together. I was expected to be always on call while times of rehearsal were changed by the hour. I yearned for a day I could call my own; longed for a resolution to their continuous squabbling. We never had a decent rehearsal, new pieces were pushed on at the last moment, I never knew what I should practice before a concert, but most disconcerting of all was the lack of joy in music making. My fear in Columbus was that I should lose heart and the lack of enthusiasm be reflected in my playing. 'Mario,' I said. 'We have a concert in the Ohio Theatre tomorrow night, perhaps 3000 expectant opera lovers in the audience. Someone must be serious about it.' He laughed and said good-night as I took up a vocal score to consider another transposition.

On the face of it transposition is easy. The music is read in the printed key but played in another. For musicians who read a single line, as a flautist or violinist does, this is relatively simple, but for a pianist a knowledge of the harmonic structure of the music is paramount. Some people have a knack, others work at it. Whichever route he takes, the cautious pianist will spend some time looking through the whole piece, ever on the alert for warning signs as the music develops into unexpected progressions that might lead to a dark forest of double sharps and flats where he could easily become entangled in the undergrowth.

This is what I was doing when Di Stefano gave me an unfamiliar song in the interval of one concert. He mistook my perusing for hesitancy, made a grunt and snatched the music off the stand. I insisted and began to play. All went well until he reached his first high note. He stopped singing, came to the piano, banged on several keys, settled on one and told me, 'This is my high note,' giving me a blank stare when I said, 'Ah, you want it transposed down a tone.' Some little time later we were on-stage performing the song. The audience liked it, but he acknowledged their applause with only a perfunctory nod, before beckoning me to share the ovation. He moved to me, grasped my hand firmly and, leading me to the edge of the stage, thrust it up into the air as a referee does the victor's at the end of a boxing bout. At that moment I felt a curious sensation, a mysterious glow of warmth, spreading from his hand to mine and up into my arm, imbuing me with a sense of well-being and a feeling of confidence. It suddenly occurred to me that this is what he gives Maria each evening as he takes her by the hand from her dressing-room and presents her to the audience, and it was this strange, invisible energy that she missed on those occasions when she sang alone, and this was the reason why she was happy to have him present even if he could not sing. It was my first experience, but proof enough for me, of the power of the healing hand.

In Columbus, as usual, Di Stefano set on Maria during the warm-up for the concert, picking on one bad note and making her repeat it so often that she lost her confidence and became depressed and worried. During the interval she asked me if he did it so that she would sing less well than he. She was irritated when he sang two Italian songs in the first half. 'It's too early for such slight music,' she complained. 'He makes it difficult for me to get the audience back to my arias.'

Mario took us directly to a Hawaiian restaurant after the dignitaries were received and the autographs signed. 'I'm going to get drunk,' Maria declared, instructing us each to have a different drink so that she could taste every one. 'Now we are just the four of us alone, and we're going to relax and enjoy ourselves.'

Di Stefano, however, was not so light-heartedly inclined, taking offence at most of Maria's remarks and raising his voice enough to alarm Mario. 'Sh, people are looking,' he cautioned as he changed places with Di Stefano during the main course in an effort to keep the peace.

'Come on, now, let's be friendly,' Maria said to Di Stefano. 'I didn't sing well tonight, but you did.' In her eyes shone the tenderness and anguish of a woman in love, longing for him to fulfil her romantic dream, realising that he never was nor could ever be that champion, but desperately clinging to the delusion. As he stubbornly resisted her coaxing, any reasonable conversation became difficult and the table talk degenerated into the telling of dubious stories and false laughter. After tasting our drinks Maria ordered a rum-and-coconut special, followed immediately by a second because she was so delighted by the multicoloured umbrellas which decorated them. By the end of the meal she was so befuddled by the rum and whatever else we had been drinking that she could hardly walk as we supported her, giggling and babbling like a teenager, on the way to the limousine.

In the hotel, as we negotiated the elevator, Di Stefano suddenly remembered some urgent business at the reception desk. Suspecting yet another test of our regard for him I held the door. He got off on the fifth floor and waved a general good-night, leaving Maria offended again. I took her to her room and Mario followed Di Stefano. 'He was in the huff,' Mario said later. 'He said he supposed you were with her so she didn't need him.'

Consuelo had been hinting that the staff in Paris knew of something but did not want to tell Madame for fear of upsetting her. They had never hidden from Maria their dislike of Di Stefano and his family, creating a continuous source of worry for her because she needed and trusted them as much as they loved and admired her. 'Poor Ferruccio,' she said. 'He has no life of his own – just lives for me.' She phoned him in Paris and in no time wheedled the secret out of him.

While in San Remo he overheard Mrs Di Stefano being reproached by her daughter Luisa. 'I know they're having an affair,' she had answered in anger, 'but we need the money.'

I suggested Maria should keep that information to herself and changed the subject to our projected tour in Japan. 'This whole tour is too long without a decent break,' she said. 'The Japs have paid the fees already but I'll tell Gorlinsky to send it back. I need some time in my home.'

'It's full moon tonight,' the hotel manager told me next day. 'Take care, New York could be crazy!'

*   *   *

Maria phoned me to say she did not want to work. She wanted to avoid 'that man' and his 'tenor tantrums'. She was gloating over an article in a Montreal newspaper accusing Di Stefano of the cancellation and threatened to give a TV interview in which she would tell the whole story to her public. 'I've fixed my cassette recorder so that I can record all my telephone calls. I'm out to kill,' she said. Her mind was restless, turning against even Mario. 'I don't know if I can trust him any longer. Is he two-faced? He's so sweet to our tenor.' I pointed out that Mario's job was to keep us all together and save the concerts. Still agitated by thoughts of Di Stefano, she phoned me again. 'Has he gone to Italy? Give him a ring, please, and ask him if he wants to rehearse at six. But I don't want to work – I'm on the warpath! I've blocked my phone so that he can't get through but it's such a pity that he has my private number.' I saw no good reason why that could not also be cut off, except that it would mean denying herself a favourite diversion when, sleepless and alone, to escape the perils of the night she would make calls to a regular choice of unmarried female admirers who, flattered at being rung whatever time it was, would gossip with her, answer her probing enquiries about the minutiae of their everyday lives and, free of ulterior motives, offer their common-sense solutions to her problems.

Dev and I were dining in an Italian restaurant when Mario arrived with Di Stefano. They had eaten in a Japanese restaurant and needed some pasta for comfort and sustenance, they said. Di Stefano was taken by a young Italian singing Neapolitan songs with a guitar. 'I've never been able to sing like that since they started paying me,' he said. The evening ended at two o'clock in Dev's Greenwich Village apartment where, non-stop, he played recordings of his favourite tenor, a glorious voice, full of virile, masculine passion. Di Stefano listened absorbed, just as Maria did when we played her records in Paris – beautiful, captivating singing.

Still on the warpath, Maria alarmed Mario next day by telling him to cancel the approaching concert and me to cancel the rehearsal with Di Stefano. Telephone calls to Vasso Devetzi in

Paris and Gina Bachauer in London had fired her discontent. She was bristling and we were apprehensive, though I sensed it was mostly bravado. Fortunately her beloved godfather, Dr Lantzounis, spoke to her, suggesting that Di Stefano might now be inciting her into cancelling so that he could sue her for breach of contract. That was the way to make sure she would sing. 'Right, Robert,' she said, 'we'll do the concert, then, but we must break his nerve if he thinks we can go on like this.'

The allegiance of the Hurok staff was now swinging in Di Stefano's direction. That day he was in the office with Mario and Sheldon Gold, arguing his case reasonably, but flaring up now and then. 'So it's come to this. I'm not wanted for my singing, I'm wanted 'cause I'm a good lay.' The excitement spread through the office. 'The whole staff is on his side now,' Mario told me. 'Maria has estranged herself from the office.'

On the afternoon of the concert I rehearsed with Di Stefano in Mario's apartment before returning to Maria. She was on the phone to Dr Parrish. 'You've got to give me a great force tonight – I've got a big fight,' she said to him, and to me, 'Stick by me, Robert, I need you. You'd better look out for trouble!'

We travelled separately to Brookville, Mario with Di Stefano in one car and I with Consuelo and Maria in another. As we were about to start the concert, the usual opening duet from *Vespri* in my hand, Maria caught sight of the *Don Carlo* duet and said, 'Why don't we do that?' We had not performed it for some time because Di Stefano was finding the high tessitura increasingly difficult. I was surprised and he was shocked, seeming unable to believe she was doing this to him. For a moment he glowered at her, apprehending her defiance, before acceding to her challenge. Unfortunately for Maria, her mischievousness backfired. Without some preparation she could not remember her words and to my astonishment I had to prompt her first entry. The atmosphere improved during the concert, however, and the audience was given some emotionally charged singing.

The duet from *Cavalleria Rusticana*, in which the wronged

Santuzza pleads with her former Sicilian lover Turiddu, '*Battimi, insultami, t'amo e perdono* (Beat me, insult me, I still love and forgive you)' was always particularly successful in a programme. That evening it was sung as though for real, shot through with an electrical tension that left my hands trembling, being particularly apt in all senses, even to it being Easter Week. Onlookers backstage could not understand why Mario, Dev and Sheila Porter were so amused when finally Santuzza (Maria) cursed the remorseless Turiddu (Di Stefano) with '*A te, la mala Pasqua spergiuro*'.

The petty quarrelling continued over dinner, both behaving like naughty schoolchildren, Maria putting ice-cream in his coffee and repeating it again when a fresh cup was served, and he retaliating by pouring the lot over her ice-cream. Snow was falling gently as we left the restaurant, each disgruntled party making for a separate limousine, and Maria furious when ours would not start and she was obliged to accept his offer of a lift. He was exultant.

For Easter Di Stefano gave Maria an enormous chocolate egg and, brought from Milan, a Colomba, a panetone-like cake in the form of a dove, symbol of peace. Gorlinsky, just arrived from London, was with Mario at the rehearsal and I was pleased that in their presence Maria reacted well to Di Stefano's coaching. It augured well for a peaceful evening. When we left Mario said we would know if things went well because in the morning Consuelo would be in a bad mood. He duly phoned me early the following day with the welcome news that Consuelo was furious; they had put the chain on the door to prevent her coming in. When I met her later she was still seething. 'Huh,' she spat out scornfully, 'he may think he's got something to show off – it's not as big as *Mon Oncle*'s.' Whatever Onassis and Di Stefano had in common it was not modesty.

Maria did not appear until late afternoon, looking very relaxed and contented. A changed Consuelo was also much in evidence, happy and excited because it was her birthday and as a treat Maria had promised her permission to phone Ferruccio in Paris. Consuelo was unlikely to know that Hurok was paying the telephone bills. Mario, whose trials included keeping the peace between Maria and Di Stefano, was relieved to see her in a good mood.

Later Di Stefano returned to rehearse the duet from *Otello*, Maria singing so well that after only half an hour he said, 'Right, that's enough. I don't want to spoil anything.' I left them happy together.

The following day Sheila Porter, Di Stefano and I lunched at Sardi's, the New York theatrical restaurant where signed photos of the famous customers hang, frame to frame, on the walls. Di Stefano talked about Callas in the old days when she appeared in the major opera houses of the world and he was frequently her partner as they sang some of the great romantic roles together. Who knows what mark that left in their relationship? He told us how wonderful she was to work with, how thoughtful, careful about musical perfection and how excited he was the first time he sang a duet with her – 'Hey, this woman sings like a man,' he remembered thinking – but how she changed when the audience applauded. On 28 May 1955, at the Teatro alla Scala, the first night of a now famous production of *La Traviata* directed by Luchino Visconti, he had felt she was being unfair. 'If you take another curtain call alone I leave,' he had warned her, as the audience roared its approval. Next day he left and another tenor took over the role of Alfredo. 'She swept me out of the way. She forgot everyone else when she heard that applause,' he said. 'It was like the effects of a drug.'

Early on the tour I had asked Maria if she enjoyed hearing the applause again. 'Well, I get it anyway from society,' she answered, referring to the occasions when she was hailed by the audience when seen in a box at the opera; even being recognised in the street was a kind of applause. But she admitted that a packed hall of exhilarated people, on their feet, cheering and screaming her name after a performance was a different matter. Now, on the tour, when she was given a similar reception before she had sung a note, she often returned to the piano, still smiling brilliantly, to say to me, 'I wish they would wait till after I've sung.'

On Easter Monday Di Stefano came to Maria's apartment before the concert in Carnegie Hall. He began the rehearsal singing like a frightened man. Instead of warming-up the voice got worse, a strange hollow sound devoid of resonance, as though he himself was preventing the notes from coming out. As he wept in frustration, Maria told him to rest while she sang but he said, 'No, I'm going back to my hotel.'

Maria looked at me in alarm and pleaded with him, 'But I can't do another concert on my own.' He was adamant and left.

I went after him and as he waited for the elevator tried to reason with him. I told him everyone has to warm up, he was not unique in having vocal problems before a concert. 'And in any case,' I said, 'there are only us three on the platform and we're on your side.' This seemed a new concept to him and as the elevator doors closed I said, 'See you at the hall.' At least he did not contradict me.

Dr Parrish was waiting when Di Stefano arrived, perspiring and not yet in his tails. After examining him Louis sent Mario to fetch something from the pharmacy. Our tenor had a temperature of 102. He sang only two solos, charming Neapolitan songs, but no concert of the whole tour was more exciting. In the *Cavalleria* duet, again the high point of the evening, I had to muster all my will-power to remain in control of my fingers. The audience went wild.

When I returned to the hotel I found Consuelo in tears. 'How can she do this to me,' she cried. 'This is my reward for protecting her night and day. He has his wife and family but she has only us.' She was talking at such a rate I had difficulty discovering the source of her distress. For her birthday present Ferruccio had told her that Elena was on her way to New York to replace her. She was broken-hearted.

The agent in Cincinnati rushed Maria to be interviewed at the airport, anxious for publicity to improve his ticket sales. Usually a large photo and article would do the trick, but an over-zealous reporter ended a flattering article with the erroneous throw-away line that the concert had been sold out for three months. Disaster for the agent. The comment, intended to exalt the star, the concert and, incidentally, the writer, cost him $10,000.

In the audience on the night was Isaac Stern who came backstage at the end with a conductor who had invited us to an after-concert dinner party. 'He's another social climber,' Maria said. 'He only wants to use me so that all the rich people will come to his party.' We missed the party.

'What a spoil-sport,' Di Stefano complained, 'and she calls my wife suburban.'

Supper was arranged instead in Maria's apartment, but Di Stefano came only to say good-night, leaving Mario and me with Maria. She was too disturbed to eat. Later, at 2.30 a.m., Di Stefano wakened me to ask if I knew where Mario was. I had just settled back to sleep when Maria phoned, also asking for Mario. She managed to trace him and kept him talking till 5 a.m.

Our programme at the Music Hall that evening did not start with the usual duet, Di Stefano saying he could not sing. Maria plunged in with the dramatic aria from *La Gioconda*, a daring piece to begin the evening. As usual, the audience was extremely enthusiastic, but the hall appeared only half full. I had never seen so many empty seats at a Callas concert. Backstage, while Di Stefano was 'getting his breath', I gazed at my music spread out on the long table, wondering what he would choose as his first solo. The break after Maria's solo was stretching longer than any audience could fairly be expected to tolerate when suddenly he turned to Maria saying, 'Oh, I'm not ready, you go and sing something.' Maria had not expected to sing a second aria without having a rest. She looked up at me. 'What shall I sing?' she asked, but before I could answer he said, 'Sing the "Habanera".' We were on the stage before Maria had time to gather her thoughts. Half-way through the first verse I could hear she was struggling to find the words. She stopped singing and with an apologetic girlish giggle, shrugged to the audience, came round to me at the keyboard and leaned on my shoulder looking at the score. Knowing that she would see nothing but a blur I gave her some lines and we began again. This time she was word perfect.

When we left the stage she apologised to me. 'Why didn't you just carry on and invent some French-sounding words,' I asked. 'Few would have noticed.' It is a practice not uncommon on the operatic stage.

'Oh, no,' she said. 'That's cheating. I can't do that,' thrusting out her open palms with such a forceful gesture that I pulled back. 'I must *give* my words to the audience.' She was surprised next day when a critic wrote that 'Callas stopped her pianist because he was going too fast'. 'Surely she heard all those wrong words,' Maria said, apologising to me again. 'They can write ridiculous stuff sometimes, Robert, but don't let it worry you. Often in the past they've been hard on my colleagues. If you're with Callas they're out to get you.' There was grit in her voice.

As in Cincinnati, we were told the ticket sales in Portland were so slow that the concert was in danger of being cancelled. 'If they don't want us why should we go?' Maria said. 'Why should we allow ourselves to be humiliated in such a way?'

In Seattle a rehearsal had been arranged for six, but just as I arrived Di Stefano said he did not feel like working. 'You two can work while I sleep,' he said, disappearing into one of the bedrooms. Instead, we watched a Bette Davis film, Maria talking incessantly about his rudeness. It was true, he was teasing her now continuously, grasping every opportunity to be sarcastic. 'Well, have you been working?' he asked me when he returned. I tried to avoid answering but he knew what that meant. He sat down with us to watch the end of the film, eating chunks of Parmesan and raw spring onions, and blowing his breath in Maria's direction because he knew she hated that smell. 'It's a pity they invented TV and the telephone,' he said, 'otherwise you might have been singing these last nine years.' Maria made a show of pretending she did not understand what he meant. He then invited me to stay for some of Elena's pasta, which she made fresh each time with flour and eggs. 'She's good,' he said to me. (On another occasion Maria phoned Elena at two-forty-five in the morning asking her if she would mind getting up to make Signor Di Stefano some pasta. Believing she knew Maria well enough, Elena said she did mind and went back to sleep. She was lucky. She was not sent back to Paris. Mario said Elena was the angel of peace, Consuelo the angel of war.)

In the meantime I suggested to Maria that we do some work. 'Well, just for the words,' she replied.

He said, 'That's a good idea. I might forget my words, but I never stop,' referring to the Cincinnati incident. Elena brought in two plates of her delicious pasta as he tipped up a shopping bag on the table. Brown bread, blue cheese, and tins of ham, corn, chick-peas and tuna toppled out. A bottle of wine had been opened and we set to as though we were having a picnic, each fending for himself. Maria made a sandwich of tuna and cheese, and started to eat some chic-peas out of the tin. He pointed to her: 'America needs gas' and she retaliated, 'Your poor wife, I suppose in bed she has to suffer that.' I offered her some pasta, she gave me her chick-peas and, not to be outdone, he gave me some corn, then annoyed her by pouring himself a glass of wine without offering any to her.

Casually addressing the air in the luxuriously appointed room, I asked, 'Why are we eating out of tins and foil plates?'

'Because I bought them,' he replied. Patriotism raised its menacing head as the puerile bickering went on: 'The Italians are better than the Greeks.'

'Not the ancient ones – the Greeks were much greater than the Italians.' I felt uneasy in this undercurrent of strife and determined to get away as early as possible.

'Where are you going this evening?' Maria asked. She had a distinctive way of looking when asking a question, almost aggressive, commanding the truth, a fixed challenging gaze, as though she expected deceit. I was never dishonest, although in the interest of a peaceful life I sometimes resorted to a diplomatic answer. I decided to be candid.

Wherever we travelled in America we frequently passed cinemas advertising a film which had become notorious. That it was banned in some States had made it even more tantalising for curious cinema-goers who normally would have had little interest in that form of entertainment. Even Jackie Kennedy was caught by the paparazzi leaving a cinema where it was showing. The film told the story of a woman who suffered a freakish physical anomaly, an essential part of her reproductive anatomy not being in the normal place, but in her larynx and effective only when her throat was wide open. 'I'm going to see Linda Lovelace in *Deep Throat*,' I answered Maria.

'I'm coming with you,' Di Stefano called immediately.

Maria must have known of the film. 'What's it about?' she asked innocently, then, with the voice of a petulant child, 'You men can't leave me all on my own.' After some friendly banter I told her if she went I would expect a detailed account of the scenario. She smiled and lowered her eyes. I did not see the film.

In the morning Di Stefano greeted me with, 'Wow, that was a terrible film you sent us to last night,' while Maria fussed with a pile of music. 'We stayed only ten minutes,' she said, avoiding my eyes. I never did learn the story-line.

I was on my way to Maria's suite for the appointed rehearsal next day when I met her, with Di Stefano, warmly wrapped up against the weather, on their way out shopping. I was glad that he had persuaded her to go out of the hotel. Most days she rose about midday and spent the rest of the day mooning about the rooms, playing with her make-up, changing dresses, telephoning or watching television, seldom leaving the apartment.

I saw them later. 'The weather here is too cold to sing,' Di Stefano said. 'Why don't we meet in San Francisco.' That would mean he would miss Seattle, Portland, Vancouver and Los Angeles. After he left Maria said he was scared of our next concert the following day. 'Tenor nerves,' she said. 'They always create a scene before every performance. I can't go on like this. It's worse than being in the war.' I saw an opportunity of changing the subject and asked about wartime Athens.

* * *

In 1941 the occupying Italians were bearable because, like the Greeks, they were Mediterranean and, not being indoctrinated by racial theories, saw no great difference between themselves and the defiant people they thought they had overrun. They got on reasonably well. But when the Germans took over, believing themselves superior to both, the difference in physical type and life-style made it easier for them to sustain the belligerence they had been taught. Life for the Greeks became even more difficult. There was always a shortage of food and if Maria and her colleagues sang they were rewarded with the basics for survival: sausage, potatoes, beans and other dried legumes, and bread. 'We sang for a loaf of bread,' was Maria's dramatic exclamation.

Maria, her sister Yacinthy and their mother experienced their share of adventure when they were asked by a captain of the Greek underground to shelter two young escaped British officers, a dark-haired Scotsman and a blond Englishman. At 9 p.m. every evening Maria sat at the piano singing loudly while they listened to the forbidden BBC news. After some days the men, bored and restless in the confinement of a small room, welcomed a plan put to them by the girls. The hair of the blond was died black and the two boys, dressed in borrowed clothes, were taken out for a walk. In the role of two happy young couples, arm in arm they strolled the streets, ignoring the danger of passing enemy soldiers, and praying that no fellow Greek would speak to them and discover their daring secret. They were fortunate in not being found out, but mother Kalogeropoulos was relieved when after a couple of weeks the two servicemen were moved on by the partisans. Although the penalty for harbouring the enemy was certain death, the escapade had brightened the lives of two headstrong girls surrounded by fear and deprivation. 'I have always found it difficult to be nice to Germans ever since,' Maria said, looking back with unexorcised memories of those troubled times.

In Seattle, for the first time ever, we agreed a programme, jotted down by me on a piece of scrap paper. When we reached the end of the evening I was surprised to discover that we had actually stuck to it. At dinner afterwards the old feud was revived, but the technique was new. Accusations were addressed through others. 'I can't understand people who pretend to love one but only show it by being rude,' said Maria in a loud ingenuous voice to her table partner. 'Don't you think that's awful?'

Further down the table Di Stefano could be heard repeating his well-rehearsed bluster: 'The Italians have always been better than the Greeks.'

'Why are singers so bitchy?' Maria asked. 'We're a terrible race, you should keep clear of us.'

In the morning, panic stations. Maria instructed Mario to book her on a plane that afternoon for Paris. 'I've had enough,' she said.

Searching for any source of help, Mario called Vasso Devetzi in Paris, Gorlinsky in London and Sheldon Gold in New York, alerting everyone to the crisis. Maria was giving up. At one point during the day he expressed his own despair; he could not continue like this, he said: 'I feel like telling her just to go home, then.' I was sympathetic, though I knew he was unlikely to do so. It mattered a great deal to him, *vis-à-vis* the Hurok office, that he save the tour.

Di Stefano wanted to go on, despite his bad notices. 'That's gratitude for you,' he said. 'Everybody does everything for her. Look how the public adores her and she selfishly ignores them. She wants to go home now just because I would not spend the night with her.' Some time after leaving her he had phoned and was alarmed not to get a reply. He went to the reception desk, made an excuse to get another key for the apartment and found her unconscious on the floor of her bedroom. She had got out of bed but had fallen asleep while attempting to adjust the humidifier. Elena told him Madame had taken two sleeping pills. Since I had often seen the potent and speedy effect of the pills on her this was no news to me.

In the afternoon Di Stefano came straight into her bedroom when he arrived. 'Oh, what do you want here,' Maria said. 'Go away. I don't want ever to see you again.' I had never seen her so rude to him. She did not break off from talking on the phone to

Sheldon Gold, telling him that she could not go on with 'Mr Di Stefano' because of his insulting behaviour. 'You ask Dr Parrish about how I'm being harassed.' Di Stefano stood at the end of the bed during the call, now and then shouting out his version at the telephone. Later Mario set up a 'conference call': Gorlinsky in London, Gold in New York and Maria in bed in Seattle, Mario and I present. All the old ground was covered, each suggestion by Gorlinsky or Gold brushed aside by Maria, until eventually she agreed that the American tour would be completed by the last five concerts, but Japan cancelled. There would be no contact between the soprano and tenor, Mario always present when Di Stefano was near her and any business between them conducted solely through him. Di Stefano left and Maria said, 'You two must stick by me.'

Despite that, and aware of the abuse Di Stefano had suffered, I did not think it unfair nor disloyal to visit him. I saw in his room much evidence of a troubled mind. A Bible lay on the bedside table, not the Gideon which is found in every American hotel room but his own leather-bound and obviously cherished personal copy. Lying open on the desk was André Maurois's *Art of Happiness*, surrounded by various frivolous slogans intended to cheer. 'Look,' he said, showing me the medallion he was wearing on a gold chain around his neck. 'I am not an ordinary opera tenor, you know. Toscanini gave me this. It's for Achievement in Opera. I sing the words and find the music in them. The composer sets the words, he doesn't think of the music then find the words.' He had brought the award from Italy. 'She owes it all to me,' he said. 'She couldn't sing a note when we met again. I taught her and now this is how she shows gratitude. She was a lonely, sad woman and I thought to put music back into her life. I thought when she began to sing again she would be happy. I did it for her . . . Why don't you and I drive together to Portland?' he suggested. 'We can have some fun.' I was not too keen on the idea because we had so little in common but, having learned on this tour that nothing was ever certain, I concurred quietly.

Maria was up and dressed when I returned. 'Sit down off that foot,' she said, dragging a stool over to my chair and lifting my right foot on to it. A few days earlier, after tripping in the street, a doctor had advised me to use the foot as little as possible. I suspected Mario was hiding something from me but at the back of my mind I was content to leave it at that. I was never shown the result of the X-ray, but later learned that it revealed a hair crack in one of the small bones. Of course Mario kept it from me, the last thing he needed at that time was the problem of finding a substitute accompanist, but I did wonder how my foot would respond to the continuous use of the piano pedal during a whole recital. 'Your poor foot,' Maria said in solicitous tones. 'Let's take the weight off it.' I lay back and wallowed in the motherly fussing I had seen Di Stefano enjoy on a calm day. 'Mario told me it was quite serious but he kept it from you so as not to worry you.' While she was on her knees at my feet I tested her on the proposed drive to Portland. She jumped up. 'Oh, no you don't. You stay with me. I want you with me,' she insisted. Mario was annoyed at missing a respite, however short, from Di Stefano. I was relieved.

'We three will have dinner together,' Maria announced, but having made such a fuss of my foot she was obliged to agree when I told her I must rest. I excused myself, looking forward to a quiet read in my room. I was unlucky. Di Stefano phoned asking me to have dinner and see a film with him. Knowing that in the morning he would be disappointed when he learned that I would not be driving with him I could hardly refuse. It was mostly a dreary evening, the conversation halting, but with a little encouragement he talked about his youth and that kept him busy and amused. An admirer who heard him sing in a café agreed to give him money each week for singing lessons. Soon learning that the teacher 'adored' his voice, he told him that he could not afford lessons any more, guessing correctly that free tuition would be on offer. Each week he collected the fee from his admirer and pocketed it. Fortunately for me, he was so amused by his own cunning that a comment was unnecessary.

*   *   *

No one drove to Portland. Di Stefano took a plane in the morning and Elena, Mario and I flew in the afternoon with Maria. Sitting beside her, I was amused to discover why the copy of *Vogue* she carried was as thick as a jumbo edition. Inside was hidden another periodical, *Seventeen*, a magazine giving advice to adolescent girls on all the problems they might encounter while growing up. The usual fashion and make-up tips were peppered with headings like, 'We've demystified that scary first visit to the gynaecologist', or 'How far do you go on a first date?'. 'I like the horoscopes,' Maria said, but I was happy to see her reading an article that caught my eye: 'Why you fight with your boy-friend'. I hoped she would digest it well. At the airport, looking as though she lived in a world of blue skies and roses, she gave the press a lively interview. There was a lot of fuss in the hotel getting Maria settled – which bedroom should she take? – there was no telephone near the bed – the manager and assistant arriving with the welcoming flowers and fruit – electricians scuffling about changing the bulbs, followed by Mario with the dimmers, the contents of his gadget box spread out on the floor – was the TV remote control long enough to reach the bed? – Maria telling me to sit down and take the weight off my 'poor foot' – Elena anxiously asking for her pasta machine. In the hubbub I escaped to unpack.

Later, when Mario asked me to dine with him and Maria, I suggested she might want to talk business with him, but he was reluctant to be left alone with her, asking me to 'pass by', the Italian politesse for visit. I went down to find Maria standing alone, unnoticed and looking vulnerable, in the foyer. She immediately assumed I would join her and Mario. We had an excellent meal and mostly we managed to keep off the subject of Di Stefano, Maria's comments only now and again betraying where her thoughts lay. 'I'm so happy now that it is finished,' she said. At that moment Di Stefano appeared, complaining that we had abandoned him while we three enjoyed ourselves. Maria turned away her head with a look of disgust and despair. As he sat down and ordered something to eat Maria said, 'My art is sacred to me. I don't know how you can expect me to perform when you behave like this to me.'

'Treat me like a god and I'll treat you like an angel,' he replied. 'Let me command . . .'

'No,' Maria interrupted. 'No, no one commands Callas. That always leads to trouble. That's why I broke with Onassis. He always tried to command me.'

Di Stefano became angry, but when he went as far as threatening physical violence Mario protested. 'Your job is to look after tickets and hotels,' he was told. 'Mind your own business.' He ignored the steak which had just arrived, stood up and walked out without another word.

Maria let out a tired, bewildered groan and asked wearily, 'What is it all about? It's so unmanly. I don't know what he wants of me. I've done all this for him. He would never have had that Festival Hall concert if it wasn't for me. But he never knew that. I told Gorlinsky I wouldn't do the tour unless he was OK. I wanted to be sure that he still had an audience.' I told her it would be better if he never knew. We took her up to the apartment but she was worried about security and afraid to be left alone. 'He might do something desperate,' she said. As it was impossible to double-lock the door Mario chose a sturdy chair and showed her how to put it under the handle to prevent the door being pushed open. He left, but Maria asked me to stay – 'Just another few moments' – then talked ceaselessly about her future, how I would help with the voice and she would return to opera. Elena came in asking permission to retire as it was already 3 a.m. 'Please don't leave me yet, Robert,' Maria pleaded. 'We must work something out.' She 'worked out' that Elena would sleep on the floor in her bedroom and I would sleep in Elena's bed.

In the morning Mario was surprised to discover me pulling up my trousers in Elena's bedroom. She heard us talking and came out of Maria's room. 'Madame is sleeping now,' she said, heavy-eyed, with a sigh of relief. All night she had been kept awake. She did not bother even to remake the bed where I had slept before climbing in. I left the apartment to shave and shower in my own room, promising Elena that I would return at two-thirty as planned, to take Maria to her doctor's appointment.

Di Stefano called, asking me to come and pick up something for Maria. It was a feeble excuse to question me about her movements, where she was going and with whom, all the while looking out of the window in case she was leaving the hotel. He asked me to take a joke pin to her – 'Chauvinistic Female' it said, over a pig's face. 'It's only a joke,' he said. 'Tell her it's only a joke.' She thought it was stupid. Mario persuaded her to allow Di Stefano to accompany us to the doctor. While Maria and Di Stefano sat at one table, Mario and I were eating lunch with the chauffeur. Mario had to visit their table several times to ask them to lower their voices and not gesticulate so much. They separated when they returned to the hotel.

'He's complaining about you now,' Maria told me after dinner that evening. Not only could he seldom reach Mario late at night, he said, the previous night he had rung me at 2 a.m., when he assumed I would be at home. Of course, at that time I was in Maria's apartment. 'They're always out on the town,' he said. 'Those boys are leading double lives.'

'What would he say if he knew the truth,' Maria said.

'The truth is *you* are our double lives,' I answered.

It was growing late and I looked at my watch. 'OK,' Maria said, 'bedtime. I'll just take a couple of pills to get me to sleep.' 'Only two,' I teased quietly. She grasped immediately my gentle allusion to the New York crisis and became defiant. 'Sure, I took an overdose,' she said, 'but I would tell the newspapers if he brought it up. I'm not afraid.' By the time I left, she had calmed down, taken two sleeping pills and was very sweet. 'Would *you* like a little soothing pill?' she asked in her little-girl voice as I made for the door. I had seen enough of the effects of Mandrax to know that it was not for me.

Our chauffeur in Portland was introduced to us as Caspar Schmand, a handsome lumberjack in his twenties and an ardent Callas fan, who had persuaded Mario to allow him to drive the great diva around while she was in town. Dressed to the nines in a smart suit and tie, Caspar appeared regularly each day, so thrilled to be in Maria's company that he never stopped smiling. Maria was amused. 'Are we travelling incognito?' she asked when she saw his battered two-door Chevrolet Impala, but was delighted with the spaciousness of the interior and the comfortable back seats. After a few days Caspar told us that he was embarrassed to have to use his robust 'logging-road' Chev because his Cadillac had been involved in an accident, and revealed that though he did sometimes work as a lumberjack he was, in fact, vice-president of his father's logging company and managed his own forestry business – a real 'Timber Baron'.

Camellias always featured among the flowers Maria received, so strongly did the fans identify her with Violetta, Alexandre Dumas's Marguerite in his play, *La Dame aux Camelias*, source of Verdi's *La Traviata*. When a lady gave her some with longer than usual stems Maria said, 'These can't be from a florist.'

'No, they're from my garden,' her admirer told her. Caspar was soon driving us to visit the suburban home where the proud gardener showed Maria her glossy-leaved bushes blooming with showy white and pink flowers.

Di Stefano was smoking when he arrived for the warm-up before the Portland concert. It did not help his singing, especially in the *Don Carlo* duet. In a very apologetic voice he said he would not be able to sing it in the original key and asked if we could do it in the transposed version. 'No,' replied Maria. We took up a different duet without another word, but when he stopped her to make vocal suggestions she said, 'Please do not do that before a concert.' Like him, I had not expected this reaction, although recently she had been grumbling to me again about his manner. 'He has no subtlety or discretion,' she complained. 'Maria' could take it when the relationship was going well, but with her developing confidence 'Callas' resented it.

When Maria and I reached the concert hall her mind was not

on the music she was about to perform. 'Go to his dressing-room and make sure he hasn't got a knife,' she told me. I knew what she was thinking. In the final bars of the *Carmen* duet, the distraught Don José, in a moment of obsessive madness, kills Carmen by stabbing her. It seemed a far-fetched idea and I could not imagine being allowed to frisk him, but to please her I went and while he was in the bathroom fixing his tie I searched his tails. I found no knife.

The concert went well, no *Don Carlo* and more Italian songs, much to Maria's annoyance. 'Those little songs are only encores,' she said. 'I feel embarrassed when I have to go on after them.' When I followed her on that evening my usual sprightly gait deteriorated step by step into an aching hobble. I felt no pain while I was playing, being involved in the music, but I could swear the shoe on my right foot was shrinking as I pumped the sustaining pedal.

Introducing the *Cavalleria* duet, Di Stefano ended by pointing to Maria. 'Santuzza – Greece,' he said, then, indicating himself, 'Turiddu – Italy.' In a broad gesture Maria swung round to me and called 'And Scotland'. She had an unfailing instinct for the right moment. At the beginning of a concert when we three walked on to a platform, the audience saw a single figure, Callas, only gradually becoming aware of the tenor and later still the pianist. Maria had chosen the ideal time in the programme. She came over to me, leaned across the piano like a night-club entertainer and said, 'Come on, Robert, get up.'

At dinner afterwards, Mario and I were subjected to the usual behaviour; the bickering seemed to have become a way of life but at least they were talking and we felt confident about leaving them together as we went 'out on the town'. We were mistaken. A very frightened manager met us when we returned. Mr Di Stefano had been so difficult he was about to phone the police. According to Elena, he was furious when he went to the apartment and found the door double-locked, Maria refusing to let him in. He claimed that he had come peacefully to apologise for his bad behaviour, but she insisted he had come for another, more personal reason, which she did not want any more. When he started to shout and scream, and kick the door, she called reception and complained that a man was trying to get into her apartment. 'I'll send for Mr Di Stefano,' the manager said.

'But it *is* Mr Di Stefano,' Maria cried. Mario and I arrived just in time to prevent the manager phoning for the police. Mario took Di Stefano to his room and I listened to Maria for two hours while she related the evening's events. 'He's finished now, you know,' she said, her eyes flaring. 'Gold and Gorlinsky don't want him any more, and neither do I. He says he loves me but I think it's only the work he wants and the money. Why does the man do this to himself? He's self-destructive. All his behaviour since Washington has been moving to this, and now I've had enough. Can't he understand that I don't want him any more?' Despite everything, I could not help feeling for Di Stefano.

I was alone with Maria for the following two days. Di Stefano flew to San Francisco, insisting that Mario accompany him, much to Maria's displeasure. 'So long as I am with him I know you are safe,' Mario assured her. I had a session with him on cars, plane tickets, luggage and they were gone. All was quiet.

Only once did I leave Maria alone in the hotel, looking calm and beautiful. When I returned after an hour she was a different person, strained and agitated. Di Stefano had phoned. I gave her a glass of port, her favourite tot late at night or in the interval of a concert (always disguised in a soft drinks bottle), and we settled down for a quiet evening together, dinner, TV, memories and reflections. She talked about life on the *Christina* with 'my boy-friend', her lack of sex education and Women's Lib. Onassis had charming idiosyncrasies which endeared him to his employees. Wherever he happened to be in the world, his shirts were regularly sent to a favourite retainer on his own island of Skorpios. He liked the way she laundered them and she, no doubt, was honoured by the compliment.

I found it hard to believe that Maria was eighteen before she learned how a baby is born. I asked her how it was possible to work in the theatre, of all places, and not discover that from her colleagues. She was too busy working, she said, at the academy and in the theatre. At home, sex was a forbidden subject – Greek girls must remain chaste until they marry. 'But on the whole I was not particularly interested,' she said. When sex did come into her life, tenderness and romantic love in the winning over mattered most. As for Women's Lib, that was unrealistic. In the Seventies the Women's Liberation Movement had grown strong. They had been trying to enlist Maria's support since her arrival in the States, mistakenly believing they would find in her a great icon for their cause. They would have been angry to learn of the old-fashioned beliefs of the real Callas and her willingness to sacrifice all for the right man. 'Of course it's unfair if a woman doing a man's job is not paid a man's rate,' she said, 'but equality? No. God made man the hunter and woman to be the mother of his children – and He knew what He was doing.'

Di Stefano forgotten for a while, she ended the evening talking of the other man in her life, the one she really loved: Onassis. 'He married on the rebound, you know. He did it just to prove to me that he could get such an important woman. We lived as man and wife for nine years, then eight days after he married her he was at my door. He phoned and said he was coming and I said "You are a married man – I don't go with married men, don't come." But a little later I heard him whistling down in the street outside my bedroom: three little whistles, his signal. I pretended not to hear so he went to a public phone. He said I was making him look ridiculous and if I didn't open the door he would tip off the photographer.' He left in the morning.

I never once heard Maria use the name Jackie Kennedy. The wife of Onassis was dubbed 'The Gold-digger'. 'She made one or two very big mistakes with him. I could have told her. One was when he came to Paris and took me out to Maxim's, and she turned up the next day. He was furious. And then she tried to redecorate the boat. I wouldn't have dared! That was his creation, his world. Now the marriage is all breaking up. He's gone to Egypt without her. That's the first sign. The divorce will come soon. And another thing, she's always away playing the *grande dame* at some American memorial or other when he wants her. HE'S MARRIED A NATIONAL MONU-MENT!' she exclaimed, flinging her arms up in the air.

We moved to Vancouver, where everything went smoothly until Mario arrived with Di Stefano from San Francisco. Maria's greeting was friendly but formal. He did not like her manner and left the hotel without telling anyone. Mario searched all day in vain and went to bed wondering where he was. Next morning he phoned: 'I'm ill. You've got to get me to a hospital.' He appeared to be unconscious when Mario arrived, an empty pill bottle on the bed-side table. The doctor thought he was play-acting but even so was 'pretty shaken up'. When Mario brought him back to our hotel Maria was like a mother to him, cuddling him while he wept con-tinuously and we tried to comfort and encourage him. He told us when he woke up in the hospital and saw the doctors leaning over him he thought they had operated on his skull, spluttering through his tears like a small, frightened boy. We reacted as outraged onlookers might when the shenanigans of someone else's wayward child results in calamity. Sympathy ousted our anger.

Later Maria asked if we thought it was all an act. 'Yes,' replied Mario, 'but how convincing.' Whatever we thought, Di Stefano desperately needed love and appreciation.

That evening he drove with us to the Queen Elizabeth Theatre where the audience was told he was ill. Daniel Pollack would play solo interludes. But the sound of the applause seemed to stir Di Stefano. As we came towards the end of the first half he told us he would sing the *Carmen* duet. Although he had plenty of time to change he sang in belted flannel trousers and a black jacket. It made a better effect. As we left the stage I saw him notice a small table, stick out a foot and stumble. 'Oh, Pippo,' Maria cried, grabbing him as he appeared to fall. In the second half he sang a couple of Sicilian folk-songs and two Neapolitan songs, afterwards telling the audience effusively how much he wanted to thank 'our pianist'. They could not know the thanks were for more than my playing.

After the concert Mario and I, with Daniel Pollack who had played Chopin so beautifully, and the local agent, dined in a nearby restaurant, leaving Maria alone with Di Stefano. We hoped their private dinner might lead to a lover's reconciliation, but not a late night, because of our early start for Los Angeles in the morning. Our plane at midday would mean an unusually early rise for Maria.

She was very sleepy when I saw her, sitting up in bed, next morning. She threw up her arms and cried, 'Well, I'm a virgin!'

In the airport lounge Di Stefano was curious about my drink. 'What's that?' he asked.

'Buck's Fizz,' I replied.

'I want one.' Before we boarded the plane for LA he had drunk three and once in the air I was dismayed to hear him order gin and tonic. Inevitably, as the mixed alcohols took effect, he became aggressive and began to argue with Maria. Suddenly he said he felt sick.

Maria helped him to the toilet and waited outside. She leaned a shoulder against the door and threw back her head, like one of her woebegone operatic characters. 'Pippo, are you all right?' her frightened little-child's voice asked, as now and then she tapped timidly on the door with the knuckle of one finger. No sound from within. 'Pippo . . . ?' At last he came out and was led to a curtained-off area in the cabin, where Maria helped an ashen-faced stewardess take out the arms in a row of four seats. Another rushed up with an oxygen mask while Mario strapped him in and George Fowler, the West Coast representative of Hurok, looked on, knowing nothing of our running battle, flabbergasted, completely at a loss, and unable to understand how Mario and I could take the dramatics with such equilibrium.

Maria, suspecting that once again he might be play-acting, whispered in the gangway to ask if I thought so too, but even in doubt she looked truly distressed. In the short time from take-off she had aged ten years.

Soon we would be landing. Mario made a plan. While he took Maria straight to the waiting limousine and the hotel, I was to detain Di Stefano on the plane until all the other passengers had disembarked. I would keep him away from newspaper photographers and bring him as soon as possible to the Bel Air Hotel, one of America's most luxurious.

As the cabin door opened two paramedics, tanned, scrubbed, pristine in crisp starched whites, rushed in. One thrust a little bottle under Di Stefano's nose. 'OK, you're gonna be all right, Surr,' he said, as Di Stefano's head jerked back. 'Now, Surr, have you had any emotional upset, Surr?' he asked, making the routine checks while his partner unfastened the straps. As I leaned over Di Stefano to encourage him out of his daze, he opened his eyes and cried out, '*Caro Roberto!*' threw his arms around me and ostentatiously kissed my lips. The two medics exchanged a knowing look, an idea too ridiculous even to embarrass me. 'You're very lucky to have such a true friend, Surr,' one told him.

From the plane we pushed Di Stefano in a wheelchair to the limousine, where he opened one big, grim, dark eye to survey the situation for a second before falling back again into his 'collapsed' role. He came to life as we drove off, insisting that he did not want to stay at our hotel and we should stop at the first motel, but was nonplussed when I told him he needed care and there was a doctor awaiting him at the Bel Air. The car stood for a long time in the driveway as we attempted to persuade him into the hotel. Mario described how beautiful his suite was, then Maria came and pleaded with him for twenty minutes. When at last he came out of the car everything seemed all right, until the manager showed him his suite. He took one quick look at the windows and said, 'I'm not even going to put my bag down on this floor.' The elaborate window hangings were in various shades of lavender and purple, the colour dreaded in Italian opera-houses. He walked out and the palaver began all over again. Eventually Mario took the offending accommodation, Elena was given a nearby room and Di Stefano took her bedroom in Maria's suite.

A new kind of peace reigned next day, Di Stefano courteous and deferential, Maria well-mannered and self-effacing. She did all she could to delay the moment when she must sing, fussing with cushions and the fire. 'Leave that fire and start singing,' he shouted, but then she found it necessary to change the lamp on the piano because, she said, it was bad for my eyes not to have a good light. He brought a more suitable one while she got down on her knees under the piano to plug it in. 'That's our prima donna.' He laughed, pointing to Maria's ample backside sticking out from under the piano. It was clear why Mrs Di Stefano referred to her, out of earshot as '*Quella culona!* (the one with the big arse)'.

In the afternoon Mario, always alert to interesting situations, took us to visit the great German soprano Lotte Lehmann, who had settled in nearby Santa Barbara. Walter Legge and his wife Elisabeth Schwarzkopf happened also to be in the area and were invited. Her house was decorated with a mixture of heavy *gemütlich* German furniture and vividly coloured tropical wicker work. She was happy, she said, to have the best of two worlds. *Kaffee und Kuchen* were served, the menfolk in one area of the living-room, talking business, while around the tea table Lehmann, Schwarzkopf and Callas, three legendary prima donnas of concert hall and opera house, discussed the weather.

On the West Coast we saw a lot of Ava Gardner – a strong, lively personality, she often came to dine with us. In my youth I knew her as one of the more versatile of the glamorous actresses of the silver screen. Off-screen, she was intelligent and witty, and if sometimes her wisecracks were enlivened by enough expletives to make a lorry driver blush, her vivacity and sense of fun brightened our lives. Perhaps the feminist movement, disappointed in Callas, would have found a role model in her independent and colourful spirit.

Our concert in Los Angeles was in the Shrine Auditorium, a vast, hangar-like place that held 6300 people. Home of conventions and the Academy Awards, it was at that time the largest public hall in America. During our visit on the morning of the concert, Maria put on her glasses to look out over the wide expanse of seating. 'Don't worry,' said a technician, 'we'll have you well miked.'

'Miked?' said Maria, her scornful look and shake of the head showing him what she thought of that idea.

'And spots?'

'Spots?!' As Maria pronounced it the word sounded like an insult. She pulled herself up to full height, turned profile on and silenced him with, 'A prima donna does not need a spotlight!'

She was less confident at the beginning of the concert that evening, her voice so hoarse that I wondered if she might give up. 'Callas never apologises to an audience,' Mario told her, a piece of encouragement that probably saved the concert.

During the 'Habanera' some of the audience laughed at her witty delivery of the words. 'Yes, I liked that,' she said when I remarked on it afterwards. 'Carmen's not just a *femme fatale* as they all sing her. If you look back to the book you'll see she also has humour.'

Despite a tremendous reception, her singing of 'Suicidio' was technically not one of her best and when we came off Di Stefano let her know it. '*Aperta, la gola*, I keep telling you. Why don't you open your throat!' He paused and in his eyes I saw a devilish idea growing. 'You ought to take some lessons from Linda Lovelace,' he said. 'If you could do what she does you might sing better.' On the other side of the curtain the audience roared their 'Bravos' and the fans screamed 'Maria! Diva!'.

Ronald Reagan, then in his second term as Governor of the State of California, came to the concert with his wife and a party. In the green-room afterwards cameras flashed as he congratulated Maria and chatted informally. I reminded him of the 1949 tear-jerker *The Hasty Heart*, in which he played the role of the Scotophobe who thought that pipers always marched while playing because they wanted to get away from the sound. He had forgotten the line but soon realised I was Scottish. 'I didn't really mean it – what a

Carnegie Hall, 5 March 1974. Curtain call.

The tour continues.

Consuelo attends to Maria's hair.

(Below) Maria in a frivolous mood.

Mario with Elena.

(Below) Arrival in Vancouver.

Mario counts twenty-seven suitcases, the tour luggage.
Only twenty-one were Maria's.

(Right) see page 219.

Dear Robert –

So fine – morning!
My! What fast progress
clear than ever – Don't
feel anymore –? do you
see, must close my ground –
must get all the mail –
was that went on –!

I thank you again
for everything now that
I feel much better –!
Could I ask a favor
from you –??

About your big
two sheets gothic paper
and when you look or
someone else comes here –
It's a special paper to shine

James –

I have to ask you
to do this for me that
I forget that time I came
to London – this jeweler
is a fine crippled who
had been long nice to
me – I will introduce you
when you come here –

You know I'm many
and work again – always –?
I was aged –
any show from holidays –
see my best regards
dear Robert –

Yours –
Maria –

One of the last concerts of the tour.

(Above) Tokyo, 12 October 1974. After the first concert in Japan. Mr Nakajima in back row, second from left.

On the tourist trail.

Maria shows off the 'Pappagallo' dress.

Pixie's birthday is celebrated
in eighteenth-century Italian grandeur.

Maria wearing a favourite caftan in the music room at Georges Mandel.

Spring 1979. A sombre moment before the commitment of
the ashes to the Aegean. Front row left, Ferruccio and
Bruna; extreme right, Vasso Devetzi; behind on her right,
Yacinthy, in dark glasses, gazes out to sea.

A tourist postcard. Maria's home has become a place of pilgrimage.

Maria Callas
36, avenue
Georges
Mandel
Paris 16ᵉ

gorgeous country Scatland is,' he said and, turning to Maria, 'Let me give you my boys to see you home, Maria.'

His boys were a group of imposing young security men in three-piece suits, bulging with muscles and firearms. As we left the stage door they scanned the roof-tops for snipers, while on the ground Mario, Caspar Schmand and I surrounded Maria, protecting her from a mob of grasping, screaming fans who all but knocked us over as we headed for the limousine. In a kind of religious frenzy they wanted to be near her, to touch her hand, her dress, anything – and sometimes more. In the rumpus I noticed a mink-clad woman on my right reach out to grab a pearl ear-ring. Maria jerked away as I stabbed my left elbow into her ribs just in time to save her pearls and perhaps a torn ear. 'Oh my, oh my,' Maria repeated, shocked at how aggressive her public had become.

We were a large party for dinner afterwards: Maria, Di Stefano with some local friends, Mario, agents, John Coveney, recently arrived from New York and Ava Gardner who, high on cocktails before we sat down, spent the evening flirting outrageously with Di Stefano. Slurred speech or not, her brazen attentions must have been a boost to his fragile ego. He resisted and after dinner returned with us to our hotel.

Nothing much changed in San Francisco, our next destination. Di Stefano escaped again, leaving Mario to ring round all the likely hotels, fearing he might have gone to Las Vegas to gamble. Maria was mixed up, her feelings confused, the woman wanting him and the professional looking on him with disdain. 'It's not manly, how he behaves,' she said. 'How can I love a man I don't respect?' She was very tired of travelling, her hiatus hernia giving trouble, and spoke longingly of getting home to Paris. She was working on Gorlinsky to postpone the tour in Japan, which was due to start only ten days after the Montreal concert, the final one of the North American tour. 'When I get to Paris I will be able to get rid of him at last,' she said, though she was dreading what he might do when she told him their affair was finished. She talked again about her stage future and seemed to be seriously considering *Carmen*. When I asked her if she needed the adulation of the public she answered, 'No, I just want to work.'

Di Stefano did go gambling in Las Vegas and while he was there Maria and I worked on 'Tu che le vanità', the aria she sang when he was not around. On his first night back with the Callas entourage he woke Maria at 3 a.m. and did not leave until 6.30 a.m., creating enough noise to waken Elena with their shouting. Maria took a couple of pills and slept until late afternoon. 'He wants me to write to his wife,' she told me later as she covered all the old familiar ground. 'He's *pazzo!*'

Burdened by all this distress, there was little hope of Maria being in best vocal form that evening. Backstage during the concert the atmosphere was cool, little conversation between the two, but the ever present competitive spirit much in evidence, each drawing the other's attention to the length of applause after a solo.

Robert Commanday, in the *San Francisco Chronicle*, found Maria's singing embarrassing and posed the question whose answer he could not possibly have guessed. 'The will to perform and the emotional commitment that made her a unique diva came through. Yet it was inescapably sad to think that Miss Callas so needs to relive the past glory and cherish the adulation that she will put herself through this experience.' He asked why anyone was willing to pay out so much for a seat that night at the Opera House: 'Why? Anyone who sincerely loved her art would only want to cherish the unspoiled memory, and spare the pain by not attending. Yet the large percentage of the audience, too young to have experienced a live Callas performance in her prime, had to satisfy curiosity and be there for the big event. Necrophilia and not a little exhibitionism.' One thing he found satisfying: '. . . the irresistible Callas excitement was there, her projection of mood and personality unerring. That's what it was all about. The indefinable "It" . . . Di Stefano still shows his style,' he wrote, 'his exceptional stage manner and his capacities to project feeling. He did this with great poise, informality and humor. Still, the Evening with Maria Callas and Giuseppe Di Stefano was a personality show, not a recital. When it was all over, it was like the fading image of the Cheshire Cat: only the smile remained.'

In the *San Francisco Examiner* Alexander Fried pointed out that 'Miss Callas's voice began showing wear and tear years ago, and its loss of reliability has been a terrible problem to her' and went on: 'Her celebrated personality showed itself ambivalently. Her legend is that she can be tigerish. She imparted this phase of fierceness subtly when she performed Carmen's "Habanera" and dramatically in the glare-to-glare emotions of Carmen and Don José in their last scene, or Santuzza and Turiddu in *Cavalleria Rusticana*. At the same time, her stage appeal involved gentle, almost timid looks. How could she know what her long-strained voice might do to her next? But her smile and handsome eyes bespoke feminine confidence.' His final paragraph illustrated the wide range of Maria's appeal. 'Musically the concert didn't make much mature artistic sense. I saw almost no sign anyone found fault with it in an audience ranging from middle-class people to oddies like a man who was garbed in sequins and fiery red and was made up like a woman while he wore a thick dark beard.' Neither Di Stefano nor Maria mentioned the reviews to me.

'This could have been a return date, the booking is so busy,' Mr Koudriavtzeff, the agent, told us when we arrived in Montreal. He was still very sore with Di Stefano for cancelling in March. We did not see Di Stefano all day. In the evening, after dining in Maria's suite, I was showing Elena how to double-lock the door when I noticed Di Stefano, in dressing-gown, standing by the ice dispenser in the hall. He saw me, began to stagger and played surprised when I approached him. Once again I wished I had taken more notice of Ivor's advice on travelling with stars. 'Always take a room on another floor,' he had urged me, 'otherwise whenever you come out of your room they will surely be there. You'll never have any privacy.' Di Stefano invited me in, made a few huffish remarks about Maria, then dropped the bombshell that his wife was coming next day. That was bad enough – I feared her presence would ruin

Maria's performance – but then he asked me if I would do him a great favour and pick her up at the airport. I should not tell anyone but take the limousine because that was his right. I had only just reached my room when Maria phoned, asking what had happened, Elena had seen me with Di Stefano in the hall and was he smoking? I did not mention his request.

I tinkled perfunctorily as I practised next morning, my mind on the implications of Mrs Di Stefano's arrival. I was uncomfortable with the thought that Maria would certainly consider me disloyal if I picked her up, but mostly, despite Maria's new independence, I feared a repetition of the New York crisis. Mario solved the first problem, insisting that I tell Maria I was intending to pick up Di Stefano's relatives – but not his wife. 'We must keep that from her,' he said.

'Oh no, Robert,' she said. 'You're my pianist and I need you by me. You shouldn't be tiring yourself out like that on the day of a concert. Tell him you will be rehearsing with me at that time.'

All day we were silent on the subject until Maria tricked John Coveney into a *faux pas*. 'Where will the meeting take place?' he asked her.

'I knew you were all hiding it from me!' Maria cried, but was not as upset as we had expected, only indignant and piqued. 'That woman must not be allowed backstage,' she commanded Mario. 'Do you know what that kind of woman is called?' she asked me. 'A *bitch*!' she exclaimed in a rasping voice. Extraordinary how much meaning she could get into a simple word – it was laden with venom.

The concert, on the whole, went well. During the afternoon I had encouraged Maria to do some breathing exercises and she was in good voice. Di Stefano practised the 'Flower Song' from *Carmen*, but did not sing it nearly so well in the concert. They were quite friendly until Maria announced the *Werther* aria to me. He told her she would be better singing 'Suicidio', but she refused, the first time I had seen her deny him so abruptly. She then sang the 'Habanera' to tremendous applause and wanted to return immediately with the duet, effectively cutting out his 'Flower Song'. It is difficult to know if it was a deliberate attempt to provoke him, an example of the bitchiness in singers of which she had warned me, or simply forgetfulness in the face of her great success with the 'Habanera'. She had heard him sing the aria in the warm-up, implying he intended to perform it in the concert, but he could not have sung it after the final duet of the opera. Fortunately Mario came to the rescue, coaxing her to allow the aria in its logical place. Di Stefano left the hall immediately after the final duet of the evening, without signing programmes, presumably to meet his wife, and did not accept Koudriavtzeff's dinner invitation to them both.

It was very late when we all, John Coveney, Louis Parrish, Sheldon Gold, Mario and I took Maria back to the apartment, accepting her offer of a nightcap, enjoying the light-hearted atmosphere when a concert is over and tensions spent. Suddenly, unannounced, Di Stefano was in the room. He had been drinking and wanted to speak to Maria alone. As we all made for the door Maria said, 'Stay, Robert,' in a defiant voice. While Di Stefano settled in a chair opposite Maria, she asked me to let down her hair. This had always been one of his pleasures and I knew I was being used as I began to undo the intricacies of her hairdo. The long hair fell over her shoulders and as she sensuously rolled her head against it his big black angry eyes watched me like a cat ready to pounce. He looked in the last moment of control before an explosion. I was glad Maria was between us. In another situation I would have run. Long silent pauses were broken by stilted conversation until Maria suggested it was time for bed, indicating that I should stay. He went quietly and as I shut the door behind him I felt a sudden rush of compassion and a deep sadness. I waited another half-hour before saying goodnight.

'You were my saviour last night,' Maria said in the morning. I wondered what the consequences of my leaving might have been, but said nothing.

Mrs Di Stefano was not received at all by Maria during her visit. I met her when I went down to the hotel entrance to say goodbye to Di Stefano. I was the only one there to see them off. We had a short, friendly conversation and even feigned jolliness, but it was a sombre farewell. The rest of the day was spent packing and preparing for our journeys, Maria and Elena to Paris, me to London and Mario, with all the gadgets which were now his 'inheritance', to New York.

Maria was happy at last to be going home to her Paris apartment where there was no need to be a celebrity and she could unbend. In the airport we took our final stroll around the duty-free shops, devoid of the usual excitement, only a matter-of-fact discussion of whether it was worth carting a couple of bottles all that way for the sake of a few dollars. Maria decided it was.

10

PARIS DIARY

21/5/74

36 Avenue Georges Mandel
Parish 16ᵉ

Dear Robert

I'm fine – recovering! My blood test proved better than ever.
(Don't tell anyone!) So you see, work does one good – even with
all the madness that went on!

I thank you again for protecting me that last evening!

Could I ask a favor from you. Could you buy 1,000 sheets of
this paper and [bring it] when you come or someone else comes
here? It's a special paper to shine jewels.

I hate to ask you to do this for me but I forgot last time I
came to London and this jeweller is a fine cripple who has been
very nice to me. I will reimburse you when you come here.

You know I'm missing our work again – already!

All my best thoughts dear Robert –

Yours
Maria

In the first days of my return to London the anxieties and vexations
of the tour slipped away. I went to bed at night confident that my

sleep would be undisturbed and in the daytime I was soon enjoying the simple pleasure of playing the piano. The American tour had been a progression of exhilarating and sometimes nerve-racking experiences. Life was not easy with two egocentric operatic giants, volatile temperaments attracted to each other but separated by opposing forces. I was a sounding-board for the wrath of one while the other was absent and a butt between them when they were together. Yet I knew that to share the ups and downs of Maria's private emotional life was the price I had to pay for the musical excitement of working with her. She phoned me before I received the letter of the 21st, still talking of Di Stefano and her future without him, and could I not please come over to Paris earlier. She wanted to work.

Before I left I met Di Stefano, who had come to London to discuss a duet recording which Caballé had invited him to make with her. The Far East tour was very much on his mind. The Koreans had first asked him to sing alone, then withdrawn their offer and now everything was hanging fire until September–October. He was still hoping that Maria might agree to go, but she was adamant, backed by Gorlinsky, who said he had had enough of Di Stefano. Gorlinsky, one of the many who early on had encouraged me to keep a diary, was growing impatient with Maria's procrastinations. 'Will she work seriously?' he asked me. 'I can't keep sending you over there if she doesn't work.' And, with a glint in his eye, he added, 'By the way, have you got any amusing stories?'

En route to the airport I turned on the car radio and heard Caballé singing 'O mio babbino caro', her much praised 'ravishingly beautiful pianissimo', which she vaunted so often with amazing poise and breath control, filling the car. My driver, a lover of music, but not an opera buff, remarked, 'Very nice, but nothing on Callas!'

Maria was standing in the middle of the room, fingers twitching, when I arrived. I could see she was upset, tense and agitated. She had heard of the proposed Di Stefano–Caballé recording and was furious that the items to be taped were mostly those on our programmes. I tried to reason with her – it seemed perfectly obvious to me that those were the only pieces currently in Di Stefano's repertoire and he was not inclined to learn anything new. But Maria saw it as an insult, an act of disloyalty if not revenge. I had known her long enough not to be surprised by this reaction, but I sensed that there was more to it than professional competition. I detected something new in her voice, a tinge of suspicious possessiveness, the pangs of the green-eyed monster. This outburst was not so much about singing as about a soprano and a tenor – and the threat of a rival woman. Some time passed before she was relaxed enough even to think of singing.

The rest from travelling had done her good and, as after the Christmas break, she had made further strides in technical control of the voice. We worked only half an hour before she began to resuscitate the turbulent dramas of the American tour and I was plummeted back into the turmoil of her love life. After London, Di Stefano had waited in Paris for three days hoping to see Maria, but she had instructed Elena to tell him she was abroad. I began to wonder if in a curious, distorted way, Maria was enjoying these battles with Di Stefano, any contact, however unpleasant, being better than nothing for a frustrated lover, pain better than no emotions at all; and, after all, she had told me of her unhappy childhood, brought up by a belligerent mother in a domestic situation where the normal mode of communication was angry shouting. She was moving in familiar territory.

We talked until after midnight, when I returned to my hotel, wondering what Gorlinsky would say to half an hour of work and remembering his exhortation, 'No matter how tired you are, get something down on paper before you go to sleep.' I took up my pen again.

PARIS, 15 June 1974

Elena took me straight into the kitchen where Maria and Ferruccio were sitting at the scrubbed-wood table poring over dozens of photographs. Some wonderful shots of Maria, on- and off-stage. She knows how to be photographed – looks straight into the eye of the lens. I suggested she should publish a photographic record of her career. 'John Ardoin's doing that already,' she said. 'He'll get all the money and I'll get nothing.' She had looked on him as a friend, had talked to him confidentially, but now considers he has 'betrayed' her with an article he wrote after the Dallas concert. I asked about an autobiography. 'How can I write my autobiography? I must tell the truth and if I did that there would be a lot of trouble. If I told all I know there would be many raised eyebrows in every part of this world.'

We listened to the long-awaited tape of the Boston concert. Poor quality, but Maria pleasantly surprised. 'If I had known it was as good as that, "Tu che" and "Sola perduta" would have been in more programmes – despite our tenor.' She thinks he was afraid such big singing would have outshone him.

We ate in her bedroom, watching television. The little $3 dish from Madison Avenue lies on her bedside table, holding a bottle of pills.

16 June

No work because Maria has a bad stomach. If it gets any worse she says she will make herself vomit by tickling the back of her throat. 'Don't be shocked, Robert!'

Di Stefano rang to say that he had returned to New York to relive their meeting and try to understand all that had happened. It suddenly came to him how wrong he had been to take her for granted, and now he was a self-contained man again, in control, etc. He will change planes in Paris, *en route* for Milan and could Ferruccio meet him at the airport to take a present to her. He would not disturb her by visiting the house.

She says she never wants to sing with him again, but I wonder . . .

17 June

Maria finds it impossible to sing without becoming involved in the text. She has not been able to sing the B flat in 'Vissi d'arte' for days. This morning I invented an exercise which included the high B flat. She sang it freely and beautifully, until she recognised the sequence of notes as being that of the last page of the aria.

Last night she had another long telephone conversation with Di Stefano. He thinks that now he has solved his problems the tour together should continue in Japan in September. She told him 'No'. He said she was so famous and powerful that she could tell the impresarios they should give him work. Again she said 'No'. He became aggressive, 'You can't sing without me!' She told him I was with her. 'What's he doing there! I need him here!' If ever he had a chance of recovering his position, which sounded likely yesterday, I think he has lost it now. Telling me this made her furious and determined to practise, 'Even to spite our colleague!'

'I'm going to ask you something which might shock you, Robert. I don't know how to put it.' I was rather scared of what might come. Lots of distracting fidgeting, then, 'I don't know if it's worth my while singing when Caballé is doing so well. She has such a beautiful voice.' She seemed genuinely uncertain, unsure of herself. I told her of my driver's comment: 'Very nice, but nothing on Callas.' She jumped up. 'Why didn't you tell me that earlier!' Confidence restored.

'Another' soprano on the radio singing a Callas role. 'That's the kind of singing I dislike. All those runs that mean nothing, just notes. When I sang, the coloraturas expressed what I was thinking.'

We had a good session today, Maria excited when I played back the tape. Her high notes had the body and brilliance of her early recordings.

She became somewhat aggressive as she searched out some of Di Stefano's scores. 'What else can we find to send back to him!'

Princess Grace has invited her down to Monaco to stay at the palace for the weekend. A Gala in aid of the Red Cross. 'I don't really want to be bothered with all that socialising, but the publicity will be good,' she said.

During her years with Onassis Callas struck up a lasting friendship with the Princess. Two career girls who gave up everything for their Prince Charmings, they had much in common. They could confide in one another. Grace, the film star daughter of an American multimillionaire and a domineering mother, married Prince Rainier and brought Holywood glamour to a fading principality, happily playing the fairy-tale princess with innate dignity and elegance – until she discovered it was a role for life. She learned that, even in the early Seventies, when feminism was a flourishing power and women's expectations were changing, she was obliged to turn down tempting and challenging film roles. They were always unsuitable for the ruling Princess of the House of Grimaldi.

In 1968, when Maria was shattered by the news of Onassis's marriage to Jackie Kennedy, Princess Grace stood by and supported her. The gesture of loyalty reinforced their friendship. The media, of course, wanted to know what Maria thought of the marriage. Not surprisingly, she sounded bitter. 'The Kennedy woman did well to give her children a grandfather. Ari is as beautiful as Croesus,' summing up her life with, 'First I lost my weight, then I lost my voice and now I've lost Onassis.'

When Onassis first began to entertain Jackie Kennedy, then wife of the President of the United States, on the *Christina* the puritanical White House required that his mistress should not be aboard. Maria was very hurt, the pain exacerbated by a telephone call from a henchman of Onassis on her birthday saying his boss knew it was a special day but was too busy to do anything about it. Would Madame Callas like to go shopping? Maria bought the most expensive ocelot coat she could find. 'I would have been happier if he himself had just gotten me a single rose,' she told me.

20 June
Maria flies to Monaco this evening. She said she is feeling guilty about leaving Paris instead of working. We agreed to start at three, so that we would be sure to achieve something before she left at six for her seven-thirty plane. Instead, she gossiped and spent time on unnecessary fussing so that when six came we had done no work. We listened to a pirate recording of the Berlin *Lucia*. She remembered how Karajan angered the soloists by repeating the sextet without warning them. As we listened to the encore she said,

'You can hear how angry I was! And I still had the mad scene to sing! I told him afterwards at dinner that he dare not do that again on me or there would be trouble.' We listened to the mad scene, an amazing performance. She was visibly impressed. 'I don't know how I did it. I just don't know how – and to think that I wept after that performance because I thought I was so far off my aim.'

I had difficulty in expressing my reaction. Such a combination of controlled technical brilliance and artistic imagination was astounding. I attempted it with, 'It's marvellous singing.'

'Marvellous? Marvellous?' She pulled herself up in the sofa. 'It isn't marvellous, it's bloody miraculous!'

An article in my English newspaper today about the Kray brothers, the twins who dominated organised crime in the East End of London in the Sixties, terrorising and murdering their way to a kind of celebrity, and partying with politicians, film stars and the rich. It caught her attention. One of the brothers, Ronnie, was said to be a paranoid schizophrenic.

Maria thinks it is not uncommon. 'My mother is a bit mad like that, but I have never said so to the newspapers, that's one thing I couldn't tell them. It's not right. And Onassis too – he's a bit like that – those sudden changes from being sweet and charming to terrible fits of anger! He knew where to hit you till it hurt and it wouldn't show in the morning.'

She has always been interested in psychology. 'They don't do enough for mental illness these days. All this stress on cancer, but they don't spend enough money for the mentally sick.' We talked about the Church. 'Your destiny is there and there is no way of avoiding it. It's time the Church changed, pulled itself together. People are better educated now, they're more sophisticated. It needs modernising so that it can mean something to them. I don't think it's necessary to go always to church. God is a superior force which is inside you, all the time. It's up to you to use it to the best of your ability. It's a duty you have to God.'

Monday, 24 June
Maria did not return today as she said she would. She talks so much about working and how guilty she feels when we don't, but she makes no effort. Latest is that she will not be in Paris till tomorrow evening.

Wednesday, 26 June
Maria has a black eye. Flippantly I said, 'Wow, somebody's given you a whopper there.'

She put a finger to her lips and whispered 'Sh', then loudly told me she had slipped in the bathroom, her story sprinkled with unnecessary and unconvincing detail, describing the beautiful marble, but how dangerous it was when wet. In the morning, so she said, a maid came to open the curtains, saw her asleep, head and pillow streaked with blood, and woke her with a scream. It was only a small break in the skin, she said, but a night of tossing and turning had spread the blood all over, giving the impression of a more serious wound. 'She thought I had been murdered.' She finished her colourful little drama with a flourish and shot me a defiant look that told me clearly, 'Don't dare ask any more questions.'

She is having terrific misgivings about continuing to sing. 'Why should I bother when there is Caballé? She's just had a big success in Moscow with *Norma.*'

Our work was fruitless. Every piece an effort. I told her something was missing, the *élan*, the pleasure in singing, the 'wanting to'. 'That's just it, I really don't want to sing. I've really got to make a big decision soon. I stopped enjoying my singing about the time of the Rome affair. It began to mean just awful rows and fights. Then Onassis was never very interested and seldom came to a performance.' She learned the Chopin D flat nocturne to amuse him. 'I took great liberties and he liked to hear me play it. It soothed him.'

Although it's a piece I know well, I asked, 'Which nocturne do you mean?' She played the opening bars. Good professional tone

[226]

and a beautiful cantabile, but with her long finger-nails clicking on the keys she stopped. 'You're too good a musician to hear what I do with it. I pulled it about so much, you would be offended.' I told her how she 'pulled it about', her rubato was exactly what I longed to hear, but could not persuade her to go on.

The Rome affair Maria mentioned happened in the Opera House on 2 January 1958. There had been scandals before in her life, but few so widely publicised and none which left such an ugly blemish on her career. The opening night was to be the greatest event in the Roman calendar. President Gronchi would be there, in his wake the rich and famous, politicians, state dignitaries, film stars, producers, designers and the glitterati. Great expectancy filled the air.

Maria arrived from Milan with her husband on 27 December and began rehearsals in an unheated Opera House. Despite protests from the singers nothing was done about it; one of the principals became ill and withdrew, leaving the performances to her under-study. Maria also caught a cold. Surrounded by sprays, inhalations and hot compresses, she told the Opera House they must be ready with a substitute, but they did nothing, intent only on pressurising her by stressing the importance of the occasion. Against her inner feelings Maria agreed to go on. It was soon clear that she had made a mistake. She struggled through the first act, then asked the management to bring on the substitute. They had not engaged another singer, even though it is the usual practice in an opera house. 'There *is* no substitute for Callas,' they told her.

'I know that, but can't you find someone to sing the notes?' she asked in a hoarse whisper. Soon her dressing-room was filled with pleading, entreating, begging officials. The General Manager appealed to her loyalty to theatrical tradition – the show must go on – and hinted that only in Italy could she have become the greatest singer alive. She should show gratitude by singing tonight and save everyone's face. The conductor told her a great artist owed it to her public. The producer suggested she begin the next act and, before the whole house, collapse in a faint. 'That's one thing I wasn't going to do,' Maria said to me, 'that would be dishonest.' By this time the interval was stretching to nearly an hour and the audience were becoming restless. The management had to admit defeat. They gave no explanation, other than quoting the old 'reasons beyond our control' excuse and announced that the performance must be abandoned. Without an explanation the audience reacted with anger, cursing, shouting insults and threatening to lynch Callas. She had 'walked out' on them and on the President, an affront not only to Rome but to the whole Italian populace. Next day two doctors, sent by the Opera House, agreed that Callas was too ill to sing, but somehow this information never reached the newspapers. Front pages were stripped of other news to make space for indignant and merciless attacks on 'this insolent foreigner', and deputies in the Italian Parliament castigated her insult to the President and the Nation.

Although she was willing and well enough, the Opera House refused to allow her to perform the remaining dates in her contract. Seeing this as blatantly unfair, as well as illegal, Callas sued. Litigation came to an end only in 1971 when, the affair now a burnt-out squib in the eyes of the press, Callas was exonerated by the Supreme Court of Appeals and awarded damages against the Rome Opera.

'It's been like that all my life,' Maria told me sixteen years after the event. 'I was never allowed even to have a common cold.'

Sheldon Gold phoned from New York during our evening session. Maria asked him to find work for Di Stefano, saying he needed it badly for the sake of his self-respect – he was still capable, but no longer with her. 'Gorlinsky says he's finished with him, but surely you could find him some work.'

I told Maria Gorlinsky was asking if we were working hard. 'Oh, he makes me angry. Why should I have to answer to him, after all, I can just pay you myself, Robert, and tell him to put it on the account. After all I can afford it.' She feels pressurised by Gorlinsky, who is arriving tomorrow and wants her to agree to a London date with orchestra in November, and to settle the Japanese tour. She does not want to commit herself. 'He'd better wait a bit unless he wants a negative answer, for that's what it'll be if he gets it tomorrow.' Insists she does not want to go to Japan, though she recognises the importance of appearances there for her record sales. She is surprised how the royalties have shot up during the tour, normally about $4000 per quarter, but now in the region of $12,000. She fought when negotiating the contract. 'I knew what merchandise I had to sell.'

Now she is saying it would be a dirty trick to sing the concerts in Japan without Di Stefano because he had arranged them in the first place. Is she softening?

When I left she asked, 'So you really think I should keep on singing?' Elena saw me out, whispering that *La Padrona* had seen Di Stefano at the weekend.

27 *June*

A much more optimistic Maria today but, annoyed that Gorlinsky is in town, she instructed Ferruccio to tell him, whatever time he phoned, that she was working. Angry again at the thought of having to justify to him my expenses. 'Why should I feel obliged to him.'

Invited me to come sailing round the Greek islands, but in July, when I have already made other plans.

I was surprised to see the piano standing in the middle of the room, looking awkward, as though waiting to be put away after use. 'It's dear Ferruccio,' she said. 'He shifts things around just to keep me amused.'

28 *June*

I was in the apartment two hours before we started work, without enthusiasm, although the voice sounded good. Later, when Maria thought we had finished I opened the score of *Il Pirata*. As I played the intro to the final scene she became excited and began to sing, surprised and elated by the result. John Coveney rang from New York and the first thing she told him was how pleased he would have been to hear her.

She does not want to see Gorlinsky. I do. He has promised to bring me cash. Maria says I should not worry about money, she will give me some and in future we should make our own arrangements.

Gorlinsky came down the grand staircase in the Georges V with a beautiful blonde on his arm. She got the push when he saw me. I was earlier than he expected. In his room he poured whiskies and started in on Maria. He is offended. He thinks she should have seen him at least out of respect for their friendship – twenty-three years. 'In all those years she has never once given me a present. She asks me to offer dates and now she refuses to see me.' He is very proud of the fact that when Maria and Di Stefano asked for more money at the time of the Tebaldi London concert he made them give him a contract in return. The money they asked was peanuts as far as he was concerned. According to him, without the contract the tour would have finished early on in America. He told Maria that Di Stefano would sue her for a couple of million dollars if she cancelled. He is tired of Maria's behaviour. 'She's irresponsible. Who needs that? I have enough artists and anyway the opera houses are cagey about having her now.' He was on his third whisky and seemed genuinely upset. I said nothing of the black eye, which is probably the real reason she is holding him off. 'She needs a bully. Meneghini was a bully and look at Onassis. When I was on the boat it was embarrassing to see how he treated her. She behaved like a slave. Bloody Greek women! It was those gossips Gina Bachauer and Vasso Devetzi who caused all that trouble over the Tebaldi concert.' As I left, some welcome francs in my pocket, he asked me to tell Maria he was very busy with incoming calls while I was with him.

Went straight to my favourite local restaurant, where I found Elena and Ferruccio. He appeared uncomfortable in his chair. 'It's his poor back,' Elena told me. 'She knows he has a bad back but she's always asking him to shift heavy furniture.'

As usual, the talk centred on 'Madame'. '*Mon Oncle*' phoned Sunday, was told she was with Princess Grace, came back with an irate, 'What's going on. Are you trying to hide something from me?' Princess Grace told me she has left.' Ferruccio had an idea where he might find her and phoned the Di Stefano house in San Remo. He was right.

29 June

Planning to hear Margaret Price in *Così fan tutte* this evening, I said I must leave at six-thirty. 'Oh, that's all right', but there was so much telephoning and chit-chat that we did not start work until five-thirty. It went so well that she did not want to stop. Could I not go in the interval? Eventually, when I was already dressed to leave, she asked me to sit down again to give my advice on a problem facing her this evening. Vasso Devetzi's boy-friend has made a pass at her and they are due for dinner and cards, but Vasso will be late, which means Maria would be alone with him. If she asks Vasso to tell him to arrive later she would be curious and perhaps suspicious, and Maria does not want to hurt an old friend. 'Why should he make a pass at me? I'm an old woman of fifty. I wonder if it's me, or just my name.' I told her what she wanted to hear and gave up on *Così*. I will phone Margaret in the morning.

Sunday, 30 June

The work pattern continues. Nothing for the first hour or more, then after prompting, some half-hearted singing. Weary sighs and 'I really don't want to sing' have become a refrain.

The proposed holiday cruise is still on the cards, a later date in August suggested. 'You could come then, couldn't you, Robert?' It's an attractive idea.

Soon after I arrived she said, 'Don't be surprised if you see Di Stefano in your hotel tonight. Keep it quiet, though, I don't want anyone to know. I told Elena because she will have to know anyway, but the others hate him. My poor Ferruccio, I haven't seen him all day. Friends came and took him away.' Probably by design.

Bruna, Maria's favourite maid and confidante, whom I have not yet met, is still in Italy caring for her ailing mother. 'I wish the old woman would just die,' Maria sighed.

Di Stefano was signing in when I reached the hotel. I went

with him to his room. He took his Toscanini medallion out of its box and toyed with it while he harangued me about the tour, complaining about Maria's use of Mandrax. He thinks it partly responsible for her behaviour to him. He tried it, but stopped because 'They are really drugs. They will make her mad. It's what the kids were taking for kicks ... She asked me why I can't be more British – me, a Sicilian! She's nuts, that's one of the things I like about her.' The telephone rang. It was Maria. As they fell into their lovie-dovie baby talk I slipped out.

1 July

Consuelo came to my hotel to ask me not to come this morning. Work at 5 p.m.

Not a word from Maria about Di Stefano, though Elena told me he has gone to London.

After a couple of Bellini songs Maria attacked 'Una voce poco fa', which she found difficult. Mostly the usual block: lack of desire. She said she was scared. When, like this, she just does not want to sing I find it increasingly difficult to know how to encourage her. She sings better when the tape machine is not running. We gave up and listened to some recordings. A pirate of the Gala opening night of *Poliuto*, the new role she had chosen for her return to La Scala on 7 December 1960, after an absence of more than two years. In earlier years a Callas opening would have been an interesting musical event. By then it had become the highlight of the Scala season, an international social event. Onassis was there, with a high-life coterie, Prince Rainier and Princess Grace, the Begum Aga Khan and Elsa Maxwell among them. I remarked that she sounded nervous. 'Who wouldn't be with that lot there!' she replied. She did not mention the others in the audience, the music critics, her ardent admirers, nor the disparagers waiting for an opportunity to vilify her with their boos and catcalls. 'I sang better the second night,' she said, taking *Anna Bolena*, another pirate recording, out of the cupboard. 'Wait till you hear this – this is singing.' She saw me smile at the expressiveness of her ornaments. 'Ah, my grupetti.

I took so much trouble with them. I really loved them.' Played the duet with Giulietta Simionato as Jane Seymour. 'That's not a pretty voice, but the woman has guts!'

Maria ate some raspberries to keep her going until dinner. Said she was eating out later, but she did not tell me, or Elena or Ferruccio, where or with whom, which is unlike her and rather suspicious. I learned the reason why when I returned after dinner to my hotel. A cab was waiting. Maria and Di Stefano were leaving to dine out, Maria very definitely 'dressed down' for the occasion. She bowed her head, looking up at me with sheepish eyes as though expecting a parental reprimand. I could only feel happy for her. Perhaps we will have a reconciliation – if only for a few days.

Maria has been talking of her first feelings of dissatisfaction with her husband, Meneghini. She wanted to ease her heavy work-load, take the pressure out of her engagement calendar. He drew her attention to the large financial commitments they had, the house in Milan, a villa at Sirmione on Lake Garda, servants, etc., then made the bad mistake of unwisely commenting, 'You've got to keep us in the comfort we're used to.' She asked Onassis for investment advice. 'How much you got?' Not knowing, she returned to enquire, only to find out that Meneghini had cunningly arranged the banking so that he had control of all her earnings. 'I never saw any of it,' Maria said, 'even after the divorce.'

'Onassis could be stingy too.' She complained one day that he did not send her flowers as he had in their early days together. 'Flowers? You belong to me now, you're part of me. Why should I send myself flowers,' was his pasha-like response. 'But he knows where to give presents when it can mean a good business deal. A Mercedes here, an Alfa Romeo there. And I helped to choose the jewels for the wives.'

She is thinking of buying a villa in the South of France. Two are on offer at four million and three million francs, which does not please her. I suggested she remind Onassis she has a birthday coming up. 'Don't you think I've tried that? Don't worry, when we were together several of my little schemes matured. But sometimes he can be cunning. When I bought the Mercedes 600 he said what do I want with a big car like that. I have to have it, I said, I'm a prima donna and people expect me to travel like that.' She smiled and shrugged her shoulders when I remarked that it was also a particularly comfortable mode of transport. 'When I had it for a while he said he would buy me a new one if I gave it to his son Alexander. He told me to go and choose the new one. But I wasn't going to fall for any of his tricks. He phoned me a week later and said where's the car and I said, 'Oh no, you're not going to catch me on that one. I don't buy the car till your money is in my bank.'

Tuesday, 2 July

Breakfasted with Dev, Di Stefano's friend from New York, before we went to see him, still in bed. He suggested we have lunch together, 'The Three Musketeers'. I don't want to be a Musketeer; nor to spend the day coaching him in the duets he is recording with Caballé in September.

The 5 p.m. session with Maria cancelled. Instead, Dev brought me up to date with the latest complication. Last night Di Stefano returned from Georges Mandel at 4 a.m., then talked with Maria on the phone till morning. Mrs Di Stefano had rung to say that the Japanese agent told her Maria was singing the concerts alone. This was the first he knew of it. A tense moment for Maria when he confronted her. Dev's task was to persuade Di Stefano to make a friendly visit to Georges Mandel before he leaves this evening. He succeeded and Di Stefano is now driving with Maria in the Bois de Boulogne, enjoying, I hope peacefully, this lovely weather we are having. Paris is nearly as beautiful as London in the early summer.

Friday, 5 July

Fine display today of 'La Callas' putting her agent in his place. Maria has discovered that for the concerts when Di Stefano did not sing Gorlinsky had transferred only $10,000, instead of $15,000, to her account. According to the contract Maria was to be paid

$15,000, out of which she would pay Di Stefano $5000. No fee for the solo pianists who played in his stead came near that, at the most $2000. Gorlinsky was quietly pocketing the difference. She phoned him in London. 'Look,' she said, 'make sure Robert gets some money.' Went on to tell him she did not like many things about his behaviour since all this return to singing started. He does not show her the contracts, though he signs for her. In the past he always discussed every detail with her. Now he goes ahead and leaves her to find out from the newspapers. That was how she learned that the USA tour was definitely on. Sounds to me it was his way of pinning her down.

Maria was incredibly blunt with him. 'Don't ever do anything like all that Tebaldi business on me again. We artists have hearts and are sensitive, you know. I don't know if you can understand that. So don't do it again.'

I could hear Gorlinsky struggling. 'I know you love me and I have worked for you so long, we are like brother and sister.'

'Well get this, brother dear, I want those contracts! You've known me long enough to realise that if you trick me now you will only have to pay later and I'll get you. You said our concerts were a circus – well, it was your idea and I am hurt by that expression.' To escape the flak he asked to speak to me. Di Stefano's solo tour in Australia has been confirmed for October. He wants me. Gorlinsky told him I might be free if I am not in Japan with Maria. All news to me.

Little work done. There is a definite offer of a boat for August. Much talk of the fun we are going to have swimming and eating in island tavernas.

She gave me 1000 francs to settle my hotel bill. When I promised to repay her she said, with a kiss, 'You don't owe me anything.'

CUMBERLAND TERRACE, LONDON, *9 August*

Call from Maria this evening. 'Well, Japan is on, with the Sicilian.'

She wants me to come to Paris, 'as soon as the bastard Gorlinsky'

– sounding like Di Stefano – 'has arranged everything. I am raring to go now, Robert, not like I was when I saw you last. I want to show a certain soprano, you know who I mean, a thing or two.'

Plans for the Aegean cruise have been abandoned. Onassis said we must not sail. There will be a war. Turkey is preparing to invade Cyprus.

PARIS, *14 August*

Work in full swing when I arrived at Georges Mandel. Few preliminaries, shook hands with both. In his presence Maria made no attempt to kiss me as she does when we are alone. He struts in the role of teacher, she calls him '*Amore*'.

15 August

Here we go again! I met Di Stefano returning to the hotel, tired and dishevelled, as I was leaving for our 1 p.m. appointment. 'We'll work after I've had some sleep,' he said. 'She's a stupid woman who lives in a world of her own. I have my work to do and must protect it. I took her back for Japan, but she's not serious. She won't work enough. She says *Il Guarany* [an opera by Carlos Gomes] is rotten music just because I'm singing it with Caballé.' He is offended by Maria ridiculing his fee for the Australian concerts, $4000. She told Gorlinsky it was a 'rotten deal'. Embarrassed, Di Stefano phoned Gorlinsky telling him not to take any notice of her, not to give up the tour, only postpone it, 'You never know what might happen.'

'Gorlinsky's a bastard, but he always got the biggest fee for us,' he told me.

To Georges Mandel at three. I do not know how either can expect results when they work as they did today. She had promised to help him learn his part in the *Il Guarany* duet, singing the soprano, but she had not taken the trouble to learn the notes, could not be bothered to sight-read it, could not hear me playing her part because he was singing so loudly, and annoyed him when he tried to conduct and she could not follow his beat. All through this he was criticising her technique. I was glad when the session came to an end and I could escape.

[236]

16 August

They were already working when I arrived at 5 p.m. Maria in much better voice, therefore Di Stefano happy.

It is nearly a year since I first came to Paris to work with them. What a difference! How close they were, trusting and sometimes, in the freedom of their reactions to one another, oblivious of my presence. Now, when he is able to control his temper, there is a tone of respect, deference even, when he coaches her. I do not see much of the girlish timidity which was so surprising in the 'Legend' I first met.

I repaid Maria the 1000 francs. She took it without a word. Gorlinsky told me she was shocked when she heard how much it costs to bring me over. Even more when he told her my expenses were set against her personal account, not the tour.

Sunday, 18 August

No rest for the wicked? Yesterday and today we had long, successful periods of work. No Sabbath. Days of the week, Holy Days even, do not exist.

When Di Stefano repaid me some old debts Maria offered to lend me some cash. She is friendly to me but formal while he is around, but if he should step out of the room she quickly asks if I think he is doing her any good.

She is scornful of the duets Caballé has chosen for the record with Di Stefano.

19 August

Session devoted to 'Vissi d'arte' and 'Tu che le vanità'. The voice continues to improve. He continues to badger her. She becomes distressed and looks to me with enormous, anguished eyes.

Generally, the results were excellent. If only she had worked like this last year, how different the crits would have been.

Tuesday, 20 August

Terrific shouting match tonight. He would not let her sing without continuous correction. She got exasperated and the shouting started. He: 'Don't get angry.' She: 'Who's angry?' 'Be modest.' 'I am modest – get another soprano. You tell me Caballé sings beautiful and I'm awful, well take another soprano to Japan.' 'What are you saying!? We are professional singers and we have a job to do. Are you going to open your throat or not?' – shouting at the top of his voice. Eventually, when things have quietened down, we start again. I had remained at the piano even when he cried, *'Buona notte, Roberto.'*

While Maria was out of the room, he said, 'What do you make of her? The most phenomenal singer in the world and she doesn't know how to open her throat! People would not believe it.'

Before the end of the session she was singing better. Discount the clashes of Mediterranean temperaments and it could be called a successful evening.

Elena told me that before Di Stefano came to Paris this time he twice phoned Consuelo to apologise to her for his behaviour in America. Even so, she and Ferruccio have been sent off on holiday to Spain so that only Elena, whom Di Stefano likes (definitely not reciprocated!), will be in the house with them.

Thursday, 22 August

Di Stefano left yesterday for a holiday with his wife in San Remo. He is hoping that she will not come to Japan if he spends time with her now.

This evening we returned to the easy relationship which Maria holds at bay when he is around. 'You know, Robert, I think I really do hate singing.' We had been trying to get her going; the voice is stronger than ever, but she just does not pull it off. I suggested she needed a big auditorium and an audience, reminding her of Boston when she just had to produce a performance. Now her technique is more secure and the voice stronger, but tonight she could not manage even 'Comme autrefois', the aria from *Les Pêcheurs de Perles*. She gave up at the cadenza. It is curious, though, how her musicianship shines through. Good or bad notes, her legato, phrasing and grace notes were a delight. But I could not pull her out of depression. She emanates her moods so powerfully it is difficult not to empathise, to overcome the feeling of being drawn in, like swimming against a rapid current to escape drowning. If she does not want to sing, why does she? Simple. Maria needs and wants Di Stefano's love and this is how she can get it. The problem is he seldom pleases 'La Callas'. Elena and the other three staff believe that he is using her to get himself work. Maria spoke to Mrs Di Stefano today, in answer to a letter asking to be friends once more. When she came off the phone she said to me, 'Pippo and I are planning a holiday somewhere on the way to Japan, but keep it quiet. I don't want her to know.'

I wrote to Ivor Newton, this being the anniversary of the day he introduced me to Maria. She asked me to include her greetings.

24 August

Vasso Divetzi is a frequent visitor, often calling in unannounced. She seems determined to ingratiate herself, continuously flattering Maria in an overly anxious obsequious manner. Today, while still in the hallway taking off her coat, she called, 'How beautiful you're looking.' Maria, in the music room, lifted her eyes to the ceiling and shrugged her shoulders. 'She's company,' Maria admits, though I can see she does not always welcome it. I suppose being Greek together is a solace to Maria.

Sunday, 25 August

A newspaper predicts that this year will see Jackie Kennedy winning the biggest ever divorce alimony. 'Not likely,' Maria said. 'He can be very mean. He'd keep her as a wife rather than give her alimony.'

Maria is singing better since Di Stefano left. She gets easily depressed by a few weak notes, but elated when all goes well. Even a remark of Elena's about how much she has improved gives her terrific encouragement. She now has two distinct attitudes to Di Stefano, one as lover and the other as competing singer. 'I have to admit I still need him to help me along, but after Japan – finito.'

He has been telling Maria that Mario De Maria is a close friend of Caballé. 'I don't think we can trust him,' Maria said. 'He's a lover of sopranos. Massages her feet,' she sniffed. I can hear the timbre of Di Stefano in her voice. He has always been jealous of Mario. Now he is putting the knife in. Maria is even suggesting Mario was responsible for much of the trouble in America.

She has been excited all day in anticipation of the film on TV this evening. 'They're showing *Camille* tonight,' she told me, as though it were a very special treat. I returned for dinner and the movie. We watched, unusually, in almost complete silence. While Garbo was on the screen Maria never took her eyes off her. She was weeping when, strings quietly quoting Verdi's *Traviata* melodies, Garbo, in Robert Taylor's arms, signals the moment of death by suddenly opening her eyes, just as Callas would do in the famous Visconti *Traviata* at La Scala in 1955. 'Poor Violetta,' Maria said, 'she was so noble.' Her eyes dabbed dry, she told me, in the naïve voice of an awestruck schoolgirl, 'Do you know, the critics actually compared my *Traviata* to Garbo's.'

In the salon there is a silver-framed sepia-toned print of Maria as Violetta, looking like a nineteenth-century diva. It is the only photograph of Callas anywhere to be seen in the apartment.

Monday, 26 August
Half an hour of work before Maria received M. Gérard Vée of D'Entraide aux Handicaps et Blessés, who wants to arrange that she sings again for the charity. She has a soft spot for the handicapped.

I left and returned to find Maria livid. 'Wait till you hear what I've just learned!' Gorlinsky sold the Paris concert to Vée for $25,000, paid Maria $10,000 and Di Stefano $5000. His only expenses were for his wife and himself, so he earned the same as Maria and twice as much as Di Stefano. 'And to think I invited *him* to dinner afterwards!'

It is 'that' time of the month. She is not too energetic in her singing, but the technique grows and she is now aware of the fabricated sound which had become a habit. We notice it particu-

larly in the late recordings. Some commentators have called it her
'bottled-up' sound.

Di Stefano rang from the airport. Like a teenager expecting her
first date, she ran to change and make herself beautiful.

Tuesday, 27 August

Di Stefano left early. Maria came to take him to the airport. At
9.30 a.m.! The result is she slept most of the day and now, at
6.30 p.m., says we won't practise this evening. Another lost day for
me.

Wednesday, 28 August

Our appointment for 1 p.m. Maria appeared at 2.15 p.m. I have
rarely seen her so agitated; riled by Di Stefano's association with
Caballé. 'Her singing is all beautiful sound but nothing else. It
means as much as a shopping list. Am I crazy? I refused to release
my *Manon* for two years because I took the easy way out on some
notes and sang piano, AND SHE MAKES A CAREER OF IT!'

(I had the pleasure of accompanying Montserrat Caballé only
once, in a castle near Munich, a recital with José Carreras, Agnes
Baltsa and Boris Christoff, where I experienced the beauty of her
pianissimo and her extraordinary breath control at first hand.
Enough to give an accompanist a heart attack. By post, in 1974,
she received a present from Maria; the ear-rings Visconti had given
her to wear as Norma. Maria had treasured them as a good-luck
talisman and wore them in every subsequent performance. Out of
respect for Callas, Caballé could never bring herself to wear them
on stage.)

'I have a nice neighbour upstairs who has offered me the use of
a room for you. It would be so much nicer than a hotel,' Maria
said today, 'and we could be close.' The thought of being on twenty-
four-hour call is enough to convince me that, however limited the
space in my charming little hotel round the corner, I will hold on
to it. I managed to deflect another ploy. 'I had such a sweet pianist
who used to come over from Covent Garden and play for me and,
you know, she didn't ask any money at all – did it out of love for

me.' I pretended not to understand. To be here with her I have given up important dates, as well as regular work with other artists. I cannot afford the position of unpaid keyboard lackey, however glamorous it is to be treated as a celebrity, travelling first class around the world and living in luxury hotels with a superstar. I hope I will continue to be paid by Gorlinsky. Tomorrow I will see him in London.

Good news. We can have the use of the Théâtre des Champs-Elysées in the daytime. We will work there when I return from London. I am looking forward to a break from this life of waiting in Paris, rarely knowing whether or not I am free from one part of the day till the next.

8 September 1974
Maria in positive, happy mood. Di Stefano has finished his recording with Caballé.

Another hint today about the saving of expenses if I took up the 'nice neighbour's' offer. Again I side-stepped a positive answer. Later Elena divulged the name of the neighbour upstairs. My struggle for independence has cost me the fun, at a dinner party perhaps, the subject of French film in the air, of nonchalantly dropping the teaser, 'I once lived with Catherine Deneuve.'

9 September
Maria unsettled but willing to work. She wants to show Di Stefano what she can do when he comes tomorrow. His association with Caballé has done more for Maria's singing than any amount of shouting and bullying.

She has been wearing her hair up in a bun during the day, so unlike her glamorous platform image. It amuses me; an air of the schoolhouse around the place.

Our work was disturbed by the sound of raised voices at the door. 'It's that Japanese girl again,' Elena said.

'But I've written to her,' Maria protested. 'Three letters is enough.' We continued our work, watched TV with dinner on our laps and I prepared to leave. The Japanese girl was sitting on the stairs when I opened the door. Begged me to let her see Madame Callas. I returned to Maria and told her how distressed the girl was. 'What shall I say to her?' she asked, looking alarmed. 'Don't go away, Robert.' I walked with her to the door, where the Japanese girl let out a scream that so frightened Maria she jumped back into the music room. I calmed the girl and took her in to meet Maria. We were confronted by a school headmistress, tall and radiating authority. Maria stood, holding her specs in clasped hands, very erect and dominant, but her voice was warm and gentle as she invited the trembling girl to sit, offered tea and asked, 'What do you want in life?' The young woman told her story. Rich parents, against her being a singer, but might relent if the great Callas would give her lessons. 'I don't teach.' Then could she be her servant? 'I already have my staff, enough to look after me. Whatever you want in life, you must work for it. Don't let anyone put you off. Stick to your guns, and work.' Ferruccio brought a photo to be autographed, then Maria guided the girl to the door with an arm around her shoulder. She left in tears of happiness. 'Oh, dear, how I sympathise with her,' Maria said, as she closed the door behind her.

Di Stefano is expected late tonight. Maria reminded me of the last night in Montreal, when she asked me to let down her hair. This made him very jealous, she said, and he has not forgotten it. Did she do it deliberately to upset him? 'Yes,' she admitted, giggling like a naughty child.

10 September

On the way to the Théâtre des Champs-Elysées we picked up Di Stefano at his hotel. In the car he teased Maria by telling me how wonderful it was to work with a real professional again, of the long phrases she could sing without taking a breath and how nice to be near a soprano with big tits. Maria stretched her left hand across to her right shoulder and looked out of the window.

His apartment in the hotel is so grand he might give a party to show it off. I asked him what was wrong with the couch in Maria's studio. 'That used to be my room, but I've been thrown out,' he said.

Maria retorted, 'Oh no, he took all his things out and when people do that, that's it. They don't get back in again.'

Worked for nearly three hours in the theatre, where Maria's voice blossomed and amazed us all. She was very happy and asked him repeatedly if he saw the progress she had made while he was away and she worked alone with me. The idea that I might have had a hand in her progress did not please him. Today's performance would seem a vindication of Maria's contention that she needs a big space to sing in. Says she has never been any good in a rehearsal room. Maybe, but I wonder how much of it was the need to show Di Stefano what she could do? Again and again he called out bravos.

11 September

Théâtre des Champs-Elysées. It was not easy for Maria today. The sound good, but she stopped often, complaining of being tired. Too little sleep, I suspect. Occasionally, she asked my advice. He seemed peeved.

Gorlinsky has changed the dates. We play Korea before Japan. The news came out casually in conversation. Now my plans must be altered.

12 September

The theatre again, singing and replaying the tape, phrase by phrase, to a lot of the usual abuse. The newspapers have been tipped off and photographers surrounded us as we left. Maria quickly took off her glasses and Di Stefano buttoned up his jacket.

On the phone Gorlinsky told me that the Korean dates were changed so that Di Stefano could have his tour in Australia. He wants me, but Gorlinsky told him Maria says she will need me in Paris. Neither has spoken to me about it. It does not seem to matter what I think.

13 September

Di Stefano left today. After all the pacts and agreements about behaving themselves, nothing has changed. More misunderstandings and arguments. Maria is hurt by the language he uses. Now she is afraid the concerts in the East will turn out like the American tour. She thinks he is jealous of her singing.

She returned after seeing him off, tired, nervous and angry. At the airport he told her she was not yet ready for opera and talked of more concerts. 'Nobody tells *me* what to sing!' she exclaimed. She consented to singing some exercises. Just to keep her breathing muscles going, I told her.

On the 21st they are going to Chicago, where Maria will take part in a conference on Verdi, organised by the Italian Instituto di Studi Verdiani and the Lyric Opera. Musicologists and Verdi experts from all over the world will be there. I asked Maria if she will read a paper. 'Not likely. I'll let them ask questions.' Di Stefano has not been invited. He will be in the audience. Afterwards they will fly to Honolulu *en route* for Seoul, where I will meet them at the end of the month.

Maria is planning to spend a holiday in Tahiti with Vasso Devetzi after the tour. 'You'll be free to go to Australia with our tenor,' she said. Am I flattered by her possessiveness, or annoyed?

Kissed me good-night. 'We mustn't do this on the tour, otherwise there will really be trouble. He hasn't forgotten Montreal!'

Saturday, 14 September

I have not realised how far the disputes had gone. Maria is talking of cancelling Japan.

Di Stefano has been asked to make another recording with Caballé. More of the duets from our programmes. She thinks they are trying to 'show me up'. I said the opera public would not think much of Caballé for playing such a trick. 'Stop being such a musician, Robert, I know the public. They wouldn't care a damn. But I could do a better one with someone else, just as we killed Tebaldi's *Tosca*. It was supposed to be the greatest thing on record – until we did it with de Sabata. They're asking me to do *Cav* with Domingo, but I don't like his singing.' I was taken aback by this remark since, having previously worked with him I knew Domingo to be an unusually perceptive and musicianly artist. She noticed my surprise. 'Well,' she said with a shrug, 'I don't really know him.'

In the afternoon I practised while she visited a couture house. I had hoped to be free by six, for a dinner date at eight, but she did not return till nearly seven. However, when we started work on *Carmen* she became so involved and elated by the new strength in her voice that we worked on until after ten. She was very appreciative that I stayed. I really think this time I could have left, but the work was so exciting that I could not possibly have brought it to an end. Dinner postponed until tomorrow.

On his latest visit Di Stefano was curiously subdued, as though engrossed in heavy thoughts. Maria thinks he is becoming aware of the end of his singing career, which is bad enough, now that she is starting a new one. The complications are unceasing.

He never talks of his daughter Luisa, but I think she is always on his mind.

15 September

Maria was in a hat, ready to leave, when I arrived this morning. To the Air France Medical Centre for cholera and typhoid jabs. 'Why should I pay my doctor the money he expects, when I can get it free?' We agreed to meet at three.

At four she appeared, making it difficult for me to get away by seven. No work, but we listened to the sessions with Di Stefano in the theatre last week. She is not always convinced by his suggestions and the tapes sometimes prove she is right. They also show the demoralising and depressing effects his coaching can have. He phoned, asking her to come to Milan, even for one day. He said she could visit her dressmaker, Biki. 'He just wants me to make it up with his wife,' Maria said.

We were to have a rest day tomorrow. She has asked me to come in, if only for one hour. I agreed, but asked for a definite time. The nearest I got was that she would let me know in the afternoon. I am so tired of hanging around my hotel, or phoning from wherever I happen to be in Paris, waiting for her to make a decision.

16 September

She was out when I phoned expecting to be told the hour of 'our appointment'. Exasperated, I decided to leave it until the morning. After an hour I felt so uneasy I gave up and went round. She was listening to Joan Sutherland singing 'Ernani! Involami' on the radio. Before it finished she had taken out the score, opening it at the aria. She told Elena to sit down and me to play. She sang it well. 'See,' she said. 'I can do it better.' No opinions were asked.

She admits Di Stefano has helped her, but says I have also. She prefers how I work, says I inspire her to sing, but he depresses her. 'He's saying he is the great teacher. He'll never be a teacher. He hasn't the manners ... *Nobody teaches Callas.*' Maria on her high horse.

Ferruccio is amazed that 'Madame' took so much from Di Stefano in the theatre. In the past, he said, she would have thrown the score at him. She's getting near to that. 'Nobody teaches Callas' but I wonder what she calls the work of the last year or so.

17 September

Maria has been weeping all night at the news of Larry Kelly's death. Cancer of the liver. She is all in black today. 'How can fate be so unfair. He was only forty-five.' When we saw him in Dallas he asked her to sing *Carmen* in 1975. 'Seventy-five? We might all be dead by then,' she had told him. 'Am I a seer or some kind of witch or something?' she asked me, taking off her glasses to dry the tears on them and her eyes. She talked of Kelly as being like a brother, and how well they had worked together in Chicago and Dallas. She says she suffers more from his death than she did when her father died. 'I wasn't very close to my mother or father.'

Di Stefano wants to sing the *Faust* duet again. Neither of us can understand why, it always sounds so difficult for him, and he belts it out fortissimo even in the very tender opening. Maria says she was embarrassed singing 'Oh silence' after his 'bawling'. It could be funny, except that she never takes her singing lightly.

On the phone to Edith Gorlinsky in London, Maria asked if

she would please discreetly tell her husband that when he comes tomorrow he should be careful not to say anything that might disturb her. 'We are artists, you know, and sensitive. Your husband can be terribly brutal. He's a good businessman but has no tact, and I don't want him upsetting us just before we go off on our tour again.' As she hung up she said, 'Gorlinsky drinks too much, that's why he has such a big mouth.'

11

THE FAR EAST

D<small>I</small> STEFANO was annoyed that the president of *Joong-ang Ilbo*, the newspaper sponsoring our two concerts in Seoul, was not at the airport on their arrival from Honolulu on 30 September. 'They sent inferiors,' he complained. Maria said nothing, content to let him be her spokesman. They both looked well, he tanned and bright-eyed, and our meeting was easy, informal and friendly.

Maria was contented and very confident, saying when we were alone, 'He's become more reasonable.'

He told me, 'Everything's all right now.'

In our first session together she surprised me by telling him he must wait until she had warmed up before making any comments. 'Oh, yes,' he said, as though remembering a pact. He was a changed man, calm, gentle and polite, full of bonhomie. Gone was the quick temper that led to quarrels, accusations, recriminations and shouting. All was reasonableness, mutual consideration and peace. It was a pleasure to be working again.

Our first concert at the Ewha Women's University was attended by 4000 people. Realising Maria was in good form, I played 'Suicidio' in the original key without first warning her. She had often suggested this and was pleased when I told her. He was not happy, though, accusing me of 'playing tricks'. He was worried that

I might do it to him, a perilous gamble I would never risk. Next morning he listened to the tape, checked on the piano that I had played in the printed key, took out 'Che gelida manina' and asked me to play it in the original key. 'Suicidio' has a high B flat, but 'Che gelida manina' stretches to the higher C. While Maria listened he sang the aria, reaching the high note only just well enough to escape embarrassment. 'I'll do it in that key at the next concert,' he said, but during it neither he nor Maria, nor I, mentioned the aria.

On the night before our second concert we were the guests of President Kim and his wife in an exotic Geisha House where, after being guided to our places around the dining-table, we were regaled for twenty-five minutes by Korean musicians playing quarter-tone music on curious stringed instruments. Maria looked bored and when Mr Kim invited her to return the compliment by singing a song, she declined politely. 'Just a verse of "One Fine Day",' he pleaded, unaware that Callas did not sing on social occasions. As a child she was made to perform on demand for any visiting relative or neighbour who could be persuaded by her mother to act as an audience. A grown woman, she still resented it. Even Winston Churchill, sailing on the *Christina* where his every wish was personally attended to by a deferential Onassis, was not granted such a request. Maria shot me the cool, still look I had seen during the interview in New York when, off camera, Barbara Walters asked, 'Madame Callas, is there a little childhood lullaby, a little simple song that you could just sing very sweetly and quietly towards the end of the programme?' Maria's glance to me seemed to ask if the lady were mad, or just naïve. 'I don't remember one at all,' she replied, very sweetly and quietly.

Like Barbara Walters, Mr Kim gave way. On a nod, dozens of little dishes began to arrive. We were sitting around a large table, which seemed to rest on the floor, little stools with low backs for the Westerners, and two girls in national costume intent on caring for my every need. While one stroked the inside of my thigh her ally fed me delicious morsels of seafood on chopsticks. Seeing me enjoy the pampering, President Kim sent one of his entourage to whisper in my ear that it was my choice which one of the two beauties would spend time with me later. I told him I would return home with the lady with whom I had set out.

At the end of the evening we were each presented with a volume of Korean folk-songs and a velvet-lined box containing a miniature nacre-and-brass decorated lacquer cabinet, its beauty marred by the slogan '*Joong-ang Daily News*. Tong-Jang Radio. TV. FM.' Di Stefano flicked the pages of the folk-song album and excited the Koreans by promising to sing one at the next concert. Poor deluded souls.

Seoul's skyline was not the most arresting of the cities we had played. In 1974 they were too busy catching up with the Western world to worry about architecture. We saw little of the centuries-old royal palaces, pagodas or temples nestling among the high-rise office blocks. Our time in the city was made memorable by our visits to the home of the French Ambassador, Pierre Landy, a man of great taste and a long-standing friend of Maria. Delicious French food, in surroundings of sophisticated Western culture, it was an island of repose in an ugly city.

'I think I shall be flying back to Paris,' Maria told Mr Nakajima, the Japanese agent, when she saw the accommodation he had booked for her in an ultra-modern hotel whose design suggested it was built on the redundant plots of adjoining sites. Inside, the oddly shaped rooms lacked character, charm, or any other attribute that might enhance an extended sojourn. Di Stefano took charge, castigating Nakajima for his insensitivity and demanding a better hotel, 'Even if it does cost more.' Japan was important for Di Stefano. This was where the idea for the tour took root. He was not prepared to see Nakajima let him down. We sat beside untouched suitcases most of the day, while they searched, eventually settling for the Hilton.

Next day began a campaign of publicity which dogged us all through Japan. We were photographed in gardens, visiting temples and shrines, in a park with an astonished mother and child, standing by important buildings and in streets so crowded that the pavements could barely be seen. Wherever we went we were accompanied by Nakajima and his partner, Madame Kobayashi, a former opera singer who in her day had starred as Cio-Cio-San in *Madama Butterfly*. Buxom and ebullient, she laughed and bowed a lot, and at meals drank only neat Suntory whisky, the very acceptable Japanese version of Scotch.

The publicity drive began with a conference for the national press and TV on the day after our arrival. Maria, Di Stefano and I sat at a table perched on a high platform so close together that I could feel their apprehension. Di Stefano was more nervous than Maria. When she was asked about singing technique she simply spouted all that he had been telling her, the open throat and so on. Fischer-Dieskau had recently given a lieder recital in Tokyo, had she thought of doing the same? 'I don't belong there. I don't sing lieder,' Maria replied politely, dispelling any lingering hopes I had in that direction. Asked about modern opera composers she mentioned Cilea (*Adriana Lecouvreur*. He died in 1950) and Mascagni (*Cavalleria Rusticana*. He died in 1945). 'I don't like modern music,' she said, 'there's too much noise. I'm an old-fashioned Romantic.'

The nearest Callas ever came to singing a recently composed opera was Gian Carlo Menotti's *The Consul*, a composition firmly set in the school of Puccini, hardly eligible for the epithet 'modern' in the light of such works as Alban Berg's *Lulu*, premièred in 1937, or even Richard Strauss's 1909 *Elektra*. In the mid-Sixties the General Manager of the Royal Opera House in Covent Garden, David Webster, took Georg Solti, his music director, to visit Callas in the Savoy Hotel and put to her an ambitious plan for her to sing the title role in Berg's opera. '*Lulu?* What's *Lulu?*' Callas asked. An opera by Alban Berg. 'Berg? Terrible music,' she exclaimed. 'Why can't we do Bellini?'

On a visit in July 1975 to Yester House, his Robert Adam home in the Lammermoor Hills near Edinburgh, Gian Carlo told me how he almost succeeded in persuading Callas to sing Magda in the first performance of his new opera in Milan. Antonio Ghiringhelli, General Manager of La Scala, told him he could pick his leading soprano, another friend suggesting he hear 'that new Greek girl who is singing in Rome'. Menotti thought he had found the ideal Magda in Callas, discussed the role with her and was happy when she agreed. But Callas had one condition. She would sing Magda only if she were engaged also in one of her traditional roles. She had replaced Tebaldi in three performances of *Aida* at La Scala in April 1950, hoping it would open its door to her, but nothing further came of it. Later, in 1951, when she was asked again to take over *Aida* from Tebaldi she refused. Once as a replacement was enough. Callas desperately wanted to perform in the grandest of opera houses in Italy, some say the world, but on her own terms, in the planned programme of the season. To sing at La Scala would be the ultimate affirmation of her success. Ghiringhelli, who never liked Callas nor hid his hostility, had been resisting this for years. He told Menotti that the only way she would ever sing at La Scala would be in the subsidiary capacity of guest artist. Menotti's hopes were dashed, but Callas won when, by force of public demand, Ghiringhelli was obliged to include her in his 1951–2 season. Callas inaugurated one of the greatest periods in the history of his house with seven performances of *I Vespri Siciliani*.

Our first concert at the NHK Hall in Tokyo was recorded by television cameras. The plan was to edit the best from two concerts and make a programme to be shown later. Di Stefano was rather hoarse and did not do too well up in the higher regions, but on the whole it was a good concert. Maria, as usual, was rapturously received. The concert was introduced by Madame Kobayashi, wearing a black Western-style evening dress. We recognised our names, Callas-San, Di Stefano-San, Sutherland-San, nothing else, but judging by the laughter from the audience her opening remarks must have been witty. After the interval she appeared again, this time in a magnificent kimono. She probably spent all of the first half of the concert being dressed in it. The kimono itself was made of elaborately embroidered silk, and the obi, the broad stiffened length of rich fabric that acts as a waistband, was tied in an enormous bow at the back. Beautiful in its own right, it did not seem to matter that the colours clashed with the kimono.

After the concert we returned to Maria's apartment which, in our absence, had been decorated for a party, colourful streamers hanging from the ceiling and the tables dressed for a festive buffet. On a long side table bottles were meticulously set out in three groups. Italian wines and aperitifs, Greek ouzo, retsina and Metaxa brandy, then Suntory whisky, Scotch whisky and three different malts – evidence of a touching thoughtfulness. I arrived first with Madame Kobayashi, wondering how I would be expected to behave in the rigid social etiquette of Japan. We were alone. She was the agent, she was 'uchi-no' (of the inside, i.e. the household). I was the artist, I was 'gaijin' (outside person, i.e. foreigner). I was in a quandary. I decided to be British, gestured across the length of the table and asked if I might pour her something to drink. She made a low obeisance, which I imitated and, in her high-pitched voice she squeaked, 'Alcohol.' I opened the Suntory.

Maria arrived with Di Stefano, Nakajima and some assistants, and the party was on. She looked tired, managed to convey the impression of enjoying the occasion, but when it was over said she was relieved.

Next morning, when Nakajima and Madame Kobayashi came to take us out for more photographic exposure I made piano practice my excuse. They were held up in traffic on the return journey, not arriving until seven, Maria impatient to start singing. She immediately produced 'Mi chiamano Mimì' and 'Un bel dì', two arias not listed on our printed programme. We had been working only about half an hour together when Di Stefano came in asking if we were ready to go. The EMI Eastern representative had come to take us to dinner at Tokyo's Maxim's. Among framed diplomas and letters lining the entrance hall my eye was caught by the familiar letter heading of 36 avenue Georges Mandel, Paris. Maria had written to wish them well for the opening. Di Stefano kept us amused with his tales during the meal, but Maria was quiet, clearly wishing to be elsewhere.

In avoiding the photographic sessions I sometimes missed out on more interesting trips. 'I looked for you,' Maria said. 'We were taken to see something special. It's all quite clear when you've got the gist of it.' They had been to the Kabuki theatre, where in a highly stylised spectacle, traditional age-old plays are performed by an all-male cast. When they returned after a Japanese dinner, Maria looked tired and complained again of the pain she was suffering from her hiatus hernia.

Di Stefano's tour in Australia had become a matter of continuous discussion, on one day, off the next. On an off-day the contract was unacceptable. He would not go, he said, because the Australian agents were stingy, allowing only tourist fares for his accompanist, but of course, that was not the real reason. Since the summer Maria had been persistently nagging him that it was 'a lousy contract'. On tour with her his fee was clear of all expenses. In Australia he would be paid less, have a much tighter schedule and be liable for my expenses. Originally he had agreed because he needed the work, but now he had come round to her way of thinking. 'It's an insult,' he said. It certainly was insulting of J. C. Williams to send him a new contract cash-on-delivery, $20, which he was obliged to pay. 'We're not going,' he told me, 'and I'm not going to tell them. We just won't turn up.' His pique lasted only a day, when he remembered that in addition to his normal commitments he had the cost of Luisa's medical care.

In the meantime Maria cancelled her much-talked-of holiday in Tahiti. She had planned to recuperate there and wait for him to join her after Australia. Their relationship was very calm and secure, and he was confident enough now to use her Christian name when talking to me of Maria. He wanted her to come with us to Australia, he said. As the possibility of travelling together became more real, and we worked on some arias and songs to fill a whole programme, he said to me, 'Hey, why is it you don't call me Pippo? Everyone else does.' There had been occasions when the diminutive form of his

Christian name would have been pertinent, as in New York when I had comforted him, weeping, in my arms. But when he made Maria unhappy, Mr Di Stefano better expressed my feelings. He had never invited me to use his nickname and in conversation, or work, it is not difficult to avoid using any name. If it depended on his moods I would have been switching from Pippo to Mr Di Stefano regularly. I said, 'OK, Pippo.'

'About time,' he answered.

In Japan they have a charming custom of exchanging gifts, their value of little importance, a gesture of respect being the intention. The method of receiving gifts is prescribed, the two hands held together with open palms, accompanied by a bow commensurate to the status of the giver. Neither Maria nor Pippo ever showed interest in this, though no day passed without flowers, chocolates, Geisha dolls and other charms being bestowed on them. They began to ask from Nakajima something more ambitious, a radio, a tape machine, or some other piece of electrical equipment. If they knew that reciprocity is an integral part of the custom they never showed it. 'La Signora likes to take, but not to give,' Consuelo whispered to me.

I was embarrassed by the lack of respect in their attitude to Nakajima as their demands grew. In the morning he would be greeted by Pippo, 'We want...' Maria asked for an expensive under-water watch, which prompted more from Pippo. 'You must have Maria's watch repaired,' he told Nakajima. 'It was in your car she lost the diamond,' as though that made him culpable. The strap of the watch tapered in graduated diamonds towards a small clasp and one of the smallest stones was missing. Nakajima tried to pass the claim off as a joke, but Pippo was insistent. 'You're lucky it's at the narrow end,' he said.

Some time later the watch was still on Maria's mind. 'No diamond, no *Tosca* next year,' she threatened poor Nakajima.

At dinner after the concert in Fukuoka, Nakajima was not let off the hook. 'There are too many photographs,' Maria told him. 'After a certain amount of photos my fee goes up.' She was feeding Pippo from a plate of soup which he had refused when we ordered and liked the look of when it was served; he simply took Nakajima's plate. As Pippo laughed at Nakajima's bewilderment, I wondered what ancient Japanese custom he might have breached.

Our third concert in Tokyo, at the Bunka Kaikan, was probably the best sung, by both singers, of the whole tour – Maria's voice stronger, more focused, the high notes firmer and the wobble, which had long been a problem, coming under control. Not one angry word in the warm-up, no petty bickering, and during the concert he encouraged her before each solo and kissed her afterwards. She sang 'Mi chiamo Mimì' for the first time, rather heavily but was rapturously received. He also sang a new aria, 'O Souverain, O Juge', from Massenet's *Le Cid*, with a brilliant high B flat which brought the house down. Everyone was feeling good. In the interval Pippo tried another song new to me, 'Aye, Aye, Aye', in three different keys before deciding on his highest note. After we performed it he took me by the hand, presented me to the audience and was still holding it firmly when we reached Maria backstage. I could not help being touched by his warmth. The evening was flowing smoothly until at one point, in Madame Kobayashi's usual speech before the second half, the audience stopped laughing and we heard, 'Callas-San ... *Tosca*.' 'How dare she announce *Tosca* now,' Maria cried, turning to Pippo and me as though looking for an explanation. 'I have not agreed yet.' She had not given a definite answer, but she had teased them, when asked to sing Tosca's 'Vissi d'arte', by saying she would save it for next year. After hearing her that afternoon the possibility that she would be able to sing *Tosca* in a year's time did not seem so unreasonable.

There was a minor clash of prima donna temperaments later in Maria's apartment as we ate an informal buffet. Around the room several bouquets, presented to Maria on stage, had already been arranged in vases by Consuelo. Madame Kobayashi told us she would be visiting the Prime Minister that evening and, as she got up to leave, lifted a bunch of roses from a vase. 'What are you doing?' Maria asked her.

'The shops are all closed now,' Madame Kobayashi answered. 'I will take these for the Prime Minister. I cannot arrive without an offering.'

'Oh, no you don't,' Maria said. 'Your Prime Minister is not getting my flowers.' Madame Kobayashi's face was blank, unreadable, as she left without another word.

That evening, *à trois*, we watched the TV presentation of our concerts. With the exception of Pippo's 'Catari' the programme was taken from the concert on the 19th.

Unbeknown to us we were filmed backstage, which we found amusing to watch, although Maria said they had cheated on us. The camera was hidden. It is a short scene but it encapsulates the essence of circumstances backstage during a Callas–Di Stefano concert, Pippo continuously on the move, annoying Maria with his loud vocalising while she attempts to revise the words of her next solo and remonstrates with him, Consuelo politely showing her exasperation, the hot-drinks thermos and mugs on one table, and me gazing over another table spread with sheet music and vocal scores. As we move towards the stage Maria makes the sign of the Cross, in the Greek Orthodox manner, and Pippo accompanies us to the edge of the flies. Maria appeared in a gown she enjoyed wearing, 'the Papagalo dress' she called it. Full-length, encrusted with multicoloured sequins, it was covered completely by a diaphanous mantle of red chiffon, the sparkling sequins suggesting something spectacular underneath. Only at the end of the concert did Maria satisfy the curiosity of the audience by lifting the chiffon to reveal the brilliantly decorated dress. It always produced a scream of delight.

Our viewing of the TV programme was accompanied by a barrage of comments and criticisms from both singers, the smallest weakness excused, explained, or regretted and any rehearsal-room difficulties successfully overcome greeted with compliments all round. 'They should have taped us today,' Maria said. 'It was much better. But, for a fifty-year-old and a fifty-three-year-old – not bad!'

Maria did not appear in the morning, I thought to allow Pippo

and me to rehearse for the Australian tour. He was unusually subdued and after only a few minutes sat down with his head in his
hands. 'She's started the New York scenes again,' he told me. 'We're
going to have a rough time from now on.' I was aware that Maria
had bought some beautiful cultured pearls as a reconciliation present for Mrs Di Stefano and intended that he take them home to
her. That was as far as she was prepared to go, refusing when he
asked her to phone his wife in Milan. Tension grew, tempers flared
and a shouting match ensued – tirades of recriminations and self-
justifications. The entente cordiale had collapsed.

In the evening Maria joined us, looking careworn and every one
of her fifty years. To my relief we reached the end of the practice
session without any fireworks, although while Pippo was singing a
solo she surprised me by interrupting him in her little-girl voice,
'May I say something?' He paused, a puzzled look changing to one
of patronising indulgence, but Maria's technical suggestion was met
with a barrier of excuses and justification. Unlike Callas, Di Stefano
could not tolerate anything that sounded like criticism, however
well intended.

On the morning of our concert in the Osaka Festival Hall Maria
complained of being unwell. She had been sick during the night
and as she came into the sitting-room in a drab caftan, fragile and
wearing almost no make-up, there was no sign of a smile. Nor was
there any enthusiasm in her singing. For almost an hour she took
his coaching without comment, almost automatically, as though she
did not hear him, then her patience broke and we were thrown
back into our usual state of belligerence. That he was not in good
voice either did not help matters. To his suggestion that we should
cancel the concert Maria dithered between a Yes and a No but
after some truly disheartening work she left, saying, 'Sorry, Robert,
I can't sing.'

In a panic, Nakajima brought in a throat specialist and some
other people he thought might give consolation. Maria addressed
them with the feeble whine of a sickly child: 'I won't be able to do it'
(tearfully); 'Do you think I'll be all right?' (hopefully, but implying

that the responsibility for the success of the concert lay on their shoulders). The time of the concert was approaching; Nakajima had a lot at stake. At last, after much pleading, Maria agreed to sing, if Madame Kobayashi would make an announcement.

The performance started quite normally, the spirit of competition high. Pippo was concerned and, although Maria and I had agreed on the original key, he advised her to sing 'Suicidio' in the lower key, 'to be on the safe side'. I followed Maria on, staring into the score and mentally transposing the aria back down. As usual, a great roar greeted us for the solo, Maria moving about, acknowledging the applause for some minutes and I grateful for the extra time. I had just got my brain functioning in the lower key when Maria swung back to the piano, flashed a brilliant smile in my direction and said, '*In tono, Roberto.*' A nightmare! Only by knowing the piece so well did I get through it. The Great Automatic Pilot took over and carried me through the maze of conflicting accidentals success- fully to the end.

'It was *in tono*,' were the first words Maria said triumphantly to Pippo when we came off. He did not answer her, but turned to me and said, 'Take *Le Cid* – *in tono*.' The aria has a high B flat – shades of Irving Berlin's, 'Anything you can do . . . anything you can sing, I can sing higher.'

Trouble started after the interval, when Maria, unable to decide what to sing, asked me to bring not only 'Sola, perduta', but also 'Tu che le vanità'. I sat at the piano waiting for the applause to subside and her announcement, only to see her eyes turn implor- ingly to me for a decision. Remembering what had happened that morning I knew either aria was a gamble. I mouthed 'Sola'. Her high notes were flat, she forgot some of the lyrics and as the audi- ence applauded I could see she was angry. I was already gathering my music to leave the stage when, to my amazement, I heard her announce 'Tu che le vanità'. No prima donna on best form would sing two such taxing arias without a considerable period of rest. She was too tired to achieve a satisfactory performance, of course, but she made a brave effort. As they applauded she showed the audience a glamorous, happy, face – and burst into tears as soon as we were out of sight. She was inconsolable. Pippo and I stayed with her as long as possible before continuing the concert with a group of Sicilian folk-songs. When we returned there was no sign of Maria. She had gone to her dressing-room to weep unseen. We thought the concert was at an end, but she came back and we went on to finish with the *Cav* duet. Pippo sang 'Catari', but Maria refused, for the first time on the tour, to sing an encore. Not since Milan had I seen her so distressed by her singing.

She had no heart for the festive dinner after the concert, barely tasting her almost raw Kobe steak before asking Pippo to take her home. He was polite enough to return to the restaurant afterwards.

In the morning I told Maria how surprised I was to hear her announce the second aria without taking a break. 'I'm a racehorse,' she said. 'I just had to go on and show them I could do better. Singing is a lousy business.' No one mentioned work that day.

An opportune diversion came in the form of a call from the captain of the *Artemision II*, the ship partly owned by Maria, a business investment set up for her by Onassis. She was docked in Yokohama. Perhaps we might change our travel plans and stop over in Tokyo to visit the vessel. Pippo was filled with the enthusiasm of a small boy expecting a new toy, all for it. But Maria was apathetic. She corrected me when I remarked that I had never been on an oil-tanker. 'Oh, no,' she said. 'I'm not rich, it's only a little ship, loading dry cargo. Onassis is the one with the oil-tankers.' Without enthusiasm from Maria nothing came of the visit.

Our next destination was Hiroshima, the city that was flattened in August 1945 by the first atomic bomb to be used in warfare. The only building partly surviving, and made the focus of the Peace Memorial Park, was number one on the publicity route. Maria was photographed laying a wreath and looking appropriately grave.

Afterwards we went shopping. I intended to buy some yukatas, part of the traditional kimono which serves well as a light dressing-gown. Formerly, in Japanese hotels, a freshly laundered yukata was laid out each morning for the use of guests, that is, until the onset of tourism, when too many were taken home as souvenirs. In 1974 they were available only on request. In the shop Maria said I would look good in a red yukata, until the three shop assistants broke out in fits of giggling when I tried it on for size. How were we to know that I was breaking an age-old convention that the colour red is traditionally reserved for women? I should have been trying the blue. Maria's thoughts were on another aspect of the purchase. 'Why bother to pay for these when you could just swipe a few from the hotel?' she said, her rhetorical comment sounding more like a suggestion than an enquiry.

Maria took some time to get over the emotional shock of the Osaka concert on the 2nd. She was afraid even to try out the voice with a few easy phrases. 'I'm scared,' she said, but to our relief the infection had passed, she was free of any pain, the voice healthy again. For three hours we worked, Pippo never allowing one weak note and often losing his temper. 'Please don't be angry, Pippo. Temperament, yes, but not angry,' Maria would say, suffering, but knowing the work was good for her. When not shouting, he fidgeted with one or other of several pieces of hi-fi equipment they had gathered in homage gifts.

'Why don't we do some operetta here? There's a lot of money in it.' Pippo had been trying to interest Maria for some days, but he was underestimating her image of Callas the prima donna who, despite not having appeared in an opera house since her *Tosca* at Covent Garden on 5 July 1965, remained Queen Regnant of Grand Opera. This attitude had always influenced her choice of role. So many times she was asked to sing Carmen on stage, so many times she refused. Others offered explanations.

Perhaps Elena knew the real reason. 'It was nothing to do with her fat ankles,' she told me. 'The society ladies of Milan said Carmen was a brazen slut and beneath her dignity. La Signora thought more of what princesses and countesses said than anybody else.'

'You can bring one of your girl-friends,' was Maria's disdainful answer when Pippo tried again, alluding to an affair he had had with a young German operetta soprano.

'I'm in your hands, Pippo,' Maria said at the beginning of the warm-up for the concert next evening, but before long, when she said, 'I can't, Pippo,' he burst into a temper, shouting 'What do you mean, can't. You are Callas, I know you can do it, don't tell me you can't,' crying out like a man at the end of his tether.

He directed her every move during the concert, dictating and encouraging before an aria, criticising and praising afterwards. She was on good form and sang with a freedom I had seldom heard. I rarely saw him so happy.

Afterwards, as I travelled in the hotel lift with Maria, five bouquets between us, she told me how relieved she was to be free of the troubles of the Osaka concert. 'I'm glad I didn't cancel,' she said. 'Well, it would be stupid to come all this way and not get the money.' When Maria repeated the words of another person the colours of the voice could be heard in hers, she could not help it. This was pure Di Stefano. When telling him something I had said there were even hints of a Scottish accent. She must have registered my surprise at hearing these words, quickly pulled herself up and, switching to her *grande dame* voice said, 'Well, it wouldn't be right to disappoint the poor public.'

Our journey from Hiroshima to Sapporo, with a change of planes at Osaka, was long and tiring. Maria had again been sick during the night and she was distressed by the news from Paris. Onassis had been admitted to the American Hospital suffering from myasthenia gravis, an incurable disease brought on by stress, alcohol and fatigue. 'He's scared to go into hospital 'cause he thinks he will never come out again. He needs to know I'm thinking of him, but I can't phone, or even send a telegram, because it would soon be all over the newspapers. We have a basic understanding. He can talk to me about his business problems and he knows there's always his favourite champagne in my house.' She reminisced for some time, even mentioning 'The Gold-digger'. 'She doesn't understand him, never was right for him. It's hard work keeping a man happy.

She's away too much. She tried to change his whole way of life, tries to redecorate everything. It's like taking away his past. I never did that. That was his.' She was sad and we were all tired. I left her for an early night.

Much to Pippo's annoyance, Maria made me laugh out loud during our session next day. He had stopped me in an interlude and was trying to suggest something he could not express in musical terms. Maria saw I was puzzled. So was she. 'Do you want him to play it faster or slower?' she asked. He was not amused, but from his recent friendliness and the compliments she had been paying me I knew I was secure from any repercussions. He had accepted me as a member of the family, even to the extent of calling me into the bedroom one morning when they were sitting up in bed together. 'He knows what's going on,' he said, as he puffed up his chest and she pulled the sheet over hers.

Nakajima was very worried in Sapporo – a poor box-office. 'Oh dear, I suppose that means more photos,' Maria groaned. 'I told you, who wants us in Sapporo?' They went on the rounds of national monuments and shrines that day and the next. In the evening, looking exhausted, Maria told me that, rather than sing and make Pippo angry, she would only go through the words, but that was never right for her and she was soon singing full voice. Sure enough, there was a row. She stopped singing and spoke the words in time to the music. When we finished she sat down with a deep sigh and said, 'Well, tomorrow's the last one.'

Pippo was still trying to persuade her to come to Australia with us and as usual she would never give a positive answer. A 'Yes' in the morning easily became a 'No' in the evening. 'I'm sick, I need to go home to Paris, to my nest.' She was thinking of Onassis in that Paris hospital.

Consuelo said, 'Well, tonight Paris – tomorrow, we'll see.'

The concert in the Hokkaido Koseinenkin Kaikan went well despite the hoarseness which blemished some of Pippo's high notes. The newspapers had done their job and we had a full house. A light-hearted air backstage throughout the evening extended into the performance when Pippo, in the *Carmen* duet, broke Maria's concentration and brought a smile to my lips when I should have been looking very serious, by changing his words. Instead of Don José's '*J'implore, je supplie, notre passé je l'oublie. Nous allons tous deux commencer une autre vie, loin d'ici sous d'autre cieux* (I beg you, I entreat you, I will forget all that has happened since we met. Let us begin another life together far from here, under other skies)', he sang '*loin d'ici, en Australie*'. Maria's answer was Carmen's '*Tu demandes l'impossible!* (You ask the impossible)', but she also could not restrain a smile.

'Well, tomorrow's the last one,' Maria had said. Prophetic words. Maria Callas, the brightest operatic star of the century, bowed out of her awesome career on 11 November 1974 in Sapporo, Hokkaido, a nice town but a modest place, which had shown no great enthusiasm to hear her. She never sang again in public.

12

THE ROAD ENDS – THE LEGEND

FLOURISHES

In the morning we all flew back to Tokyo where Pippo and I changed for Australia and Maria, with Consuelo, took a plane to Paris. Her blood pressure was low; she was ill, exhausted and homesick.

On 23 January 1975 she wrote to Dr Parrish in New York:

Dear Louis,

I'm sorry I'm late in answering your letter but as usual I got involved – this time I had tooth problems . . . My last tour was fantastic all the way round. I mean all was well – <u>fine</u> with Pippo. He sang very well too. We had no one around and therefore no gossips or other nonsense. It's very difficult to be near to artists without consequences unfortunately.

Only I had a bad attack of my old Hernia in the stomach. So my whole tour was a torment of weakness and great pain – I was terribly thin – and though I <u>love</u> to be thin – I got frightened I was so thin and wan. Of course the reason was that the damn hernia also bled internally.

I finished the tour very well but arriving in Paris I collapsed – and I'm not joking. They couldn't wake me up (and I had taken no pills). I'm off them as they are not on the market and coming back after such a long trip you certainly don't need pills to sleep. On the contrary – you need something to keep you awake, one is so sleepy with the difference in hours.

But, also, leaving Tokyo I had a bad head cold and I had an unpleasant thing happen to me. As a result of the cold, they say, I had my <u>labirinth</u> [sic] disturbed [inner-ear disfunction]. I couldn't stand straight, sit straight, I had lost most of my reflexes and couldn't see for nearly 12 hrs. I'm still terrified thinking about it.

Now I'm fine – never been so well – because my doctor here called a neurologist. Thank heavens I regained all reflexes in 2 or 3 days so no hospitalizing was necessary.

He started me on pills which keep me calm so that by night I'm not all keyed up as I was (overexcited as the Dr said and he was right) very calm – clear minded – my memory even has improved.

My decision to resume singing, dear Louis, Alas, as a result of what I went threw [sic] upon my return, is very dubious.

If I didn't have this hernia and its result – maybe. But is it really worth it?

I'll never be what I used to! Why torture myself, frankly. Yes, I said, I don't want to rot. But I can occupy myself otherwise without risking my health.

I don't have the resistance anymore. Also I ask too much of my singing to be happy with even these good results. But right now – calm and lucid as I am – I think my decision will be to dub some of my best records and perform them for films so they will see Callas on stage (or nearly) and it will remain for posterity as all say I should leave documents of my acting ability. Maybe it might capture my stage appearance. This way, I keep busy – and the tension is reduced to the minimum.

I can never top those records even if a miracle happened.

This is my thought right now. I hope all is well with you – your personal life I mean!

Let me hear from you, Maria.

Three days after Sapporo, Pippo and I started the Australian tour with a concert in Perth and finished two weeks later in Adelaide. Wherever we went there were enough Italians to fill the halls, wildly cheering and applauding when he appeared and, free of any competition, he became once again the 'primo donno', singing freely, confidently and captivating his public.

I arrived back in London to find telephone messages from Maria. She had recovered from the Japanese ordeal, her blood pressure back to normal, and was impatient to start again on the voice in preparation for the Tokyo *Toscas* in the autumn. We did not work at all on the opera, she knew that one well enough, but solely on vocal technique, Panoufka exercises, simple Bellini songs, and now and then the random aria, 'just for fun'.

But all the time she was worried. Onassis had collapsed in Athens, had been recommended a hospital in New York, but had chosen the American Hospital in Paris, Maria believed to be near her. By a strange coincidence Vasso Devetzi's mother was also in the hospital, on the same floor. This was an opportunity for Vasso to observe and report to Maria the comings and goings around Onassis. Maria needed to know how he was progressing and Vasso was her only source of information. 'Fate decreed that the old woman would be ill,' Maria said, her strong belief in destiny contrasting with her exaggerated respect for the worldly, old-fashioned, lower-middle-class ethics which decreed that Onassis's family alone should attend him. Maria, the woman he knew loved him and understood him better than his wife, was an outsider who had to bear the torture of living within a taxi ride of his bedside and not have the right to visit him. Only once did she manage to outwit the newspaper reporters and slip into the hospital unrecognised.

Work had no place at Georges Mandel. Maria, with Ferruccio and Bruna, whose mother had died, leaving her free for her adored mistress, flew to Palm Beach, where, on 15 March 1975 she heard the final news of Onassis. His death was the greatest but not the only blow for Maria. Two days after Onassis, on the 17th, Luchino

Visconti, friend and collaborator in the great successes at La Scala, died; and Luisa Di Stefano, who had struggled so defiantly with cancer for five years, finally succumbed on the 19th. Some weeks later Pippo, broken by grief, joined Maria in Palm Beach on the pretext of helping her select and buy a property there. As usual, she could never make a decision and the idea was soon abandoned.

Despite these blows, or perhaps because of them, Maria was still keen to work when I saw her again in the summer, although she was becoming fearful of the *Toscas* in Japan.

Another worry was a proposed concert with orchestra at Covent Garden. John Tooley, the General Administrator, had been urging her for some time to confirm a date and offered to send a repetiteur, all expenses paid, to help her prepare. 'I don't want to be alone with someone new at this stage,' Maria told me on the phone. 'Please come over.'

I sat in the salon with the adjoining doors open, while in the music room the Covent Garden man, none other than the now celebrated conductor Jeffrey Tate, played for Maria. Knowing nothing of my work with her, he seemed amazed that Maria accepted my criticisms without complaint. After I left Paris they worked at the Théâtre des Champs-Elysée, where one day a journalist from *France-Dimanche* found his way unnoticed into the auditorium and, for the sake of a moment of dubious personal success, wrote a libellous article about the state of Maria's voice. I like to think that had his editor guessed the far-reaching repercussions of that piece it might never have been printed. Maria was devastated, all her will to work demolished. She sued the newspaper (she won posthumously) and decided to give up the forthcoming *Toscas*, her already faltering courage now shattered.

It was August and Maria, suffering from an inflammation in her right elbow, had resorted to the use of a typewriter in her private correspondence. Typically, because a piece of office equipment was being used, everything had to be as formally laid out as a secretary would a business letter.

36, Avenue Georges Mandel
Paris 16ᵉ

Paris, August 27, 1975

Mr. Robert Sutherland
4I Cumberland Terrace
Regent's Park
LONDON N.W. I 4 H P (England)

Dear Robert :

Thank you for your book. As soon as I finish my Forsyte book
I will attack your book.

I thank you for thinking of me. I hope all is well with you.

I am not practising and I am not going to sing in Japan at
least this year.

There is my news. And I am afraid, dear Robert, I cannot stand
the Wears and Tears of everyday exercisings. My nerves cannot
take it. So that is that.

All my love.

Maria Callas

I am in Paris now and stay.

Knowing Maria as I did, I interpreted her postscript, 'I am in Paris now and stay', as her code inviting me to visit.

Her decision not to sing in Tokyo presented Pippo with a crisis: he needed to find a Tosca quickly. The Japanese public were expectant. On the promise of hearing the most famous soprano in the world sing one of her most acclaimed roles, they had eagerly bought their tickets months in advance. The performances were sold out. Pippo turned to the only soprano with a reputation big enough to replace Callas, Montserrat Caballé. As he spoke to her from the music room at avenue Georges Mandel, he passed the phone to Maria, who very politely asked Caballé to sing in her place. It was a request few could resist. Caballé, always a great admirer of Callas, freed herself from other commitments and sang with Pippo the three *Toscas* in Japan.

Giving up those *Toscas* marked the beginning of the end of Maria's possibilities of a come-back. John Tooley never got his Covent Garden concert, and though we met and went through the old exercises and arias together I knew that our work was fruitless, all hope stopped with the final cadence. Appearing on the stage again had become a dream only to be talked about, but a delusion that she was ready to live with. New ideas sometimes annoyed her. 'They want me to sing the *Merry Widow*,' she said indignantly, drawing herself up with an hauteur that showed me how wonderful she would look as Lehár's Hanna. 'It's all so undignified,' she said dismissively.

Callas had always claimed it was work that kept her alive. 'I work, therefore I am,' she told an interviewer. Now she was occupying herself only with the *idea* of work, her sole pleasure the knowledge that her public still wanted her. She allowed agents and directors to make offers, to spend hours at Georges Mandel jostling from one idea to another, but the only thing which really could have satisfied her was one more chance to sing her beloved Norma and, in her heart, she knew that to be impossible. When they had gone her misgivings returned, the show of absorbed interest a pretence, her desperate way of clinging on to the anchor-line of the great battleship of opera on whose bow she had once been a magnificent, dazzling figurehead.

I began to fear what I would find each time I arrived in Paris. Maria became very pessimistic, bitter even. She had run out of spiritual energy; without that, it was hard to go on. Friends fell off, tired of last-minute changes, or the voice of Bruna on the telephone saying that Madame was unwell and must cancel the dinner appointment. Maria found comfort again in chocolate and ice-cream, and began to put on weight. As she walked she hunched her shoulders as though protecting herself. Her eyes, which I had seen so often blazing forth her feelings, had a far-away look, empty and unresponsive. Full of doubts, she had no confidence in her own thoughts, any opinion she expressed followed by, 'Am I right?' We listened even more often to her recordings, no longer 'shall we?' but 'Now, let's hear some singing'. It worried Ferruccio that, as well as Mandrax at night, she was taking amphetamines in the morning when she struggled out of bed. He warned Vasso about it and was answered with a shrug.

Sometimes Maria would call me in London late at night and ramble long about mundane things, trivial banalities, morosely dismissing one subject after another, 'What does it matter, nothing matters any more. Well, good-night, that's another one over, one more day nearer the end.' On a different call she was aggressive. 'The world is full of Jews and homosexuals,' she said. 'I hate them all' – until I pointed out that without her agents and a host of great directors, designers and conductors, many of whom were one or the other, or both, her career might have been much less fulfilling. 'That's different,' she answered. '*They* were my friends.'

She was seeing less of Pippo, he had his work and her feelings for him were changing. 'I'm tired of Di Stefano trying to manipulate me,' she said, using the intimate form of his name less often. I ventured the idea that the time had come for her to make a big decision, to shed 'La Callas', the prima donna's work finished. She should settle for Maria, start to live as an ordinary woman, put Callas into the cupboard beside her recordings and find a husband, a rich man with some personality who would appreciate all that she had achieved and be a support in a new life. I did not think there was much chance of this happening; it was something to talk about, but I was asking too much. With a distant smile she dismissed the two ideas in one answer, showing me that she could never be less than the luminary she had created. 'Where am I going to find such a man? They're all taken up and anyway, it would be difficult to be Mr Callas.'

Maria's death was sudden. On 15 December 1977 she complained of pains in her back, asked Bruna to give her a massage and to make an appointment with a professional masseuse for the next day. On the morning of the 16th Bruna took in a glass of orange juice as usual and opened the curtains. Maria greeted her with '*Buon giorno*' and she went back to the kitchen to fetch the hot coffee. When she returned she found Maria slumped on the floor by the bathroom door. '*Mi sento male* (I feel unwell),' Maria said as she tried to get up but fell back again. Bruna called Ferruccio and together they managed to lift her on to the bed. Her lips were blue, her complexion a frightening colour and she was gasping for breath. She asked for coffee, which Bruna fed her with a spoon. Ferruccio telephoned her doctor but could not get through. The line to the American Hospital being also busy, he called his own physician. By the time he arrived Maria was dead and within an hour the news had spread around the world. Rumours were rife. For some people a natural death was too ordinary for the Queen of Opera; they wanted to believe something more dramatic, suicide, or even murder. They did not know of Maria's invincible belief in God. With her fertile imagination there were no doubt times when she weighed up all the methods of ending her life, but she believed her destiny was foreordained and it did not include self-destruction, even in her state of loneliness and depression. There was no autopsy and no inquest, and some close friends, including Princess Grace, expressed surprise at the hastiness of the funeral. Perhaps Vasso Devetzi, knowing of Maria's use of Mandrax and amphetamines, feared that the evidence would be misinterpreted.

For the authorities she produced a formal death certificate, which stated that Maria had died of a heart attack, but Dr Andreas Statho-poulos, husband since 1983 of Maria's sister (now known to me as Jackie), thinks differently. 'As a medical doctor,' he told me, 'I have carefully examined all the evidence, particularly Bruna's account of the day of death and the time preceding it. The symptoms described by Bruna, the pains Maria complained of in her back and her breathlessness, clearly indicate partial infarction of the lungs fol-lowed the next day by complete infarction. I believe she died of a massive pulmonary infarction. A thrombo-embolism travelled from the legs up through the blood system and finally blocked the pul-monary artery. Maria had a lot of reasons to have such symptoms. She was a middle-aged woman, she was taking pills to sleep and pills to wake up, she was depressed and the circulation is slow in those circumstances. She had problems with her legs; if she stood for any length of time the ankles swelled up. It is bad circulation. All these circumstances – being inactive, lying in bed a lot, lack of exercise, the pills, et cetera – are usual causes of pulmonary infarction.'

'So you don't think it was a heart attack,' I asked.

'No, no heart attack, but the body should have been taken to the morgue for the official report of a pathologist about the cause of death. Vasso Devetzi took care to get the body to the crematorium quickly, without examination.'

'Why?' I asked.

'I don't know why, but there is no suspicion of Maria's death involving a criminal action. Who had the interest to kill Maria? To take advantage of an inheritance? There was no hatred around her. In criminal law we investigate the motives of the person who has an interest in killing the deceased. No one knew the contents of her will and who might inherit. There was no motive.'

'What about suicide?'

'No, no,' was his dismissive reply. 'A person who is planning a holiday months in advance, who is still looking forward to the joys of life, to swimming in the sea at Cyprus and makes an appointment for the following day, does not commit suicide. No, suicide is out.'

Dressed in an *haute couture* grey chiffon gown, Maria was laid out on her elaborately carved eighteenth-century Italian bed, her long tresses elegantly arranged and her hands crossed on her breast. Even without make-up she looked beautiful. 'She was really lovely,' Jackie remembers. 'It made a deep impression on me. I don't understand it. She was never more beautiful than she was in death. It seems that death makes you appear younger. My mother was the same, if you saw her on her death-bed you would say she was eighteen years old.'

Many distinguished colleagues and friends visited the house to pay their last respects and sign a book of condolence. Giuseppe Di Stefano, the tenor who partnered her in many famous recordings and shared some of her most glorious triumphs in the opera house, flew from Hamburg where he was singing, only to be refused entry by Vasso Devetzi. Of all her questionable behaviour after Maria's death nothing was more dastardly.

Just as most people in the Western world can say what they were doing when J. F. Kennedy was assassinated so, in the musical world, men and women can tell you where they were when Maria Callas died. I was in the Glasgow Botanical Gardens, walking the pet dog of my host, Arthur Blake, Head of Music for Scottish Television. He told me to sit down when I returned, thrust a large glass of neat whisky into my hand and said, 'The BBC want to interview you about the news.'

'What news?'

'Someone close to you has died,' he answered. It did not take me long to work out who that could be. I knew only one person whose death would warrant an interview on the radio. Before long I was in the studios being questioned by Mary Marquis, Scotland's Barbara Walters. She must have been disappointed. In a state of shock I found it difficult to express my true feelings. Any one word said about such a bafflingly complex personality would need to be tempered by another. In three or four minutes I was unable to say very much, words came slowly, and on the other side of the microphone Mary was gesticulating. How could Maria Callas and all she meant be summed up in a pithy sound-bite? Shunning the customary tired platitudes, I simply told the listeners I was not surprised by Maria's death, but I had not been expecting it.

In the evening some friends gathered in Arthur's flat for a Scottish wake. Without a body, we celebrated a life, eating, drinking, reminiscing and playing recordings of Maria Callas into the wee hours.

The funeral was at 4.30 p.m. on 20 September 1977, in the Greek Orthodox Church in rue Georges Bizet (composer of *Carmen*). The crowded church chattered noisily and watched as the photographers and TV crews battled for position. Everything and everybody was being photographed, flowers rearranged to make a better picture, an elaborate tribute in a tall, precariously slim vase carrying the name 'Christina' on a red ribbon, knocked over and left for a member of the congregation to pick up. Propped up on supports were enormous wreaths from international institutions and authorities: Covent Garden, La Scala, the President of Greece, the President of the French Republic and on the marble floor a touchingly simple rectangular cushion inscribed 'Grace and Rainier', of red, yellow and orange marigolds, the colours Maria wore on the day I first met her.

When Princess Grace arrived with her daughter Caroline the photographers fought in a frantic scrum for the best shot, cameras up close, almost in her face, hoping to capture any sign of a tear.

It was not possible to say when the service started, the mumbling of the congregation and the noise of clicking cameras and TV directors in the background drowning out the chanting of the priests so effectively that the ceremony had to be stopped while an acolyte, solemnly robed and showing signs of alarm and indignation, pleaded for silence.

The scene seemed to epitomise Maria's life: always surrounded by gossiping people, propriety and religious belief represented by

the chanting priests, who could barely be heard above the scandal-
ous intrusion of the media. In the midst of this harrowing travesty
of a funeral service the casket stood apart, on its top an icon and
a simple bunch of flowers from Yacinthy and her mother. Only
when we filed out behind the coffin, having found no solace inside,
did we find any real respect and honest appreciation. A hushed
crowd lining the street watched in silence while the coffin slid into
the hearse. As it moved off, a lone man lifted his hands in the air,
began to clap and called, 'Bravo, Callas!' Within a moment his
applause was taken up by the tense crowd, relieved at the chance
to release their pent-up feelings. Not one second of the elaborate
religious service inside the church had the impact of that sound.
In the crowd, men and women were weeping as they cried 'Bravo',
'Diva!' and other epithets of love and admiration I had heard so
often during our tours. At last the funeral meant something. Maria
would have been happy to hear their calls and applause, the part
of her fantasy world she craved most, the approbation of her public,
the only love that never let her down.

I did not meet Maria's sister on the day of the funeral – Vasso
Devetzi allowed her little contact with anyone who knew Maria –
but some months later I received a diplomatic call from EMI in
London asking if I would accept were I to be invited to dinner
by Mrs Calogeropoulos-Stathopoulos. Of course I would accept,
though all I knew of her was what I could remember from a few
snide remarks of her sister's. I met a charming, handsome woman
who looked more delicately feminine than Maria, but had a way of
moving, speaking and expressing herself which was uncannily like
her. I found it strange to be asked 'What was my sister like?' not
realising that they had met only rarely since September 1945, when
Maria sailed from Athens to America. In the company of her husband Dr Andreas Stathopoulos, an astute man with a lively sense
of humour, the dinner party went well for me until Jackie produced
a tape from her handbag. 'This is a recording of a concert I gave.
Would you be so kind as to listen to it and tell me what you think
of my singing.' My heart sank. Andreas had told me they had met

in their voice teacher's waiting-room, but I did not know that she had been anything more than an amateur.

'Of course,' I said, my mind already calling up all the tactful, kindly phrases an adjudicator may use to disguise his true opinion. I hoped after listening to the tape I might discreetly forget about it. But Jackie was determined to get an answer. They were leaving next day, she told me, and could I phone her in the morning?

At home in my flat I dutifully played the tape and found myself sitting up in amazement. Here was a big voice of unusual timbre and character, not always entirely controlled, but certainly material of professional promise. My thoughts turned to Elvira de Hidalgo's reaction when in 1938 she first heard Maria Kalogeropoulos: 'Cascades of sound, not yet fully controlled. I listened with my eyes closed and imagined what a pleasure it would be to work with such metal, to mould it to perfection.' She could have been speaking of the voice on the tape I was playing. 'My sister was furious when she heard I was giving recitals,' Jackie told me. 'She demanded that I must never use the name Callas.'

Later I spent a week with Andreas and Jackie in Athens, swapping stories about her sister, Jackie telling me of their childhood days and I recounting stories of my years with the two grown women, Maria and La Callas.

Vasso Devetzi had seemed a godsend when Jackie arrived, bewildered and alone, in Paris for the funeral. Without any authority Vasso had gone ahead, organised the funeral and arranged for cremation. She introduced herself as Maria's closest and dearest friend, (Jackie had no way of knowing otherwise, nor how deceitful and cunning were her intentions), told her not to worry, she would guide her through the tedious intricacies of French law and business, and assured her that she and her mother would be rich, because Maria had not left a will and therefore they would inherit all. In fact, Maria had some months previously drawn up a will in which Bruna and Ferruccio were the principal beneficiaries – each would be a millionaire – but, true to form Maria, who had hesitated always before signing a contract, was too superstitious to put her name to it. That would have been tantamount to signing her own death-warrant.

If Vasso thought her efforts on Jackie's behalf would be plain sailing, she was mistaken. No one had reckoned on Meneghini. He entered the arena brandishing a will which Maria had signed in 1954, while still his wife, leaving everything to him. Ironically, the two people with whom Maria had bitterly severed all contact during her life, her mother and Meneghini, were now contesting her fortune. Rather than embark on a long battle in the courts, a meeting was arranged and Meneghini, aged eighty-two, agreed when Vasso, representing Jackie and her mother, proposed dividing the estate equally. The first move Jackie made was to persuade the unwilling Vasso and a reluctant Meneghini that Bruna and Ferruccio must each be awarded a substantial amount, enough to bring security for life. Bruna returned to her Italian village and Ferruccio went to Switzerland to work for, of all people, Christina Onassis, who had always resented Maria's presence in her father's life. He was unhappy there, never having any real personal contact with his employer, who was constantly surrounded by minders. When he left after eighteen months she said to him, 'I don't understand, you've only been with me a short time and you could stand Callas for twenty-two years!'

With half of Maria's fortune now in her control, Vasso embarked on a devious campaign aimed at making herself rich. She persuaded Jackie to transfer hundreds of thousands of dollars to her bank account to enable her to establish a so-called Maria Callas Foundation, which would give scholarships to further the studies of young music students. No such scholarships were ever awarded and when confronted Vasso denied ever receiving any money. She did not live much longer to enjoy the spoils, her last major act being the solution of what to do with Maria's ashes. She petitioned the Greek government to organise a national ceremony in which, led by the minister of culture and other dignitaries, the ashes would be carried out on a naval destroyer to a suitable spot and scattered into the Aegean.

[279]

Jackie and her mother, who was too ill to attend, were invited simply as guests, while Vasso took the starring role and played hostess to the dignitaries. On the crowded deck the minister, manifestly not a seaman, opened the casket and, heedless of the blustery weather, tipped the ashes over the gunwhale. In this ill-timed moment the ashes were caught up in a gust of wind and blown back on to the faces of the onlookers and into the mouths of some who were gasping for breath in the strong wind. 'They were eating my sister,' Jackie commented. When she returned home, her overbearing mother, at eighty still demanding complete submission, compliance and obedience from her sixty-one-year-old daughter, was sitting up in bed eagerly awaiting news and details of the event. While Jackie related most of the happenings of the afternoon Evangelia reprimanded her for not checking her make-up often enough, especially in the presence of a minister and other VIPs. 'What is that grey smudge on your nose?' she asked. Jackie did not answer. 'I didn't like to say it was all that was left of her daughter,' she told me.

Many books have been written about Maria Callas, some of real worth, like John Ardoin's *The Callas Legacy*, which perceptively examines her growth as an artist, or Nadia Stancioff's *Maria, Callas Remembered*, the only book which draws a portrait of the woman I recognise. Some are updated biographies doggedly researched over years, others works of nauseatingly sentimental invention or, worse, a heap of prurient near-fiction, culled from scandal rags and other doubtful sources. Enough of the facts of her career and her private life are known. We wait now for some brilliant young psychoanalyst who, overwhelmed by the discovery of her recordings, will devour all the books and be stirred to investigate her convoluted personality. He will be intrigued by a bewildering picture: an unwanted child who was driven by an ambitious, domineering mother, denied the rough and tumble of a normal education, was incapable of developed powers of reasoning yet had an intensely alert intuition; who was obsessed by a desire for self-improvement and perfection, had an immediately recognisable voice which she drove further than the limits of normal expectation, a magnetic personality, an artistic imagination beyond the capacities of ordinary singers and a dramatic instinct that amazed the greatest stage directors of her time; an 'ugly duckling' whose desire to be beautiful put in jeopardy the great artist she had created; a woman who looked to older men for love, who at fifty read magazines for adolescent girls, never missed an opportunity of reading a horoscope, was worth $15 million, not counting future royalties, but was afraid of dying poor; a divided personality who, when not playing the role of a sharp-tongued prima donna, 'La Callas', was a rather gullible woman, Maria, who as often as not reverted further to become a repressed, insecure and frightened schoolgirl, trapped in a fairy-tale dream world of her own making, never wanting, nor able, to relinquish her romantic fantasies and grow up.

After dinner at Georges Mandel one evening we sat in the music room talking generally of Maria's career, the early struggles and the great successes. 'I have been lucky,' she said, 'because through music I have had the power to give something to the public, something that they wanted and needed. You see, Robert' – and here she made a statement which in other circumstances might have embarrassed me, or even produced a chuckle, something to be shrugged off as impious arrogance. But not with Maria. Free of pretension or conceit, but with quiet conviction, she said simply, 'I have been touched by the hand of God.' Just so.

INDEX